Reform in the
Middle East
Oil Monarchies

Reform in the
Middle East
Oil Monarchies

Edited by
Anoushiravan Ehteshami and **Steven Wright**

REFORM IN THE MIDDLE EAST OIL MONARCHIES

Published by
Ithaca Press
8 Southern Court
South Street
Reading
Berkshire
RG1 4QS
UK
www.ithacapress.co.uk

Ithaca Press is an imprint of Garnet Publishing Limited

First Edition

ISBN 13: 978-0-86372-323-0

British Library Cataloguing-in-Publication Data
A catalogue record for this book is available from the British Library

Typeset by PHi, India
Jacket design by David Rose
Cover photo used with permission of Ali Jasim/Reuters/Corbis

Printed by Biddles, UK

Contents

Part 3
Reform in a Geopolitical and International Context

Foreword

Sir Donald Hawley

This book, the fruit of a lively conference at Durham University in September 2005 under the auspices of the Sir William Luce Fund and the Institute of Middle Eastern and Islamic Studies, is a valuable contribution to the study of progress, reform and popular participation in government in the Gulf states – Kuwait, Bahrain, Qatar, the United Arab Emirates, the Sultanate of Oman and Saudi Arabia.

Political, economic and social conditions in these states are now very different from those of 1958 when I first served in the Gulf – as HM Political Agent in the then Trucial States. Undeveloped as they then were, serious journals in Britain argued that the conservative rulers in the Gulf were as doomed as Egypt's monarch had been and Iraq's and Yemen's were about to be. It was received wisdom that the area was inherently unstable and parts of academia propounded this thesis as witnessed by Professor Fred Halliday's book *Arabia without Sultans*. It was, however, only a short time after my arrival in the Gulf that I came to regard this analysis as flawed. These traditional states, moving with the times have, perhaps paradoxically, proved the most stable in the Middle East for the last 50 years or so, except when Iraq threatened Kuwait in 1961 and invaded it in 1991 and the Tunb islands were seized by Iran on the eve of Britain's withdrawal from the Gulf in 1971.

In 1958 the Sheikh's *majlis* was an open place of debate on every topic, but times and conditions have changed and, concomitant with an advance in economic circumstances and enviable social and welfare conditions, over the years more modern political institutions and popular participation in government and elections have been introduced – in different degrees – to meet the needs of more complex states. The gradual pace of change has perhaps been contributory to the resulting stability.

More recently some Western countries have sought to promote democracy of a Western type as the panacea for the countries of the wider region. Desirable as this may be in certain cases, it is not necessarily a cap that immediately fits every head and democratic institutions of this type cannot function well if there is, as the present state of Iraq shows, no security. Whilst internal and external imperatives in all the Gulf states point to accelerated popular participation in government, important questions of degree, timing and nature require separate consideration in each state.

This book helps to explain some of these factors and will, I hope, be useful to those people – practitioners of government, academics, diplomats and foreign statesmen, politicians and academics – to whom the continued peaceful existence of the Gulf states is of concern in the changed circumstances of the modern world.

I also hope that it will be of use in future forums where the subject is studied.

Congratulations are due to the authors for their contribution to understanding and to Dr Steven Wright for coordinating this project.

Contributors

His Excellency Sayyid Badr bin Sa'ud Al-Busaidi is the Sultanate of Oman's Deputy Minister for Foreign Affairs.

Dr Christopher Davidson is a Lecturer in Middle East Politics in the Institute for Middle Eastern and Islamic Studies at Durham University. He was formerly based at Zayed University in the United Arab Emirates.

Professor Anoushiravan Ehteshami is Head of the School of Government and International Affairs and Professor of International Relations at Durham University. He is also a Fellow of the World Economic Forum and the Royal Society of Arts.

Sir Donald Hawley KCMG, MBE had a distinguished public service career between 1955 and 1981, first in the Sudan and then as a diplomat in several Middle East countries before becoming the first Ambassador to the Sultanate of Oman and then British High Commissioner in Malaysia. President of the Royal Society for Asian Affairs and the Anglo-Omani and British-Malaysian Societies, he is the author of a number of books, mainly on the Middle East.

Professor Bahgat Korany is Professor of International Relations at the Universities of Montreal and Cairo.

Professor Emma Murphy is Professor of Political Economy in the School of Government and International Affairs at Durham University. She is also a Fellow of the Royal Society of Arts.

Professor Gerd Nonneman holds the Al-Qasimi Chair of Arab Gulf Studies at the Institute of Arab and Islamic Studies (IAIS), University of Exeter. He was formerly Professor of International Relations and Middle East Politics at Lancaster University.

Dr Neil Quilliam is a Senior Middle East Analyst with the Control Risks Group. He was formerly based at the United Nations University in Jordan.

Professor Mohammad Al Rumaihi is Professor of Political Sociology at Kuwait University. He was Editor-in-chief of the well-known magazine *Al-Arabi* for seventeen years and General Secretary for the Council of Culture, Art and Letters within the Kuwaiti government.

Dr Ahmed Saif is Assistant Professor of Politics at Sanaʻa University in Yemen and the Director of the Saba Centre for Studies and Research (SCSR), Yemen.

The Rt Hon. Baroness Symons of Vernham Dean is a former British Minister of State at the Foreign and Commonwealth Office. She was created a Labour life peer in 1996.

Professor Rodney Wilson is Professor of Economics in the Institute for Middle Eastern and Islamic Studies at Durham University.

Dr Steven M. Wright is Assistant Professor of International Affairs at Qatar University. He was formerly the Sir William Luce Fellow in the Institute for Middle Eastern and Islamic Studies at Durham University.

Dr Mahjoob Zweiri is a Senior Researcher in Iran and Middle East Politics at the Center for Strategic Studies at the University of Jordan. He was formerly the Director of the Centre for Iranian Studies in the Institute for Middle Eastern and Islamic Studies at Durham University.

PART 1

REFORM ISSUES IN CONTEMPORARY PERSPECTIVE

1

Political Reform in the Gulf Monarchies: From Liberalization to Democratization? A Comparative Perspective

Gerd Nonneman

After decades of being stereotyped as anachronistic exceptions amidst a changing tide of modernization and democratization that was assumed to be working its way around the world, the six states comprising the Gulf Cooperation Council (GCC) have recently begun to draw interest for a different reason. A series of reforms in the first seven years of the 21st century in countries such as Bahrain, Qatar, Kuwait and even Saudi Arabia suggested that these polities were not, perhaps, quite so uniformly and unchangeably 'autocratic' as commonly perceived – indeed that they might in some ways even hold out a more positive prospect of political reform than the rest of the Middle East. This chapter attempts to assess, explain and interpret what may be happening, and to consider what the implications might be for the future.[1]

Apart from their obvious strategic and economic significance, these polities stand out in several ways: they are, for the most part, exceptionally rich by developing world standards, but in the case of the UAE and Qatar they are rich even by the standard of the developed world; their political and economic systems are based to a significant extent on 'rent' ('unearned income' derived from the export of hydrocarbons); they are monarchies – with the monarchs and royal families exercising real power; they are, with the exception of Saudi Arabia and to a lesser extent Oman, very small polities; and they are characterized also by the prominence of traditionalist themes and *motifs* in social and political organization and in regime strategies and discourse.

Answers to questions about various kinds of reform depend very much on how one fills in the meaning of those terms. 'Democratization' can be either an intentional or a de facto series of developments aiming at, or with some likelihood of leading to, 'democracy'. It can come in any number of forms, not necessarily identified with any particular 'Western' or 'liberal' variety: the key components are (1) political partici- pation; (2) accountability; and (3) pluralism. 'Liberalization' could be defined either as applying to any kind of 'opening', from minor relaxing of government controls, all the way to the kind of reform that could credibly be termed 'democratization'; or the term could be reserved for openings and reforms short of democratization, i.e. 'freedom from' rather than 'freedom to'. Certainly, liberalization is not the same as democratization, although more advanced forms of the former may shade into the latter.[2] One question to be explored, indeed, is precisely whether in particular cases liberalization may stand in contradistinction to democratization.

The GCC States: Tradition or Modernity?

There have been two opposing but equally 'exceptionalist' approaches to the question of democracy, or political participation, in the Arab monarchical polities of the Gulf. The first painted these polities as anachronisms stuck in traditional authoritarian absolutism or oligarchy. The second equally stressed their traditional nature, interpreting them as reflecting the traditional Arabian features and values of egalitarianism, personal access, and 'desert democracy', with *majlis*es ('councils', tribal discussion and consultation sessions presided over by the senior social figure; Arabic singular: *majlis*; plural: *majalis*) as the functional equiva- lent of participatory channels. Neither are particularly useful: in fact, it is untenable to see them as 'traditional' systems at all – even though elements of tradition remain and, in part, have been consciously used by the ruling families to build state, 'nation', and political control and acquiescence. The creation of state structures in the 20th century; the consolidation of the position of the ruling families by the combined effect of foreign protection and oil revenues; the subsequent demo- graphic, social and economic effects of oil wealth, and the accompanying expansion and increasing complexity of society, economy and governing apparatus – all of this has turned these countries into what might be called 'neo-traditionalist' systems.

Some traditional values remain prevalent in society, whether with regard to religion, social status, the importance of personal connections or attitudes towards kinship – including a respect for 'leading families'. The ruling families have also consciously used these themes and instruments derived from them to build their legitimacy and instruments of control. Yet this is all taking place in societies and polities whose size and complexities, technologies and administrative systems, and linkages to the outside world, have changed beyond recognition. In that new context, various elements of 'tradition' have been reinterpreted and appropriated both by the regimes and different parts of the populations.[3] From the regimes' side, this includes new ways of using what only superficially resembles the old patrimonial style and mechanisms.[4]

Combining elements of tradition and modernity in novel ways, these states have been characterized by John Peterson as 'post-traditional'[5] – i.e. no longer even 'neo-traditional' in the sense of Sultan Sa'id bin Taimur's or Abdul-Aziz bin Abdul-Rahman Al-Sa'ud's systems. While those rulers 'sought to preserve the existing traditional society . . . by enhancing . . . the capability to control the state [but thereby] altered the nature of the decentralized political system',[6] that brief phase tends to be followed by a longer 'post-traditional' phase, where modernization of one sort or another is actively pursued, without making these systems 'modern'. These polities are therefore best labelled *post-traditional states using neo-traditionalist forms and methods*. Within this category, Kuwait and Bahrain might be classed as closer to the 'modern' end of the post-traditional spectrum than most of the UAE and Oman which are at the other end. This has important implications for our treatment of the question of democratization or political reform.

Political Participation in the GCC States in the Twentieth Century

Once the ruling families of the polities now making up the GCC were firmly in place and buttressed by oil rent, they swiftly eclipsed any domestic competitors for power. In the distant past, the concept of a traditional Arabian 'desert democracy' might have had some relevance – with small and simple entities characterized by very limited surplus resources, and fluctuating fortunes of ruling clans and individuals, combining with traditions of personal access, and ruling families less than assured either of superior resources or of certain support. Yet foreign involvement and oil comprehensively altered those dynamics. Even though all of the current monarchies have historical roots and a long-standing connection with their domains, without the resources that foreign powers (mainly Britain) and oil represented, several states or emirates would not have come into, or remained in, existence, while in those that did, the ruling family, or its ruling branches, might well have been different. There was competition from outside these rulers' realms, but also from within – witness the relative power of Kuwait's Al Sabah and the merchants until the advent of the oil age after the Second World War.[7] The situation has changed beyond recognition since then. The relative power position of the ruling family, and of the ruler and his immediate family, left any erstwhile balancing forces in society far behind.

These polities became, to varying extents, 'rentier states': their economies, and hence political systems, came to depend predominantly on the 'rent' derived from oil sales, in which only a tiny fraction of the population or domestic activity was involved. This obviated the need for taxation and lent the state (and regime) far-reaching autonomy from society, and indeed the ability to balance, foster or even create societal groups. The implied logic of the 'no taxation without representation' motto of most of the literature on democracy and democratization was thus arguably reversed: 'no representation without taxation'. On the whole, the population acquiesced in a system where, as long as government policy maintained this rentier arrangement and did not act against key values (e.g. traditional local interpretations of Islam), they had more to lose than to gain from upheaval. This was further facilitated by a traditional set of values and mechanisms assuring a sense that rulers by and large acted in accordance with the values and interests of the population. This social contract applied most strongly from the 1970s to the mid-1980s, after which a combination of the evolution of oil prices and markets, globalizing pressures in the world economy, the population explosion, social change and, from the 1990s, new external pressures for political reform, began to change the scene.[8]

That is not to say that some pattern of consultation and pre-emption of grievances through the use of personal and traditional networks did not persist – but it became a peripheral feature when compared with the more direct levers of power the rulers could employ. Kuwait was a partial exception, in its early adoption of a constitution that provided for a significant role for an elected parliament – in part reflecting a longer tradition of political mobilization (especially among the merchant class), in part related to the presence to the immediate north of the ideological and irredentist threat of Iraq, but in any case a sign of a degree of willingness on the part of the ruling family to allow political participation that was unlike elsewhere in the region.[9] Even there, of course, the parliament's actual power remained limited, and it could be suspended by the Emir for extended periods. Indeed, the attempted emasculation of the constitution after 1986 was only reversed against the background of the Iraqi invasion of 1990.[10]

In Bahrain, too, the early post-independence experiment with parliamentary constitutionalism was soon ended, and the emirate gradually took on some of the appearances of a repressive police state – its socially liberal climate notwithstanding. In the other states, political participation, or any limits on the ruling family's power, except formally from conventions of Islamic probity, were virtually absent. Oman's monarchy would, admittedly, have to wait for this position of untrammelled power until 1975 and the end of the civil war, but by then the usual combination of foreign assistance and oil rent – plus a visionary co-optation and hearts-and-minds policy on the part of Sultan Qaboos – had achieved the same result there also. In Saudi Arabia, the Al al-Sheikh of the Wahhabi establishment have often been portrayed as 'partners in power' – supporting Al-Sa'ud rule as long as the latter kept its side of the bargain of supporting the *Wahhabiya* – but in fact the latter has long since become the (very) junior partner in this relationship.[11]

Traditional forms of interaction with society were still maintained, in part in order to gauge opinion and pre-empt grievances, in part to help maintain the system of patronage and personal and tribal alliances, and in part simply to project an image of the rulers upholding traditional values. Clearly, this was not *only* a cosmetic exercise, but in the post-traditional phase of these polities, such traditional channels of communication, 'venting' or participation, as for instance in the regular *majlis*es held by senior sheikhs or princes, or indeed the ruler himself, no longer fulfilled their erstwhile function effectively. This was so both because the dynamics of the political system had changed, and both need and intention to allow genuine input from below had become vanishingly small; but also because society and economy had become incomparably larger and more complex, as had its administration: in that context such traditional channels *could* no longer be sufficient, even for the non-participatory purposes the rulers wished to use them for. Nevertheless, they remained important as legitimizing parts of the regimes' neo-traditionalist strategy – not least because they linked into the existing traditions at the societal level, as with the Kuwaiti *diwaniyyas*, for instance (informal *majlis*es at the homes of prominent citizens). Moreover, the smaller the polity, the more such mechanisms' usefulness was likely to survive at least in part.

The retention and reinvention of traditional forms of the link between rulers and ruled also formed part of a broader socio-political environment where a measure of 'social pluralism' was accepted – albeit more in some of these states than in others: these were never totalitarian systems, nor 'atomized' societies. Traditional tribal corporatism was extended into new formats in these post-traditional socio-political environments. Even if the *political* leverage of various old and new social groups was extremely limited, they remained – and in some cases became – significant in other ways, in social and economic dynamics. Indeed in the rentier state context sketched above, regimes were able to balance or form such groups. On the one hand, this was an additional means for the ruling group to manage the system and preserve their power. Yet by the same token, it helps explain the survival of 'political space' – in effect space for the development and functioning of 'civil society' – as shown perhaps most clearly by the case of Kuwait and its *diwaniyyas*.[12] Regimes could use sometimes harsh methods of repressing challenges and dissent – but they were not concerned to abolish such social pluralism, and by and large preferred co-optation and alternative means of obtaining acquiescence.

The Reforms So Far

As already suggested, changing circumstances both internal and external brought pressure for reform from the second half of the 1980s, starting from quite different bases in the different GCC states, and being responded to in various ways and to varying extents by the ruling families. The rash of reforms introduced in all GCC states since the late 1990s caused considerable interest in the region and beyond: something, clearly, was going on that seemed at first sight to break both with local political tradition and with wider Arab political patterns. These states –

or at least some of them – now came to be seen by some as the exception that would prove Arab democratization was possible after all.

This is not the place to detail the various reforms in each of the six states: the space is lacking, and much of the information can be found in a number of other sources.[13] My purpose in this chapter is to interpret and compare the dynamics of these developments and suggest what they might mean for the future. Here, some brief factual comments will suffice.

Kuwait

Kuwait witnessed an apparent consolidation and assertion of parliamentary power – the formal restoration of the constitution and a series of hard-fought elections since 1992; vigorous parliamentary questioning of ministers (and some forced resignations); the blocking of key government proposals – indeed, paradoxically, even the Emir's own decree allowing women to vote; the final enfranchisement of women, approved by parliament after a change of position by a majority of Islamist MPs in 2005; and, most recently, the central constitutional role of the parliament in the succession crisis from Sheikh Jabir to Sheikh Sabah al-Ahmad Al Sabah as Emir in 2006, and the blocking of the government's preferred electoral redistricting model (see section 6 below).[14]

Bahrain

The sudden change in the Bahraini political climate following the accession of Sheikh Hamad in 1998, turned the country from one of the more egregious examples of repression in the Gulf to one of its more conciliatory systems through the introduction of a new constitution and significant liberalization, including parliamentary elections. The changes brought about a huge surge in popularity for the Emir and the Crown Prince when it became clear that a genuine break with the past was being made. Indeed, the speed and extent of the reforms pushed through by the Emir, less than two years after his succession, can be seen as a conscious attempt to establish a new political base for his rule, and as partly neutralizing challengers from within the ruling family. Emergency laws were abolished, and long-exiled opposition leaders returned to the country, taking part in the debate and dialogue with the reforming monarchy and government, and with other political forces. In December 2000, Sheikh Hamad assumed the title of King, as part of a formal relabelling of the country as a constitutional monarchy. Yet following the initial overwhelming approval in a popular referendum of a 'National Action Charter' setting out the main lines of the new political dispensation, the Emir unilaterally adjusted the constitution to include a non-elected second chamber that would have an equal legislative role. This brought opposition objections and, in the end, a boycott by the mainly Shia opposition of the first parliamentary elections under the new system in 2002. The resulting parliament consequently contained a majority of Sunni Islamist members.[15] Much of the political struggle since then has been over the question of constitutional change and, within the opposition, over whether to continue the boycott or participate in the 2006 elections. In the end, the main opposition movement, *al-Wifaq*, decided to participate in these elections. In the event, opposition candidates did well, some irregularities notwithstanding, capturing nearly half the parliamentary seats.[16]

Qatar

Qatar has known little organized opposition, but when the Emir allowed free municipal elections in March 1999, participation was intense. The country's small population and future gas riches meant the Emir could be assumed to be under less pressure than elsewhere to open up the system. That he did so nevertheless, in quite striking fashion, a few years after ousting his father as ruler, indicates his appreciation that there was indeed a demand to be tapped into, not least among the educated younger generation staffing much of the private and public sector, including the armed forces. As in the case of his namesake, Sheikh Hamad of Bahrain, it served to buttress his power base against potential challengers within the regime.[17] Formal censorship and the information ministry were abolished, and elections for the Central Municipal Council were held for the first time in 1999, allowing women both to vote and to stand. In 2002 a draft new constitution was presented stipulating universal elections of a unicameral parliament of 45 members, of whom 15 would be appointed; the parliament was to have the right to legislate, vote on the state budget, question ministers and, with a two-thirds majority, vote ministers out of office. It could overturn an Emiri rejection of parliamentary legislation with a two-thirds majority, although the Emir reserved the right to suspend such legislation temporarily. The new constitution was approved in 2003, and became effective from July 2005, holding out national parliamentary elections for early 2007. In the meantime forceful but generic pro-democracy speeches were given by the Emir and Foreign Minister – but political parties remain banned.[18]

Saudi Arabia

Reform in the Kingdom began to take shape in the aftermath of the 1990–91 Gulf War, with the promulgation of the Basic Law in 1992 and the introduction of the appointed *Majlis al-Shura* the following year – a *majlis* that was gradually expanded and carved for itself an increasingly forceful role even behind the curtain of secrecy that officially shrouded its work, especially through the workings of the specialized committees that were established in 2001.[19] In 2005, the new *Majlis al-Shura* was expanded to 150, and several senior figures intimated that it was to be allowed to scrutinize the budget, and might eventually be two-thirds elected.[20] Almost simultaneously, a major reform of the much-criticized judicial system was announced.[21]

Although the municipal elections of 2005 were the most immediately visible sign of recent reform in the Kingdom, they came against a background of already expanded room for discussion both in the media and in the context of the 'National Dialogue' started by Crown Prince Abdullah, which had reached its sixth session by 2006. However constrained in its remit, and however limited the feed-through to society at large and to actual policy, the Dialogue was nevertheless an indication of a changing context and an awareness of a need for a different regime response (whether substantial or tactical). The very fact that a number of issues that were previously taboo could now at least be discussed, and that in the process previously 'illegitimate' voices such as those of Shia religious figures were given formal equal standing as discussion partners in a forum established publicly by the Crown Prince, was without question an important departure.[22]

But it was the municipal elections between February and April 2005, for half the nearly 12,000 seats of the country's 178 municipal councils, that drew the most attention internationally. The remaining half of the seats were to be appointed; the councils were not to deal with 'political' issues but only with local services and planning matters; women were barred from either standing or voting, albeit for 'logistical', not legal reasons; and no group campaigns, platforms or manifestos were allowed – let alone political parties. These were not in fact the Kingdom's first-ever elections: when first conquering the Hijaz, Abdul-Aziz Al Sa'ud had taken account of local sensitivities by establishing an elected *Majlis al-Shura* for the region in addition to five municipal councils for the main towns;[23] and in the 1950s, under King Sa'ud, local elections were begun, only for the experiment to be shelved when King Faisal came to power.[24]

Even so, from the perspective of the post-1960s era, the 2005 elections were a significant development, both in themselves and for the way they unfolded and the atmosphere that developed around them. Notable features were fairly low voter registration; high turn-out among those registered; vigorous competition for the seats; in many places moderate Islamist candidates sweeping the board, not least because they had been the better organized; a clear sectarian tinge to the results in the Eastern Province; clear evidence of group politics even though group platforms and campaigning had been banned; and campaigning focused mainly on real local issues of practical importance to the daily lives of local residents – not on broader philosophical or ideological issues.[25] In sum, while this was by no means a democratic breakthrough, the elections both illustrated and stimulated interest in participatory politics and in the wider issues and questions associated with it.[26]

Oman

Oman remains, in essence, an absolute monarchy: Sultan Qaboos singly remains the ultimate arbiter – with even other members of the ruling family kept at a decidedly second rung. Yet reform of sorts had been taking gradual shape with a succession of consultative mechanisms, evolving into the State Consultative Council as of 1981, which was in turn replaced by the *Majlis al-Shura* in 1991. Notable citizens from each of the provinces nominated two candidates each, of whom the Sultan chose one. Additionally, further members were appointed – increasing as the Council was expanded to 80 in 1994, when the first two women were also appointed. In 1996, the Sultan issued the Basic Law, the first time the basic outlines of the country's principles of governance were laid down. The following year, he established a new appointed consultative body – a 'second chamber' – in the shape of the *Majlis al-Dawla* (State Council) – made up by prominent figures such as tribal notables, senior businessmen and former government officials (together, the two Councils were henceforth known as the *Majlis Oman*).

When the rules for the *Majlis al-Shura* were changed in 2000 to feature direct elections for the first time (albeit still with a restricted electorate), considerable competition ensued. Finally, Oman introduced universal suffrage for the elections of 2003 – even if the resulting parliament still has only an advisory, not a legislative role, and cannot discuss matters of defence, foreign affairs, security and finance.[27] Council members also, with a few exceptions, remained quite timid in exploring the extent of their formal powers. In the event, a modest 34% of eligible voters registered to vote (262,000), although 74% of those registered (194,000) then did vote. That said, the mechanics of the actual elections themselves were professionally and neutrally handled.[28]

UAE

Formal participatory systems in the UAE remain the least developed of any of the GCC states. Each of the seven Emirs remains the sovereign power within his own emirate, although some (most prominently Sharjah) have introduced appointed consultative bodies. At the Federal level, the Federal National Council (FNC) has some of the apparatus of a parliamentary body, with special committees and established voting procedures, but it cannot initiate or block legislation, and its relevance is limited by the retention of real power by the individual Emirs. Even so, the number of subjects discussed has de facto increased since the late 1990s, and ministers (including ruling family members) have been questioned.[29] The most recent development followed the December 2005 announcement by Sheikh Khalifa bin Zayed Al Nahyan, the Emir of Abu Dhabi and President of the UAE since the death of his father, Sheikh Zayed, in 2004, that half of the FNC would be elected by the relevant council of each emirate, while it would also be expanded and see its powers enhanced.[30] These elections did indeed proceed as planned on 16–18 December 2006, even if they remained an extremely constrained affair: voters and candidates were in the end selected by the seven Emirs. In total, 6689 voters including 1189 women elected 20 of the 40 members of the Federal National Council from a slate of 439 candidates including 65 women (split between the individual emirates).[31] Any expansion of powers remains to be specified.

A Comparative Perspective: Factors Favouring Democratization

Comparative studies indicate that a varying combination of factors tend to be involved in driving liberalization and democratization. These include, on the one hand, the role of 'domestic actors', and on the other, environmental/structural factors (domestic and external) and external actors – it being understood that there is a mutual influence between these two categories.

- The relevant *domestic actors* include regimes, other groups, political parties and individuals. These act on the basis both of calculation of interest and ideational motivations.
- *Domestic factors (or structures)* include the political economy in question; the nature of the political system and its levels and bases of legitimacy; the characteristics of civil society, technology, societal factors such as literacy and urbanization, and cultural factors.
- *External factors (or structures)* include the characteristics of the international political economy and the 'Zeitgeist'.
- Finally, there is the role played by particular *external actors (or agents)*.

It is within the context shaped by the last three, that the domestic actors – not least the regimes – calculate their strategies and tactics. Below I summarize what I take to be the main lessons from past comparative work; most of this will prove of direct relevance to the case of the GCC states.

1. Liberalization/democratization tends to be driven by a combination of top-down responses and pre-emptive moves, and bottom-up pressures;[32] in turn, these occur in an external environment that may hinder or help the process.
2. Regimes when liberalizing do not usually intend to allow more than 'decompression' while retaining ultimate control, but may not be able to stop further development once the process has achieved a certain momentum and sufficient (and sufficiently organized) pressure is exerted by groups in society.[33]
3. Real democratization is never a foregone conclusion of such a process, but when it does emerge it tends to be after a lengthy process that can feature repeated setbacks.[34]
4. An independent bourgeoisie can be a major actor and factor in such an outcome, where they see their interests constrained by the existing authoritarian system, and especially when allies for reform are found within the regime.[35] Yet there is a distinction to be made between different parts of the bourgeoisie, or indeed the middle

class: 'small-scale entrepreneurs and the professional middle classes [may be] more likely to support democratization; the major owners of capital, especially those benefiting from state contracts and largesse, are much more likely to support continued authoritarian rule'.[36] Even so, cross-national evidence does present compelling evidence that the growth of the middle class *tends* to have a positive influence on the level of democracy.[37]

5.   Where 'civil society' more broadly speaking already had a significant level of organization, it is more likely that some form of democratization will be the outcome of this process.[38] A strong civil society is not a sufficient condition for democratization, however. Indeed, civil society is not necessarily 'democratic'. But even where parts of it are not, it can help constrain the power of the state. The development of civil society is itself shaped, of course, by many of the other factors discussed in this section – in particular by socio-economic development, existing political culture, and, crucially, by the willingness of the existing regime to tolerate it.[39]

6.   Compelling statistical and other evidence shows socio-economic development – encompassing economic development, literacy, urbanization, and technology – to be positively correlated both with greater levels of democracy directly and with the evolution of civil society, with the growth of the middle class and bourgeoisie, and hence again, indirectly with the potential for liberalization and democratization. Even so, these causal links are neither universal nor all-explanatory: they are neither necessary nor sufficient explanations for democratization.[40] Economic growth and increasing wealth *in itself* may not necessarily bring democratization.[41] Much depends on how that wealth is created and distributed (the 'rentier state' model is one cautionary example).[42] It also depends on how such growth and wealth, together with development more broadly, enhance 'crucial intervening variables' in political culture, civil society capability, class structure and the nature of the state.[43] But socio-economic development does widen the distribution of 'power resources'.[44] Technology proves important here both because it impacts on the economy, on international economic linkages, on social conditions and because it plays a role in the nature of communications within and outside the polity. Changes in technology thus change the distribution of power resources.[45]

7. Just as mere wealth or growth does not equate to better chances for democratization, low or reduced availability of rent also cannot, by itself, 'be considered a sufficient or even necessary condition for democratization':[46] some of the most authoritarian states have much less access to such rent than others that have been liberalizing.[47] But economic crisis, and in particular the fiscal crisis of the state, certainly can undercut the regime's power base, legitimacy, and ability to contain opposition.

8. There is no clear, linear short-term linkage between economic and political liberalization: indeed, some kinds of domestic economic liberalization may work simply to give room for selected domestic private interests while protecting them from outside competition. Even so, more far-reaching economic liberalization can have several effects that boost the chances of democratization:[48] (1) it puts resources (and networking options) in the hands of private entrepreneurs (helping to foster an independent bourgeoisie), at the same time as removing resources from the state (one part of the 'Power Resources' landscape); (2) at least in its 21st-century incarnation (World Trade Organization) it introduces transparency requirements that limit the ability of regimes to obscure their use of national funds; and (3) it often imposes at least short-term pain on certain groups, who may therefore be more likely to demand a say.[49]

9. Cultural factors, and in particular political culture, can play a significant role: indeed, elite and mass political culture – itself an evolving accretion of historical and other influences both local and external – has been recognized both as an important factor in its own right, and as an intervening variable in how other factors discussed here affect liberalization and democratization.[50] A culture of deference will tend to slow the emergence of effective, large-scale politically organized movement for reform; the same goes for a cultural preference for communal cohesion and stability over individual rights.[51] But examples abound to illustrate that this does not constitute an immovable obstacle: Diamond, Linz and Lipset – sympathetic to the notion of political culture as a factor – conclude from a wide range of case studies that 'It is misleading . . . to infer too much from the contours of a country's political culture at any particular point in time. . . . [P]olitical culture . . . is plastic and malleable over time. [It] is not destiny.'[52] The case of Latin America's escape

from authoritarianism, and the experience of Taiwan, Korea and Thailand, among others, show us as much – and in the process also demonstrate that 'religious' culture is a similarly inadequate predictor. Religion in its own right (as opposed to particular socio-politically shaped emanations) is a factor that is neither an inherent inhibitor or driver for change.[53] It is clear, however, that a political culture featuring social pluralism, as well as pragmatism and a tradition of compromise, offers more immediately fertile ground for the emergence of democratic practice.[54]

One important constituent variable in shaping political culture is colonial experience – either because in a few cases long-established colonial administration imparted both the structures and a long-term aspiration to democracy as a goal, or because in the absence of such a tradition, emerging elite politics and wider political mobilization were strongly shaped by the anti-colonial struggle rather than by any particular concern with pluralism or democratic governance. In the latter case, once state structures were captured by a post-colonial leadership, politics often contin-ued to be driven by this tradition as well as by the tendency for control of the state apparatus to be viewed as a means to ensure group or personal power, wealth and security.[55]

Political culture is also subject to the diffusion of ideas – as with the spread of democratic ideas from the French Revolution onwards, and as illustrated in the cases of Asia, Africa, Europe and Latin America.[56] Huntington and Schmitter, among others, have made the case that such diffusion (or 'contagion') tends to have the strongest effect when countries are 'geographically proximate and culturally similar'.[57]

10. The external environment, then, can have a crucial impact. This is so in terms of ideas (political, economic) from the surrounding region or beyond ('Zeitgeist'); in terms of the attitudes of particular outside actors which can inhibit or enhance the chances of political change; and in terms of the international political economy and the position of the country in question in it. The very fact of globaliza-tion – economic and political – tends to diminish the freedom of action regimes have and increases the pressures (and interests) for economic openness and transparency. Yet these external factors are not, in the main, a sufficient condition: they cannot by themselves

explain instances of far-reaching liberalization or democratization. With some problematic exceptions such as Afghanistan and Iraq, the external factors tend to work through (or are effective if joining with) domestic dynamics, such as an active civil society. They may also affect political culture in the longer term.[58]

11. Pre-existing regime types do seem to matter, both in terms of whether they are likely to allow openings to begin and in terms of how smoothly liberalization and democratization proceed thereafter.[59] A related finding is that where the economy and the system as a whole under the authoritarian phase were performing relatively well, subsequent progression from opening-up to democratization would appear to proceed more smoothly (in other cases upheaval may ensue, or, indeed, revolution).[60]

12. Elites' and rulers' calculations and actions matter. In the end, it is not just actors in society at large that are shaping developments under the influence of all of the factors listed above: it is also the elites' and the ruling regimes' perceptions, political culture, calculations and, finally, decisions that are crucial in co-determining what happens.

Both 'agency' and 'structure', then, matter; both material interests and ideational factors matter – but so do short-term conjunctural or unpredictable factors, the historical paths trodden by the societies and states in question and their external environments. The key insight should perhaps be that none of these factors is deterministic, and none of the different levels of explanation can work in isolation: all play (usually interrelated) roles, albeit in differing combinations at different times and different places.

Key Factors Relevant to Liberalization in the GCC States

Much of the above is directly and obviously relevant to the GCC states. Here, I elaborate further on the four key categories of factors: (1) socio-economic development, the middle class and civil society; (2) state and regime types; (3) cultural factors and political culture; and (4) external factors. Clearly, these categories overlap and interlink: it is precisely in their varying combinations and interlinkages that they achieve explanatory power.

Socio-economic development, the middle class and civil society

It is clear that society as a whole and the economy in particular have been changing enormously in the past few decades: polities and the economic systems they house have become incomparably larger and more complex. This has made traditional or neo-traditional mechanisms of consultation and access between ruled and rulers insufficient by themselves, leading to the necessity, and in some cases the demand, for more effective mechanisms.[61] Moreover, while oil wealth-induced change initially led to an increased hold of the state through rentier dynamics, this was cut across in two ways. First, the mid-1980s to the early 2000s saw a downturn in the demands/resources equation, something which even with current high oil prices remains a longer-term issue except for Qatar and the UAE. Second, there was a very gradual build-up of resources in the hands of wider society, increasingly visible from the 1990s – resources which, regardless of their initial roots in state distribution of rent, nevertheless became something that in turn allowed some groups to acquire some room for autonomous action. Mary Ann Tetreault has shown this to be the case for Kuwait,[62] and it is especially relevant with regard to the question of the bourgeoisie in these states.

Indeed, Giacomo Luciani has shown that Saudi Arabia has been witnessing the emergence of a genuine bourgeoisie of well over half a million people that is no longer quite so dependent on the state and that is involved in the production of value added – not merely accessing and circulating rent. The UAE and Kuwait feature a similar phenomenon at significant levels.[63] This bourgeoisie base their now significant degree of autonomy on very extensive wealth acquired initially largely from state expenditure but increasingly from productive investment and commercial activity – wealth that has in any case become a factor in its own right not dependent on government distribution.

The wealth of these polities may also make political liberalization easier and less threatening: it can help absorb some of the worst social grievances and may give regimes a window of opportunity, during which opening up the system need not lead to calls for their removal. This is compatible with Lipset's suggestion that political competition in wealthier societies is likely to be less fierce, allowing for a more consensual form of politics.[64] There is also a possible parallel with other cases of democratization that indicate that where the economy under the authoritarian phase was relatively well run, subsequent democratiza-tion processes may run more smoothly.

The growing pressures of economic globalization, combined with the desire of these states to be part of the WTO, and also with the domestic aim of achieving a measure of sustainable economic diversifica-tion, are all bringing greater pressures for economic liberalization. The consequences that this can have for political change are as valid for the GCC states as elsewhere: the demands of increased competitiveness lead to the rentier social contract being undermined, and the increased transparency required under WTO rules and international reporting requirements mean that financial management becomes more visible and open to scrutiny and protest, while the state's mechanisms for political distribution of rents becomes constrained.

Literacy, education and urbanization – factors recognized as highly signif-icant in the general literature on democratization[65] – have all increased dramatically in the GCC states over the past generation, and hence would point to a greater propensity to reform. It is true that, on their own, such factors are not necessarily a predictor for democratization, at least in the short-to-medium term, as the case of other Arab states shows: these indicators have also been rising fast in those states, without a concomitant movement up the democratization scale.[66]

Information and technology too have changed beyond recognition in the past half-century. Information has expanded exponentially, in particular through IT and other communications technology, and has thus exposed people increasingly to international and regional events and developments – even if the short-term democratizing impact remains very limited.[67] More broadly, technological development has had effects not only in this arena but throughout the economy and society, creating longer-term trends of change as seen elsewhere, and thus affecting most of the other categories of factors discussed here.

Civil society. Much of the above has a direct – both short- and long-term – impact on the nature and functioning of civil society. Civil society, as a consequence of many of the above factors and dynamics, has unquestionably been expanding and strengthening.[68] But it should be noted that this has gone hand in hand with already existing local forms of organization between the private/family level and that of the state. Kuwait has been the most studied example,[69] but forms of organized civil society life have increased in most of these states (least in Oman) in the form of journalists' associations, political groupings or platforms (even if not yet called parties), women's organizations, etc. They remain, of course, constrained, but nevertheless offer a greater potential base for political reform trends than has been the case. The development of civil society may also be influenced by some of the features of state and regime types discussed below, as well as by 'culture' and, arguably, external factors.

State and regime types: It's not just rent

Of course, these states do to a large extent remain rentier states, and regimes continue to derive from this a significant degree of autonomy and an ability to engage in 'group formation'. But, in addition to the fact that 'post-rentier' dynamics are emerging, four further features of these states and regimes could be put forward to underpin the argument that they might be more amenable to political evolution than has long been assumed of such supposedly 'anachronistic' and 'rentier' systems, and also more than 'republican' Arab systems.

i.   *Basic-level legitimacy of the states and the ruling families, deriving both from the local roots of these states, and from elements of traditional legitimacy.* There is a measure of local legitimacy for these polities, as they did not have to face the struggle faced by many of the regimes in suddenly and artificially created states throughout the Middle East and North Africa, where fierce nationalist and militarist assertion against domestic, as well as outside, actors became the norm. Even if most of the GCC states arguably owe their continued existence (and in some cases their recognition as separate polities) to protection by Britain, the latter built on local political realities. The elements of traditional legitimacy for the ruling families are linked to the above factor, and to continued rule by the founding families of these polities – a rule which consciously uses elements of tradition. The consequence of this is that regimes have less reason to fear that allowing some measure of reform need lead to upheaval and perhaps their overthrow.

ii. Except for the Saudi case, *these are small polities*, featuring *strong personal, kinship and other social networks* that cut across ideological and economic cleavages. Change may be more easily manageable here. Most key political actors will often know each other, and personal, family or social links will often connect even those who are political opponents. Such links and networks tend to take some of the edge off political conflict – arguably making for evolutionary rather than revolutionary responses to tensions. The impact of smallness on political climate has been identified by Springborg and Salamé, among others: small societies invite political participation, and their rulers can hardly suppress the intrinsic plurality by reference to some great regional leadership vision.[70] They also potentially provide a more conducive environment for the emergence of 'political moderation and accommodation at the mass level' which the earlier work of Almond, Verba and Lipset suggested are 'facilitated by structural patterns of social interaction that bring people together regularly across major social and political cleavages'[71] – something arguably facilitated further by cultural features such as the pattern of kinship ties cutting across class cleavages, the importance of personal relations, and social institutions such as the *majlis* and the *diwaniyya*. One key part of this is the nature of interactions at the elite level. Dahl suggested that the important ingredient of a political culture that features moderation, pragmatism and cooperation has most successfully been developed where, as in Sweden and Britain, 'the rules, the practices and the culture of competitive politics developed first among a small elite [connected by] ties of friendship, family, interest, class and ideology', which kept conflict manageable, before these practices and rules were gradually expanded to wider society.[72] Arguably the GCC states' elites provide the right environment for such interactions.

iii. *They are monarchies*: while this, too, has long been considered a feature predisposing a system to either immobilism or revolution, the evidence from the Middle East as well as elsewhere has in fact pointed the other way. Not only have Middle Eastern monarchies proved very resilient,[73] Kuwait, Bahrain and Qatar have shown that political liberalization and adaptation are anything but alien to these systems. Republican but autocratic presidents claiming ideological legitimacy must almost inevitably fall when their particular system and ideology is challenged either by a rival or by democratization.[74] By contrast, a monarchy may (re)fashion itself as above politics and survive democratization – especially if it is the main agent of such change and thus derives added legitimacy from it. Moreover, the *social* pluralism that has always been present and even encouraged in the small Gulf monarchies in particular, has in many ways been a factor in such dynamics, presided over, segmentally connected to or co-opted by the ruling family.[75]

iv.   A final, related factor that may cut both ways, is the extent to which these *societies and polities are structured on 'corporatist' or 'segmented clientelist' lines*.[76] On the one hand, of course, this has been argued to constitute a brake on real reform, as the entrenched (and actively reproduced) vertical divisions into 'corpora' or 'segments' leads both to potential opposition remaining divided, and to the state (the ruling family) creating or maintaining separate relationships of patronage. On the other hand, however, it means (1) that an element of pluralism is already an inherent and accepted part of the system (this goes alongside the accepted 'social pluralism' that characterizes monarchies as opposed to republican ideology-based systems); (2) that measures of liberalization are likely to reinforce this without leading the regime to fear united opposition – indeed some 'segments' of this socially plural patchwork may become de facto supporters of the wider system; and (3) that, therefore, this factor too may lead to the view that political liberalization measures can be a useful means of political 'decompression',[77] pre-empting domestic or external criticism and building new support bases.[78]

Of course, inherent in some of these factors is that it is political *liberalization*, rather than fully-fledged *democratization*, that the regimes may intend, and indeed that it is precisely because the danger of the former leading to a wholesale change of the system is low, that they are prepared to open up in the first place. I return to that question below.

Culture and political culture
A discussion of 'cultural' factors is problematic: the category contains a host of features and attitudes, differing among the populations and often competing within groups and individuals. Culture – whether local, national or regional, and whether 'social', 'religious' or 'political' – is always in flux and being created. Certainly *political* culture is also

constantly shaped by history and the other categories of factors discussed in this chapter.

The argument that 'Islam' could be an inhibitor for democratization is weak. Firstly, Islam as a category is multifarious – far more so than such arguments assume, and is only 'essentialized' at one's peril. Secondly, there is considerable work by Muslim political thinkers past and present that points in the opposite direction.[79] Thirdly, various Islamist opposition groups are demanding a greater say – even if not necessarily proposing a democratic style of government themselves, but in some cases doing exactly that.[80] And fourthly, the evidence of other Islamic countries (not least Indonesia, Turkey and Malaysia) is that Islam as such poses no obstacle; indeed, some of the most recent and most extensive comparative research based on the World Values Survey shows that 'residents of predominantly Muslim states voice democratic support at levels similar to residents of other countries [and] . . . greater support than residents of the former Soviet nations of East Europe'.[81] The extent to which particular interpretations of religious frameworks have inhibited political reform, therefore, depends on the socio-political domestic and external context within which such interpretations have evolved.[82]

Even so, other cultural factors may play a role – including a tradition of deference and the strength of kinship and tribal values as an organizing principle of society and the polity.[83] Arguably the stress on obedience to authority in Arab culture and society has at least partly shaped political culture and indeed political dynamics.[84] That this is not, however, a necessary or immutable block on democratic or liberalizing demands is demonstrated by the strength of such demands and active mobilizing behind them in Bahrain and Kuwait. Indeed, the evidence from the Arab world (as for the wider Muslim world) is that 'issues of democracy are well established in Arab political discourse',[85] even if they are by no means dominant. Of course regimes have used and played on such features of local culture to shore up their own rule.

By contrast, other features of local culture may potentially work in favour of liberalization and democratization. The cross-cutting personal, kinship and other social networks, allowing a pattern of elite bargaining and competition to evolve avoiding crisis or real strife, and the extent to which this may be more easily extended to wider society in very small polities, is one such element. Another links into political history.

Although Britain's (and later the US's) presence were certainly an important factor helping to shape the GCC states and regimes, they were never colonized. The radicalizing effect that some forms of colonization have often proved to have on subsequent political cultures therefore also remained absent (note the contrast of South Yemen!). By the same token, of course, there also was never the long-established colonial tradition, and hence direct experience, of pluralist practice that a country like India enjoyed, nor the consequent internalized aim of democratic organization of the independent polity.

Political culture as a factor of course links into that of 'civil society' and into other factors discussed in this chapter: it both influences and may be changed by them. This is as true in the states of the GCC as it is elsewhere – and both global and regional 'diffusion', 'demonstration' or 'contagion' effects may contribute to it.

External factors

Gause has argued that the survival and continued authoritarian control of Gulf monarchies – and by implication their ability to resist pressures for political liberalization – must be explained largely with reference to external protection.[86] Yet this cannot be a sufficient explanation. Not only is it precisely in some of these Western-allied regimes that reforms *are* taking place; more stringent authoritarianism in fact characterizes several republican systems that do *not* benefit from any major such external support; and several of those monarchical regimes that did fall by the wayside were supported by the US and the West – in fact they fell in part precisely because of that close Western link. We do, therefore, need to keep a prime focus on the domestic environment: the external factor can either facilitate or obstruct political liberalization, not determine outcomes on its own.[87]

Clearly the GCC regimes cannot count on quite the same level of unquestioned support and protection, regardless of domestic arrangements, that characterized the relationship with the West during the Cold War; by the same token, there has been a significantly higher level of proactive pressure from the US and, in different ways, the EU over the question of political reform. But this is limited in three ways: (1) the outside world has less leverage over these regimes than over poorer states;[88] (2) overly brusque forms of pressure, especially combined with the lack of credibility from which the US in particular suffers in the region, may be

[25]

counter-productive and may be easily dismissed domestically; and (3) the EU's level of clear and united commitment to its stated aim of fostering democratization and good governance is open to question, to say the least.[89] Even so, there is unquestionably a greater level of outside pressure both from specific actors and in wider, 'Zeitgeist' terms.

This is combined with economic globalization and the desire of these states to enter the WTO for both economic and prestige reasons. The potential political consequences are neither straightforward nor certain, but they certainly act to limit a regime's array and extent of economic resources to be deployed in pursuit of political ends, they place relatively more such resources in the hands of actors in society, they necessitate relatively greater transparency, and, through the demands economic competitiveness places on the workforce, they almost inevitably generate a greater desire for a say in how the economy and the polity are run.

The *regional* environment is important in a variety of ways.[90] The effects can either enhance or inhibit the prospects for political reform; they can do so either by affecting elites' perceptions and calculations, or by influencing popular perceptions and aspirations; and they can arise from, and affect, both material facts/interests, and ideas. With regard to the latter, it is worth, when considering the Gulf, remembering Huntington's and Schmitter's suggestion that 'demonstration' or 'contagion' effects tend to be strongest among 'geographically proximate and culturally similar' countries.[91]

Events in the wider region, including most prominently in Palestine, Iraq and Lebanon, have been making their influence felt, along with the variously interpreted shadow of Iran. On the one hand, some of these developments have raised fears over the effects of political openings and especially steps towards democratization. Ruling families and moderate Sunni reformist elites inevitably became concerned by the apparent risks of chaos (as in Iraq), a takeover of radical Islamist forces, and the rise of the Shia as a divisive factor in their own polities.[92]

On the other hand, there can be little doubt that the example of the genuine elections with mass participation in Palestine and Iraq, and the effects of 'people power' in Lebanon, may inspire sections of the population (not least, indeed, the Shia), by showing that popular power is not a complete chimera, nor simply a Western imposition. The Sunni politicians of Hamas in Palestine have set a highly significant precedent, with clear evidence of a shift towards pluralism in that organization. If allowed to succeed, this might yet create one of the most important demonstration effects of all.[93] Even in Iraq, the insurgency and the rejectionist position of the hardline Association of Muslim Scholars should not obscure the fact that neither was able to stop Sunni Iraqis participating in large numbers in the elections for the first permanent parliament. Moreover, even the Association is not against elections in principle (only 'under occupation'), and important Sunni organizations, politicians and religious leaders have come to support the new democratizing model.[94] Reliable surveys of how these factors changed perceptions at the popular level in the GCC are still lacking, but there is no reason to assume that regional developments will not add to the pressures from below.

The Limits to Gulf Openings: Liberalization without Democratization?

It is clear, then, that some significant changes have been taking place in the GCC states, and that these can at least in part be explained by reference to some of the comparative insights laid out above. Does this, however, make them more than top-down liberalization measures that can be reversed, or at least can be stopped from leading any further on the road towards democratization – defined as 'political participation, accountability and pluralism'?

It is true that wealth and some of the other regime strengths enumerated above mean that there will be temporarily less pressure to democratize in such systems. But when, as pressures inevitably rise, it *does* become judged necessary to adjust the system, these regimes have the flexibility to adapt without risking either chaos or the overthrow of the monarchy. They are less brittle, in other words, than regimes such as Saddam Hussein's and several other Arab republican systems. They are, also, not trapped in the legacy of populist authoritarianism and grand ideological claims that have typified such republican regimes.[95]

Whether they do adapt depends, of course, on a decision by the monarch and the ruling family. Yet from the evidence of recent reforms it would appear that some recognition of the need to adapt is present among most of the royal families in the Gulf. Elite choices are as crucial here as in most other cases of democratization that did not come about by revolution (and arguably there as well, through regime *mis*calculation).[96]

Evidence for the limits to reform

By the same token, there is also plenty of evidence that rulers do intend to control any change and generally do intend to limit its extent. In Saudi Arabia, the municipal elections did not impart any real power to those elected beyond functional matters of local importance, and they were balanced by the half of the councils that were appointed; all of the key powers remain in the hands of the royal family. In Kuwait, the Al Sabah remains the ultimate arbiter and continues to dominate successive cabinets, while the formation of political parties remains outside the law. In Bahrain, the King introduced a second, appointed chamber with equal powers into the constitution, thus ensuring a large measure of control (and causing the Shia opposition to boycott the 2002 elections). There were reports, also, of attempts to shape the outcome of the 2006 elections.[97]

In the UAE there was, until late 2006, no real participatory mechanism at all – except in a functional and consultative way when it comes to the business community in Dubai, in the manner of the relationship between a CEO and managers/investors. The impact of the December 2006 elections and Sheikh Khalifa's earlier announcement that the Federal National Council's (FNC) size and powers were to be expanded, remains unclear: the emirate electoral colleges that elected 20 of the 40 FNC seats were themselves appointed, rather than elected; nor is there much likelihood of the new FNC being really allowed to hold the key royal decision-makers to account or block their main wishes. The seven Emirs, at any rate, remain the sovereign arbiters of the law and political dispensation within their own emirates.[98]

In Qatar, the provision for elections in the new constitution has yet to be implemented: expectations that elections would be held in 2004 have been adjusted to 2007. In addition, statements by the two key people – the Emir and the Foreign Minister – have become markedly more cautious: strong language continues to be used about the need for democratization and the need to make this happen on a clear timetable, but at the same time, the way in which this was introduced, from 2005, has failed to be at all specific about such a schedule, while simultaneously introducing comments about making sure the implementation of reforms was compatible with local circumstances.[99] Similarly, 2004 saw the introduction of a law that severely constrained workers' ability to organize or take strike action, and in 2005 the new Associations Law made clear that societies would not be allowed to deal with political issues and all their activities would be monitored by the ministry of Civil Service Affairs and Housing. In any case, with one-third of the 45-member parliament to be appointed by the Emir, and a two-thirds majority needed to vote out ministers or to overturn Emiri decrees issued when parliament is not in session, parliamentary power remains significantly hemmed in.

In *Oman*, the elected *Majlis al-Shura* is balanced by the appointed State Council and by the limited purview of members' powers (apart from Defence, National Security and Foreign Affairs, Finance is also excluded from its remit, and it cannot initiate, only comment on, legislation). Any discussion of further opening up takes place self-consciously in a context where all key decisions are ultimately dependent on the Sultan's word; this finds expression in the reluctance of Assembly members to fully exercise the powers they do have. The limited perceived relevance of the *Majlis* may have been one reason for the relatively low voter registration for the first universal elections in 2003 (262,000 out of 800,000 eligible).[100]

There is a prima facie case, then, for accepting Brumberg's argument that what we are witnessing is intrinsically limited to the production of 'liberalized autocracy'.[101] In this view, what is happening is no more than the securing of the autocratic systems in a different garb, with greater room for the expression of social and some political pluralism but with ultimate control remaining in the hands of the rulers, in order to take the domestic and external pressure off regimes. Indeed, for the monarchies of the GCC, liberalization may not only take the sting out of immediate pressures, but may in effect serve as a 'divide-and-rule' tactic, under which the opposition or its various strands become 'submerged' in a more diverse number of social groups now given access to a limited form of political participation. The various groups and representatives may both acquire a stake in the system and continue, separately, to seek the ear and favour of the monarch, who remains the ultimate arbiter and source of authority.[102]

So reform and liberalization do not equate to democratization –

nor do they necessarily lead to it. The constraints referred to above mirror factors that elsewhere, and especially across the Middle East, have been recognized as obstructing moves beyond the limits of 'liberalizing' or 'modernizing autocracy' or 'political decompression'.[103] Three central and intimately interrelated factors are:

- evolving variants of rentierism (intertwined with segmented clientelism in the Saudi case, and more generally corporatist features);
- the limited and particular character of civil society with its own divisions, not least between an arguably illiberal majority and a liberal minority (even if both want a greater say and greater transparency); and
- a middle class lacking a united political purpose.

It is in such an environment especially that regimes may use liberalization to co-opt and/or divide actual and potential opposition forces most successfully, without intending to cede their position as the ultimate source of authority. Brumberg has argued that, in fact, 'the very success of liberalized autocracy can become a trap for even the most well-intentioned leader.'[104]

To be sure, it is indeed possible that such will be the future of the GCC's political systems, and such is indeed likely to be the ruling families' intention. One might note, of course, that some parts of these states' societies would in fact welcome such an outcome, provided demands about greater transparency and good governance were met.

A more positive spin?

Can these 'modernizing autocracies' escape this trap? While it does seem probable that they will move further in the direction of liberalization, it is not very likely that some, at least (including Saudi Arabia, the UAE and Oman), will move beyond the confines of 'liberalized autocracy' for at least a generation. Even so, there are both generic and specific reasons to think that these polities need not *necessarily* remain trapped there.

The generic reasons include that, just as happened in Europe in transitions from absolutism, and in the more recent Latin American transitions from autocracy, limited moves made by ruling elites as a tactic of 'decompression' can, in combination with growing pressures from below, lead such trends to slip beyond the control of what these elites originally intended, especially when alliances develop between key social groups and elements within the regime.[105] In some sense, this may already have begun to happen in Kuwait, and it may perhaps be in its initial stages in Bahrain. In Rustow's terms, Kuwait might be seen as in the phase of a 'pact' between rulers and political forces in society – i.e. the second of his three stages, having reached a stalemate in the first stage where the regime initially responds to pressures by tactical, polarizing use of democratizing gestures. It has not quite yet moved to the stage of 'habituation' which could bring more recognizably and sustainably democratic practice. Bahrain in these terms would perhaps just be crossing the boundary line between the first and second stages.[106]

Baaklini, Denoeux and Springborg, for the case of legislative politics in the Arab world, have suggested a slightly different scheme, which I interpret as starting from roughly the end of Rustow's first phase – i.e. when negotiated transition begins. Their first stage is in essence a 'pact' (al-mithaq) (often officially referred to as such) between rulers and other groups; a second phase is 'national dialogue' (al-hiwar); this is in turn followed by the assertion of legislative authority (they accept, of course, that reversals are possible).[107] In these terms, I would place Kuwait well into the second phase; Bahrain just crossing from the first to the second; Qatar in an advanced version of the first; Saudi Arabia in the process of working out a *mithaq* (interestingly using a non-binding process formally labelled *hiwar watani* as a means to explore what a subsequent phase might involve); Oman in the very early stages of a *mithaq*-like situation; and the UAE, perhaps, just entering the first phase – although in the latter case it should be noted that, as electoral politics are hardly the prime concern of the national population, perhaps we have an unstated, implicit *mithaq* here of a different nature.

In turn, the underlying cause for this evolution would be the combined effects of the changes wrought by economic and technological development, changing political economies and class or group formation and shifts in political culture, which may over the long term have the effect predicted by much of the comparative literature reviewed earlier. The presence of an emerging national bourgeoisie holds out the possibility of deeper and longer-term reform dynamics emerging from below. Even if there is no consensus within these societies over where such reform should lead, the common factor is a desire for greater transparency and a greater say in some form.

To put it differently, the combined effects of a changing distribution of power resources and changing political cultures – both driven by domestic as well as external factors – may well eventually result in changing political dispensations that include significant elements of political participation, accountability and pluralism. Practices and institutions that are being gradually established may take on a life of their own: there has been some evidence of this with the judiciary in Egypt, Moroccan electoral politics, the parliament in Kuwait and even the cautious drive towards a greater role in decision-making from within the Saudi *Majlis al-Shura*. Indeed, even imperfect elections and hobbled parliaments may themselves increasingly add to civil society's tools and change the flavour of politics: even where the executive attempts to control them, parliaments often seem to contribute to the process of transition.[108] It is also conceivable that a key factor in other processes of democratization – viz. allies for further reform emerging *within* the ruling elite – will become a reality in the GCC states: indeed there are such potential allies in all of them.

Yet the relatively higher levels of political and economic resources available to the regimes when compared to other non-democratic systems mean that this is indeed likely to be a long-term prospect, stretching well into the 21st century. Gradualism, in other words, is both likely and feasible. One is also reminded here, of course, of the notion proposed by Dahl, Almond and Verba, discussed earlier, that elite-level 'preparation' of democratic practice and 'culture' has historically proved a useful basis for effective later adoption by other groups in society – even if the GCC states are neither Sweden nor Britain.[109]

It is true that, just as in the European precedent of centuries, there may be frequent setbacks when the regime attempts to reverse the tide. This indeed has been the pattern rightly identified, and feared for the future, by Brumberg. But that may not be a sustainable strategy in the long run if those earlier precedents are anything to go by (they do, of course, also tell us once again that the dynamics producing real democratization may only bear fruit in the much longer term).

At a more specific level, at least *some* of the current reform evidence in different GCC states leaves room for a more positive spin than my earlier qualifications might suggest.

In Kuwait, the parliament has been able to frustrate a number of important policy initiatives of the ruling family – holding up women's right to vote (something personally pushed by the Emir) until a change of heart by Islamist groupings in 2005; blocking, for the time being, any progress on the plans to open northern Kuwait to investment by international energy firms ('Project Kuwait'); and, in 2006, rejecting the government's preferred model for electoral redistricting – leading the Emir to dissolve the assembly and new elections to be held in June 2006. Parliament had, of course, already acquired the right to question royal and other ministers, and had in effect forced a number of resignations over the previous decade. In fact, the direct trigger for the latest dissolution was a demand, for the first time in Kuwait's history, to question the prime minister, Sheikh Nasir Muhammad Al Sabah, appointed only months before by the new Emir. But a significant new feature was that a genuine popular movement emerged over the redistricting issue, headed by relatively younger figures from outside the usual political circles. It clearly modelled its tactics on the 'colour' movements in Eastern Europe and elsewhere, holding rallies (using orange) in support of a 5-district model (from 25) that would make representation fairer and also cut the potential for corruption – indeed arguably stiffening the parliamentarians' spine in the same cause (in the process, the Constitutional Court struck down a law that limited the right to such gatherings). Following the elections which brought a majority of 34 MPs into a parliament which could on some issues be associated with 'opposition',[110] the new government did adopt the 5-district model: on this issue, at least, the opposition was united, and could defeat the government had the latter tried to hold out.

This parliamentary flexing of muscles was inspired in part by the civil society support, and in part by the confidence deriving from its crucial role in the succession of Sheikh Sabah in January 2006. Following the death of Sheikh Jabir, the automatic succession of the ailing Crown Prince was blocked due both to an opposing majority within the family itself and parliamentary insistence that he had to take the oath in person in the assembly – for which he was too ill. Sheikh Saad's last-minute agreement to stand down came too late, as parliament had already voted to strip him of his title and to anoint Sheikh Sabah as his successor. This was clearly the outcome preferred by most, but the family's perceived need to seek recourse to parliament's constitutional role being deployed in managing the succession crisis is likely to have been a significant point in the emirate's political evolution. It will now be difficult for the Al Sabah to diminish or override parliament again quite as easily as happened periodically until Iraq's invasion.

That is not to say that parliament is now supreme: the Al Sabah retains key levers of power (including the key 'power ministries'), and can continue to count on a number of pro-government 'service MPs', as well as on the ex officio membership made up by the ministers. This is especially important given that 'the opposition' only really exists as a united group on a few issues. But the redistricting episode has also shown that some senior members of the ruling family now feel there is merit in reform.[111] Kuwait does gradually seem to be moving beyond the confines of the 'liberalized autocracy' model.

In Bahrain, the main, largely Shia-based, opposition group *Al-Wifaq* decided to reverse the stance it adopted in 2002 and participate in the 2006 election, judging that there was perhaps after all a genuine chance of gradually reforming the system – and at least initially already some policies and legislation – from within. Notwithstanding alleged irregularities, they won 17 out of 40 seats – i.e. all those they contested.[112] Even with the continued splits within the ruling family over the pace of reform, and the recurrent clampdowns on civil society activism, it would seem unlikely that the regime will feel either able or willing to suppress the new vibrant political society and discourse sufficiently to stop further gradual change.

In Qatar, the in-built limitations of the constitution still leave a remarkable change in place, once the parliament is up and running in 2007: legislation *can* be pushed through with a simple majority and even if the Emir sends it back if he disagrees, parliament *can* then overrule him with a two-thirds majority. While it is true that the one-third of appointed members make it less likely that such a scenario would obtain, it is by no means impossible. The Emir can in extremis suspend the implementation of such legislation for some time if he deems it in the interests of the country, but clearly, extensive use of such intervention would soon bring the system into disrepute and would presumably be avoided if at all possible. Against the background of a rather uncontentious domestic political climate (with the partial exception of foreign affairs), it is possible that the parliament will gradually begin to be allowed to spread its wings, moving in the direction of Kuwait's political system.

Even in Saudi Arabia, there is a particularly interesting development in the evolution of the *Majlis al-Shura*'s stance on matters of taxation:

in the words of one acute Saudi observer, the pattern of the Council's decisions shows it 'has taken a decision in principle not to agree to any imposition of taxes of higher fees unless they get a say over expenditure';[113] a telling reflection of the old 'no taxation without representation' maxim. The nature and extent of some of the debate in the media and elsewhere, about the desirability of expanding elections to the *Majlis*, also indicates a changing political culture and climate that may support longer-term gradual evolution.[114]

It is not beyond the bounds of possibility that even in the UAE, local experiments with partial election of emirate councils (perhaps first in Sharjah) may change the flavour of political life – exerting an effect both through electing, in turn, the members of the mooted new FNC, and through demonstration effects in neighbouring emirates. Even for the severely limited exercise electing 20 FNC members by an approved list of 6689 electors in December 2006 (turn-out among those electors was around 70%), there was real competition, along with official and semi-official suggestions that this was a trial run that should eventually lead to universal suffrage.[115] While there has been no groundswell of opinion pushing for participation, the issue has nevertheless been discussed for some years among some of the intelligentsia (and even some members of ruling families), especially in emirates such as Sharjah and Ras al-Khaimah.[116] It is perhaps telling, also, that the Secretary-General of the FNC, Muhammad al-Mazrui, felt free at a recent conference to make the hardly veiled point that 'whenever a legislature has more authority, it performs better'.[117] Sheikh Khalifa once again promised to expand the FNC's powers: for now it retains merely an advisory role.

Finally, in Oman, too, a number of tentatively positive indications can be gleaned. Even amidst the general reluctance to explore the boundaries of the permissible, there nevertheless appears to be an expectation on the part of at least *some* well-placed officials, parliamentary officials and assembly members, that the elected *Majlis al-Shura* will, within the next ten years, have acquired significantly expanded powers – possibly even beginning to stretch, according to some, into the area of foreign affairs. The fact that some dissenting voices, expressing frustration at the pointlessness of much of the assembly's activity, feel able to give their assessment quite candidly, even from significant positions in the institutions of government or parliament itself, is perhaps in itself another indication of a gradual and partial change in elite political culture. It is also certainly the case that – as in the other GCC states – some members of the royal family are genuinely reformist-minded. And the very experience in 2003 of technically fair elections under universal suffrage with quite extensive competition and at least some results not in line with expected local tribal dominance, may in itself feed into modestly changing mass political culture.[118] That said, the prospects for tangible moves anytime soon towards the key components of a democratic system – political participation, accountability and pluralism – do remain faint at best.

Conclusion

The political systems of the Gulf oil monarchies are experiencing varying levels of pressure from continuing change in their domestic and external environments. Yet their material and legitimacy resources remain relatively abundant so a sudden wholesale change is unlikely. Further liberalizing reform is likely in the short-to-medium term. The factors militating against further change may leave most of these polities trapped in the 'liberalized autocracy' stage, yet neither can the possibility be dismissed that they might eventually move beyond it as, indeed, Kuwait is already doing. As suggested elsewhere for the case of Saudi Arabia, '*If* that happens, it will come as the result of a very gradual process, driven and signalled as much by the incremental expansion of representative institutions' grip on day-to-day and technical decision-making, and of the habit-forming effect of even limited exercises in political participation and discussion, as by grand political departures.'[119] Such an evolving new politics will also doubtless continue to include a variety of specifically local features, as a result of its inevitable cultural and political path-dependence.

NOTES

1 This is a significantly revised and updated version of a somewhat longer study under the same title, first published in 2006 by Durham University as the Sir William Luce Paper No. 6 (http://eprints.dur.ac.uk/archive/00000222).
2 See Gerd Nonneman, 'Patterns of Political Liberalization: Explanations and Modalities', in Nonneman (ed.), *Political and Economic Liberalization:*

Dynamics and Linkages in Comparative Perspective (Boulder: Lynne Rienner, 1996), pp. 45–62: at 45–46.

3 See for instance Madawi Al-Rasheed, *A History of Saudi Arabia* (Cambridge: Cambridge University Press, 2002); Mary Ann Tetreault, *Stories of Democracy: Politics and Society in Contemporary Kuwait* (New York: Columbia University Press, 2000); Russell Lucas, 'Monarchical Authoritarianism: Survival and Political Liberalization in a Middle Eastern Regime Type', in *International Journal of Middle Eastern Studies*, Vol. 36 (2004), pp. 103–119; John Peterson, 'The Emergence of Post-Traditional Oman', Durham Middle East Papers No. 78 (Sir William Luce Fellowship Paper No. 5), Durham University, January 2005; Christopher Davidson, *The United Arab Emirates: A Study in Survival* (Boulder: Lynne Rienner, 2005), Chapter 2: 'The Survival of Monarchy'; Lisa Anderson on the invention of tradition in 'Dynasts and Nationalists: Why Middle Eastern Monarchies Survive', in Joseph Kostiner (ed.), *Middle East Monarchies: The Challenge of Modernity* (Boulder: Lynne Rienner, 2000), pp. 53–69; and Khaldoun Al Naqeeb, 'How Likely is Democracy in the Gulf?', in John Fox et al. (eds.), *Globalization and the Gulf* (New York: Routledge, 2006), pp. 127–140.

4 Hence the use of terms such as 'neo-patrimonialism' and 'neo-patriarchy' (see e.g. Hisham Sharabi, *Neo-patriarchy: A Theory of Distorted Change in the Arab World* (New York: Oxford University Press, 1988).

5 Peterson, 'The Emergence of Post-Traditional Oman'.

6 John Peterson, 'Legitimacy and Political Change in Yemen and Oman', in *Orbis*, Vol. 27, No. 4 (1984), pp. 971–998: p. 985.

7 Jill Crystal, *Oil and Politics in the Gulf: Rulers and Merchants in Kuwait and Qatar*, 2nd edn (Cambridge: Cambridge University Press, 1995).

8 See Gerd Nonneman, *Governance, Human Rights, and the Case for Political Adaptation in the Gulf* (RSC policy paper 01–3) (Florence: Robert Schuman Centre, European University Institute, 2001) (http://www.iue.it/RSCAS/WP-Texts/01_03p.pdf).

9 Jill Crystal and Abdullah al-Shayeji, 'The Pro-democracy Agenda in Kuwait', in Bahgat Korany, Rex Brynen and Paul Noble (eds.), *Political Liberalization and Democratization in the Arab World, Vol. 2 – Comparative Experiences* (Boulder: Lynne Rienner, 1998), pp. 101–126.

10 Tetreault, *Stories of Democracy*.

11 See Guido Steinberg, 'The Wahhabi Ulama and the Saudi State: 1745 to the Present', in Paul Aarts and Gerd Nonneman (eds.), *Saudi Arabia in the Balance: Political Economy, Society, Foreign Affairs* (New York/London: New York University Press/Hurst & Co., 2005), pp. 11–34.

12 Tetreault, *Stories of Democracy*.

13 See in particular Andrzej Kapiszewski, 'Elections and Parliamentary Activity in the GCC States', in Abdulhadi Khalaf and Giacomo Luciani (eds.), *Constitutional Reform and Political Participation in the Gulf* (Dubai: Gulf Research Center, 2006), pp. 88–131; and Giovanni Parolin, 'Generations of Gulf Constitutions: Paths and Perspectives', in Khalaf and Luciani (eds.), *Constitutional Reform and Political Participation in the Gulf*, pp. 51–87. Also Michael Herb, 'Princes, Parliaments, and the Prospects for Democracy in the Gulf', in Marsha Pripstein Posusney and Michele Penner Angrist (eds.),

Authoritarianism in the Middle East (Boulder: Lynne Rienner, 2005), pp. 169–191; and, on developments in 2005, Hassanain Tawfiq Ibrahim, 'Internal Political Developments in the GCC States: An Overview', in *Gulf Yearbook 2005–2006* (Dubai: Gulf Research Center, 2006), pp. 15–69.

14 For details see Kapiszewski, 'Elections and Parliamentary Activity in the GCC States', pp. 98–107; Parolin, 'Generations of Gulf Constitutions', pp. 61–84.

15 For details see Kapiszewski, 'Elections and Parliamentary Activity in the GCC States', pp. 107–114; Parolin, 'Generations of Gulf Constitutions', pp. 61–84.

16 *Arab News*, 16 December 2006.

17 See Andrew Rathmell and Kirsten Schulze, 'Political Reform in the Gulf: The Case of Qatar', in *Middle Eastern Studies*, Vol. 36, No. 4 (October 2000), pp. 47–62.

18 Author's observation and interviews in Doha, Qatar, over several visits between 2002–2005; Mary Anne Weaver, 'Democracy by Decree', *The New Yorker*, 11 November 2002; 'Address of HH Shaikh Hamad Bin Khalifa Al-Thani, Third Qatar Conference on Democracy and Free Trade, Doha, 14 April 2002'; 'Mideast Reforms Cannot Wait, says Emir' [Sheikh Hamad's speech to the Fourth Qatar Conference on Democracy and Free Trade], *The Peninsula*, 6 April 2004; 'Address of HH Sheikh Hamad Bin Khalifa Al-Thani, Fourth Qatar Conference on Democracy and Free Trade, Doha, March 29, 2005'; and *The Peninsula*, 29, 30, 31 March 2005. See also Kapiszewski, 'Elections and Parliamentary Activity in the GCC States', pp. 114–117; Parolin, 'Generations of Gulf Constitutions', pp. 61–84.

19 See Mohammad al-Muhanna, 'The Saudi Majlis ash-Shura: Domestic Functions and International Role' (PhD thesis, Institute of Middle Eastern & Islamic Studies, Durham University, 2005). This is also the only study to provide comprehensive detail on the nature, extent and effect of the work of the committees, and to survey systematically Majlis members' views on their own powers.

20 Strikingly also, a debate was held on Saudi TV in early April on the merits of elections for the Council (even if both invited speakers advocated gradualism, thus mirroring the majority view among members). *Saudi Gazette*, 13 April 2005; *Arab News*, 13 April 2005; SPA dispatch 13 April 2005; Economist Intelligence Unit, *Saudi Arabia Report*, May 2005, pp. 12–16; for the views of Council members themselves see also Al-Muhanna, 'The Saudi Majlis ash-Shura'.

21 Economist Intelligence Unit, *Saudi Arabia Report*, May 2005, pp. 12–16.

22 The Dialogue, which has covered the themes of national unity, fighting extremism, youth, women, 'dealing with world cultures' and education, has its own website (http://www.kacnd.org/), with an English-language version also launched in September 2006 (http://www.kacnd.org/eng/).

23 Al-Muhanna, 'The Saudi Majlis ash-Shura', chapter 4; and Abdulaziz Al Fahad, 'Ornamental Constitutionalism: The Saudi Basic Law of Governance', paper for the Sixth Mediterranean Social and political Research Meeting, Montecatini, 16–20 March 2005, Workshop 13.

24 Robert Vitalis, *America's Kingdom* (pre-publication version, 2005, posted on http://cas.uchicago.edu/workshops/cpolit/papers/vitalis.doc).

25 *Saudi Gazette*, 13 and 22 April 2005; *Arab News*, 13–29 April 2005; SPA dispatch 13 April 2005; Economist Intelligence Unit, *Saudi Arabia Report*, May 2005, pp. 12–16; 'Third Round Balloting Marks End of Landmark

Elections', on Saudi–US Relations, 23 April 2005 (www.saudi-us-relations.org/
newsletter2005/saudi-relations-interest-04-23.html) (plus the links offered there);
and *Gulf News*, 24 April 2005, 'Citizens debate Islamists' win in municipal
elections'.

26 For detail and an assessment on the Saudi reform process, see Paul Aarts and
Gerd Nonneman, 'A Triple Nexus: Ideology, Economy, Foreign Policy and the
Outlook for the Saudi Polity', in Aarts and Nonneman (eds.), *Saudi Arabia in
the Balance*, pp. 433–455, especially pp. 443–455; also Kapiszewski, 'Elections
and Parliamentary Activity in the GCC States', pp. 90–98; Parolin, 'Generations
of Gulf Constitutions', pp. 61–84; and Amr Hamzawy, 'The Saudi Labyrinth:
Evaluating the Current Political Opening' (Carnegie Endowment, Middle East
Series, No. 68, April 2006).

27 Interviews with officials and members of the *Majlis al-Shura* and *Majlis al-Dawla*
in the course of several visits in 2003–2004. See also Jeremy Jones, *Negotiating
Change: The New Politics of the Middle East* (London: I.B. Tauris, 2006),
chapter on Oman; and Kapiszewski, 'Elections and Parliamentary Activity in
the GCC States', pp. 117–120; and Parolin, 'Generations of Gulf Constitutions',
pp. 61–84.

28 Observation and interviews in Oman, October 2003.

29 The best recent description and in-depth analysis of the UAE's political system is
Davidson, *The United Arab Emirates*, especially chapter 4: 'Domestic Pathologies
and the Political Process', pp. 185–250.

30 Ibrahim, 'Internal Political Developments in the GCC States', pp. 15–16, 26–27.

31 AFP dispatch 16 December 2006.

32 This insight recurs throughout much of the literature, from Seymour Martin
Lipset onwards: see the survey in Nonneman, 'Patterns of Political
Liberalization' (incl. note 1, p. 60); also John Markoff, *Waves of Democracy:
Social Movements and Social Change* (Thousand Oaks: Pine Forge Press, 1996).

33 Adam Przeworski, *Democracy and the Market: Political and Economic Reforms in
Eastern Europe and Latin America* (Cambridge: Cambridge University Press,
1991); Markoff, *Waves of Democracy*; and N. Hamilton and E. Kim, 'Economic
and Political Liberalization in South Korea and Mexico', *Third World Quarterly*,
Vol. 14 (1993), No. 1, pp. 109–136: p. 113.

34 This emerges from any number of cases studies and historical surveys – see for
instance Diamond, Linz and Lipset, 'Introduction', in Ghassan Salamé (ed.),
Democracy without Democrats? The Renewal of Politics in the Muslim World
(London: I.B. Tauris, 1994), and Markoff, *Waves of Democracy*.

35 The role of the bourgeoisie is key in Barrington Moore's *The Social Origins of
Dictatorship and Democracy* (London: Allen Lane, 1967); see also Lipset, *Political
Man* (Baltimore: Johns Hopkins University Press, 1981); Robert Dahl, *Polyarchy:
Participation and Opposition* (New Haven: Yale University Press, 1988).

36 Diamond, Linz and Lipset, 'Introduction', p. 23; also John Waterbury,
'Democracy without Democrats?' in Ghassan Salamé (ed.), *Democracy without
Democrats? The Renewal of Politics in the Muslim World* (London: I.B. Tauris,
1994), pp. 23–47.

37 See e.g. Renske Doorenspleet, 'Political Democracy: A Cross-National Quantitative
Analysis of Modernization and Dependency Theories', in *Acta Politica:
International Journal of Political Science*, Vol. 32 (1997), No. 4, pp. 347–374.

38 Guillermo O'Donnell and Philippe Schmitter, *Transitions from Authoritarian Rule: Tentative Conclusions about Uncertain Democracies* (Baltimore: Johns Hopkins University Press, 1986); and Diamond, Linz and Lipset, 'Introduction', pp. 27–31.

39 Rex Brynen, Bahgat Korany and Paul Noble, 'Introduction: Theoretical Perspectives on Arab Liberalization and Democratization', in Brynen, Korany and Noble (eds.), *Political Liberalization and Democratization in the Arab World: Theoretical Perspectives* (Boulder: Lynne Rienner 1995), pp. 3–28: at 10–14.

40 Dorenspleet, 'Political Democracy'. Lipset, *Political Man*; id., 'Some Social Requisites for Democracy: Economic Development and Political Legitimacy', in *American Political Science Review*, Vol. 53 (1959), No. 1, pp. 69–105. For the effect on civil society and, hence, on democratization, see also Diamond, Linz and Lipset, 'Introduction: What Makes for Democracy?', pp. 22–24, 30.

41 This claim was originally made by Seymour Martin Lipset, *Political Man*, 2nd edn (London: Heinemann, 1983, although subsequently qualified in Larry Diamond, Juan Linz and Seymour Martin Lipset, 'Introduction: What makes for Democracy?', in Diamond, Linz and Lipset (eds.), *Politics in Developing Countries*, 2nd edn (Boulder: Lynne Rienner, 1995), pp. 1–66: p. 24.

42 Giacomo Luciani, 'Allocation versus Production States', in Giacomo Luciani (ed.), *The Arab State* (London: Routledge, 1988), pp. 65–84.

43 Diamond, Linz and Lipset, 'Introduction', p. 24.

44 Tatu Vanhanen and Richard Kimber, 'Predicting and Explaining Democratization in Eastern Europe', in Geoffrey Pridham and Tatu Vanhanen (eds.), *Democratization in Eastern Europe: Domestic and International Perspectives* (London: Routledge, 1994), pp. 63–96, especially p. 67. Kimber and Vanhanen constructed an Index made up of three sub-indices: the 'index of occupational diversification' (taking in the percentage of urban population and the percentage of non-agricultural population); the 'index of knowledge distribution' (taking in proportion of students, and literacy levels); and 'index of distribution of economic resources' (measured by percentage share of family farms out of total area of holdings, and degree of centralization of non-agricultural resources).

45 In Eastern Europe, regimes 'were ultimately unable to control the consequences of technological change'. Pridham and Vanhanen, 'Conclusion', p. 261.

46 Marsha Pripstein Posusney, 'The Middle East's Democracy Deficit in Comparative Perspective', in Pripstein Posusney and Michele Penner Angrist (eds.), *Authoritarianism in the Middle East*, pp. 1–18: p. 7.

47 Raymond Hinnebusch, 'Democratization in the Middle East: The Evidence from Syria' in Gerd Nonneman (ed.), *Political and Economic Liberalization*, pp. 153–167: esp. pp. 155–156; see also Waterbury, 'Democracy without Democrats?', pp. 29–30.

48 See also Richard Sklar, 'Towards a Theory of Developmental Democracy', in Adrian Leftwich (ed.), *Democracy and Development* (Cambridge: Polity, 1996), pp. 25–44: p. 39.

49 See Gerd Nonneman, 'Linkages Between Economic and Political Liberalization', in Nonneman (ed.), *Political and Economic Liberalization*, pp. 307–313.

50 See for instance Larry Diamond, 'Political Culture and Democracy', in Diamond (ed.), *Political Culture and Democracy in Developing Countries* (Boulder: Lynne Rienner, 1994), pp. 1–27.

51 Lucian Pye and Mary Pye have compellingly argued for the case of Asia: *Asian Power and Politics: The Cultural Dimensions of Authority* (Cambridge, MA: Harvard University Press, 1985).

52 Diamond, Linz and Lipset, 'Introduction', p. 21.

53 Also see ibid., and Diamond, 'Causes and Effects', in Diamond (ed.), *Political Culture and Democracy in Developing Countries*, pp. 229–249: p. 236.

54 For a survey of the literature, see Diamond, Linz and Lipset, 'Introduction', pp. 10–15.

55 See Christopher Clapham, *Africa in the International System* (Cambridge: Cambridge University Press, 1996); Robert Pinkney, *Democracy in the Third World* (Buckingham: Open University Press, 1993), pp. 40–48; Diamond, Linz and Lipset, 'Introduction', pp. 15–17; Naomi Chazan, 'Between Liberalization and Statism: African Political Cultures and Democracy', in Diamond (ed.), *Political Culture and Democracy in Developing Countries*, pp. 59–98.

56 See also Diamond, 'Causes and Effects', pp. 237–238.

57 Samuel Huntington, *The Third Wave: Democratization in the Late Twentieth Century* (Norman: University of Oklahoma Press, 1991), p. 102; Philippe Schmitter, 'The International Context of Contemporary Democratisation', in *Stanford Journal of International Affairs*, Vol. 2 (1993), No. 1.

58 Schmitter, 'The International Context', pp. 1–29; Gerd Nonneman, 'Patterns of Political Liberalization: Explanations and Modalities', in Nonneman (ed.), *Political and Economic Liberalization*, pp. 45–62: pp. 53–55; Diamond, 'Causes and Effects', pp. 237–238 (on the international diffusion effects on political culture); Geoffrey Pridham (ed.), *Encouraging Democracy: The International Context of Regime Transition in Southern Europe* (London: St Martin's Press, 1991); Geoffrey Pridham and Tatu Vanhanen (eds.), *Democratization in Eastern Europe*; Diamond, Linz and Lipset, 'Introduction', pp. 48–52; and Samuel Huntington, *The Third Wave*.

59 Nonneman, 'Patterns of Political Liberalization', pp. 54–55.

60 Tat Yan Kong, 'The Origins of Economic Liberalization and Democratization in South Korea', in Nonneman (ed.), *Political and Economic Liberalization*, pp. 229–244.

61 See also Nonneman, *Governance, Human Rights, and the Case for Political Adaptation in the Gulf*, pp. 13–18.

62 Tetreault, *Stories of Democracy*.

63 Giacomo Luciani, 'From Private Sector to National Bourgeoisie: Saudi Business', in Aarts and Nonneman (eds.), *Saudi Arabia in the Balance*, pp. 144–181. Private liquidity in the GCC according to one estimate in 2006 had risen to $1.5 trillion (*Arabian Business*, 16 October 2006), while the number of non-royal millionaires in Saudi Arabia was estimated at over 80,000, and in the UAE at 69,000 (*Arabian Business*, 9 October 2006).

64 Lipset, 'Some Social Requisites for Democracy'.

65 For instance Philippe Schmitter, 'Introduction'; Vanhanen and Kimber, 'Predicting and Explaining Democratization in Eastern Europe'; Nonneman, 'Patterns of Political Liberalization'.

66 Waterbury, 'Democracy without Democrats?', p. 24.

67 See Emma Murphy, 'Agency and Space: The Political Impact of Information Technologies in the Gulf Arab States', *Third World Quarterly*, Vol. 27 (Sept.

2006), No. 6, pp. 1059–1083; the special issue of the *Arab Reform Bulletin* (Carnegie Endowment), December 2004, Volume 2, Issue 11, on http://www.carnegieendowment.org/publications/index.cfm?fa=view&id=16242; and Giacomo Luciani, 'Democracy vs Shura in the Age of the Internet', in Khalaf and Luciani (eds.), *Constitutional Reform and Political Participation in the Gulf*, pp. 274–297.

68 Jill Schwedler, *Toward Civil Society in the Middle East* (Boulder: Lynne Rienner, 1995); Augustus Richard Norton (ed.), *Civil Society in the Middle East*, vols. 1 and 2 (Leiden: Brill, 1994, 1995); Crystal and al-Shayeji, 'The Pro-democracy Agenda in Kuwait'; and Anh Nga Longva, 'Citizenship in the Gulf States: Conceptualization and Practice', in Nils Butenschon et al. (eds.) *Citizenship and the State in the Middle East* (Syracuse: Syracuse University Press, 2000), pp. 179–197. For an interesting study of civil society in the UAE, see Davidson, *The United Arab Emirates*, Chapter 5: 'Globalization and the Prospects for Civil Society', pp. 251–292.

69 Longva, 'Citizenship in the Gulf States'; Tetreault, *Stories of Democracy*.

70 Patricia Springborg, 'Politics, Primordialism and Orientalism', in *American Political Science Review*, Vol. 80, (March 1986), No. 1, pp. 185–211; Ghassan Salamé, 'Small is Pluralistic', in Salamé (ed.), *Democracy without Democrats?*, pp. 84–111.

71 As summarized by Diamond, 'Introduction', p. 11.

72 Dahl, *Polyarchy*, pp. 36–37; Also Gabriel Almond and Sidney Verba, The *Civic Culture: Political Attitudes and Democracy in Five Nations* (Princeton: Princeton University Press, 1963).

73 See Joseph Kostiner (ed.), *Middle East Monarchies: The Challenge of Modernity* (Boulder: Lynne Rienner, 2000); especially the article by Lisa Anderson, 'Dynasts and Nationalists: Why Middle Eastern Monarchies Survive' (pp. 53–69). Also Michael Herb, *All in the Family: Absolutism, Revolution and Democracy in the Middle Eastern Monarchies* (Albany: State University of New York Press, 1999).

74 Daniel Brumberg, 'Authoritarian Legacies and Reform Strategies in the Arab World', in Brynen, Korany and Noble (eds.), *Political Liberalization and Democratization in the Arab World*, Vol. 1, pp. 229–260.

75 See Lisa Anderson, 'Dynasts and Nationalists: Why Middle Eastern Monarchies Survive'; Abdulhadi Khalaf, 'What do Gulf Ruling Families do when they Rule?' in *Orient*, Vol. 44 (20034), No. 4, pp. 537–554; and the review article by Russell Lucas, 'Monarchical Authoritarianism: Survival and Political Liberalization in a Middle Eastern Regime Type', pp. 103–119.

76 The concept of 'segmented clientelism' was introduced by Steffen Hertog, 'Segmented Clientelism: The Political Economy of Saudi Economic Reform Efforts', in Aarts and Nonneman (eds.), *Saudi Arabia in the Balance*, pp. 111–143.

77 Raymond Hinnebusch, 'Calculated Decompression as a Substitute for Democratization: Syria', in Korany, Brynen and Noble (eds.), *Political Liberalization and Democratization in the Arab World, Vol. 2 – Comparative Experiences*, pp. 223–240.

78 See also Lucas, 'Monarchical Authoritarianism'.

79 See Gudrun Krämer, 'Islam and Pluralism', in Brynen, Korany and Noble (eds.), *Political Liberalization and Democratization in the Arab World*, Vol. 1, pp. 6–128;

Charles Kurzman (ed.), *Liberal Islam: A Sourcebook* (Oxford: Oxford University Press, 1998); Timothy Sisk, *Islam and Democracy* (USIP Press, 1992).

80 In April 2006, the Muslim Brotherhood's deputy supreme guide, Muhammad Habib, posted a plea on the organization's website calling on political parties, syndicates, and associations in the Arab world 'to acknowledge that comprehensive reform can only be achieved through a political reform process based on the notions of pluralism, peaceful rotation of power, free and fair elections and separation of powers' (as paraphrased by *Arab Reform Bulletin*, April 2006, Volume 4, Issue III, on http://www.carnegieendowment.org/publications/index.cfm?fa=view&id=18233. For the original in Arabic see the Brotherhood's website Ikhwanonline, on http://www.ikhwanonline.com/Article.asp?ID=19414& SectionID=113.

81 Daniel Thope and Katherine Meyer, 'Religion and Democratic Support: Evidence from the World Survey', in *Democracy and Society*, Vol. 3, No. 1, pp. 1 and 10–12.

82 Katerina Dalacoura, *Islam, Liberalism and Human Rights* (London: I.B. Tauris, 1998); Nazih Ayubi, *Political Islam* (London: Routledge, 1988); Ayubi, 'Islam and Democracy', in David Potter et al. (eds.), *Democratization* (Polity Press, 1997), pp. 345–366; Augustus Richard Norton, 'The Challenge of Inclusion in the Middle East', in *Current History*, January 1995, pp. 1–6; Waterbury presents a more equivocal picture: Waterbury, 'Democracy without Democrats?' A balanced overview is given in Beverley Milton-Edwards, *Islam and Politics in the Contemporary Middle East* (Cambridge: Polity Press, 1999), chapter 4: 'The Democracy Debate', pp. 88–117. See also Judy Barsalou, 'Islamists at the Ballot Box', USIP Special Report 144, July 2005.

83 Waterbury, 'Democracy without Democrats?'; Michael Hudson, 'The Political Culture Approach to Arab Democratization: The Case for Bringing it Back in, Carefully', in Brynen, Korany and Noble (eds.), *Political Liberalization and Democratization in the Arab World: Theoretical Perspectives*, pp. 61–76.

84 See Sharabi, *Neo-patriarchy*; Saad Eddin Ibrahim, *Al Mujtama' wa-d-dawla fi-l watan al-'arabi* (Beirut, 1988).

85 Salwa Ismail, 'Democracy in Contemporary Arab Intellectual Discourse', in Brynen, Korany and Noble (eds.), *Political Liberalization and Democratization in the Arab World: Theoretical Perspectives*, pp. 93–111.

86 Gregory Gause, 'The Persistence of Monarchy in the Arabian Peninsula', in Kostiner (ed.), *Middle East Monarchies*, pp. 167–186.

87 This is also the strong thrust of the argument put forward by Abdulaziz Sager, 'Political Reform Measures from a Domestic GCC Perspective', in Khalaf and Luciani, *Constitutional Reform and Political Participation in the Gulf*, pp. 17–32.

88 See also Nonneman, *Governance, Human Rights and the Case for Political Adaptation in the Gulf*, p. 19.

89 Gerd Nonneman, *EU–GCC Relations: Dynamics, Patterns and Perspectives*, Gulf Papers Series (Dubai: Gulf Research Center, June 2006).

90 See also Gregory Gause, 'Regional Influences on Experiments in Political Liberalization in the Arab World', in Brynen, Korany and Noble (eds.), *Political Liberalization and Democratization in the Arab World*, Vol. 1, pp. 283–306.

91 Huntington, *The Third Wave*, p. 102; and Schmitter, 'The International Context', pp. 18–19.

92 These fears are, in various ways, expressed frequently by ruling family members and middle class reformists alike, both in a number of official comments (especially by Saudi princes) and in informal discussions. Author's interviews and off-the-record discussions in a number of GCC states, and with nationals of all six states, 2003–2006. See also Toby Jones, 'The Iraq Effect in Saudi Arabia', *Middle East Report*, No. 237, Winter 2005, pp. 20–25.

93 Alastair Crooke, 'Talking to Hamas', *Prospect Magazine*, June 2006 (also http://www.prospect-magazine.co.uk/article_details.php?id=7481).

94 Roel Meijer, 'The Association of Muslim Scholars in Iraq', *Middle East Report*, No. 237, Winter 2005, pp. 12–19.

95 Brumberg, 'Authoritarian Legacies and Reform Strategies in the Arab World'.

96 O'Donnell, Schmitter and Whitehead (eds.), *Transitions from Authoritarian Rule;* Dahl, *Polyarchy;* Rustow, 'Transitions to Democracy'.

97 See the (disputed) report by Dr Salah al-Bandar, former Chancellor at the Council of Ministerial Affairs and subsequently deported to Britain, on http://www.bahrainrights.org/files/albandar.pdf.

98 Davidson, *The United Arab Emirates*.

99 For example, the statements of the Emir and the Foreign Minister at the Fifth Doha Conference on Democracy and Free Trade, Doha, April 2005, and the Foreign Minister's response to questions. The speeches and related interviews are reproduced also in *The Peninsula*, 28, 29, 30 March 2005.

100 Findings confirmed through a series of off-the-record discussions with officials, observers, business people and members of both councils, in Oman, 2003–2004. See also Peterson, 'The Emergence of Post-Traditional Oman'. The observation that the assembly does not use all its current powers was also made in comments by Muhammad al-Mazrui, Secretary-General of the UAE's Federal National Council, at the Gulf Research Centre Conference on 'The Gulf in a Year', Dubai, Grand Hyatt, January 2005.

101 Daniel Brumberg, 'The Trap of Liberalized Autocracy', in Larry Diamond et al. (eds.), *Islam and Democracy in the Middle East* (Baltimore: Johns Hopkins University Press, 2003), pp. 35–47; and id., 'Liberalization versus Democracy: Understanding Arab Political Reform' (Washington: Carnegie Endowment, May 2003 [Working Papers, Middle East Series, No. 37]).

102 A forceful argument along these lines is made also by Al Naqeeb, 'How Likely is Democracy in the Gulf?'

103 The term 'decompression' was introduced by Hinnebusch for the case of Syrian instances of liberalization but given wider relevance (Raymond Hinnebusch, 'Calculated Decompression as a Substitute for Democratization: Syria', in Brynen, Korany and Noble (eds.), *Political Liberalization and Democratization in the Arab World* , Vol. 2 (Boulder: Lynne Rienner, 1998), pp. 223–240. Bernard Lewis refers to 'modernizing autocracies' ('A Historical Overview', in Larry Diamond et al. (eds.), *Islam and Democracy in the Middle East*, pp. 208–219).

104 Brumberg, 'Liberalization versus Democracy', p. 12.

105 See Przeworski, *Democracy and the Market;* Nonneman, 'Patterns of Political Liberalization', Hamilton and E. Kim, 'Economic and Political Liberalization in South Korea and Mexico'. This in essence is also the argument of Dankwart Rustow's three-phase progression from elites' tactical response to 'pacts' to 'habituation': Rustow, 'Transitions to Democracy'.

106 Rustow, 'Transitions to Democracy'.

107 Abdo Baaklini, Guilain Deneoux and Robert Springborg, *Legislative Politics in the Arab World: The Resurgence of Democratic Institutions* (Boulder: Lynne Rienner, 1999).

108 Baaklini et al., *Legislative Politics in the Arab World,*, pp. 5, 45 et passim; Anoushiravan Ehteshami, 'Power Sharing and Elections in the Middle East', in Sven Behrendt and Christian Hanelt (eds.), *Bound to Cooperate – Europe and the Middle East* (Gütersloh: Bertelsmann, 2000), pp. 359–375: at p. 373; and Dale Eickelman, 'Introduction', in Norton, *Civil Society in the Middle East*, Vol. II, p. xiii.

109 As suggested by Dahl, and Almond and Verba – see section 5 above; see also Diamond, 'Introduction', pp. 10–11.

110 For an analysis of the results and assessment of the size of the various 'opposition' strands (who can indeed be a real opposition on those issues where they agree among themselves, since they could outvote the pro-government MPs even including the ministers, see the article by Hamid al-Jasim in *Al-Hayat*, 21 October 2006.

111 Indeed, one of them headed the committee that initially came up with the 5-district model. Ghanim Al Najjar has suggested that the outcome of the redistricting episode 'could open the way toward a broader discussion of representation including the issue of possible legalization of political parties': 'Kuwait: Struggle over Parliament', *Arab Reform Bulletin* (Carnegie Endowment June 2006 Vol. 4, No. 5) (http://www.carnegieendowment.org/publications/index.cfm?fa= view&id=18413&prog=zgp&proj=zdrl#kuwaitStruggle).

112 See Salman Dossari, 'Round-up: Bahrain Elections', in *Asharq al-Awsat* (English edition), 29 November 2006 (http://aawsat.com/english/news.asp?section=3&id=7176).

113 Personal communication, March 2005.

114 Mohammad al-Muhanna, 'The Saudi Majlis ash-Shura'.

115 For a useful entry-point to local coverage see the *Gulf News* website on the elections on http://archive.gulfnews.com/indepth/fncelections/puffs/mid_left/10083719.html. Also *Arab News*, 21 December 2006. Turnout among the 6689 electors is reported to have varied from 60% in Abu Dhabi, to 85% in Ajman (the latter figure translating into a mere 436 voters). For the list of winning candidates with their votes, see http://uaeinteract.com/news/default.asp?ID=275 (posted 21 December 2006).

116 See also Davidson, *The United Arab Emirates*, Chapter 5.

117 'The Gulf in a Year', Gulf Research Center meeting, Dubai, Grand Hyatt, January 2005 – i.e. well before the announcement that the Council's size and role would be expanded.

118 Off-the-record interviews and observation in Muscat, Oman, over several visits in 2003–2004.

119 Aarts and Nonneman, 'A Triple Nexus', pp. 454–455.

2

Reform in the Arabian Peninsula World*

The Rt Hon. Baroness Symons of Vernham Dean

The countries of the Gulf states share a great deal in terms of politics, religion and culture, but are very different from each other not only politically and culturally, but in size, wealth, social mores and military capability. Moreover, they have much in common with, and much to distinguish them from, the rest of the region. The Arab League countries can and do act together politically, but whilst sharing a common language and some cultural and religious precepts they are arguably as different from each other as Europeans are from their neighbours; though the Europeans of the EU do at least share a commitment to democracy, to common human rights legislation as well as to a single market. The countries of the wider Middle East comprise republics, both theocratic and secular, and monarchies, both constitutional and absolute; they have enormously varied approaches to human rights and individual freedom, and, despite years of effort, they trade less with each other than they do with Europe.

Regional Influences on the Gulf

In considering political and economic reform in the Gulf, it is important to consider the impact of the rest of the region on the Gulf. Also to be considered are the further implications of an increasingly globalized world, not just in terms of political changes toward democracy – in Eastern Europe, in Latin America and the emerging democracies of Africa, or an increasingly powerful lobby on trade, and particularly on fair trade, but also in terms of the globalization of the huge ideological dilemmas; for example, the balance between individual freedom and

---

* This chapter draws from a speech delivered by the author to a conference on political change in the GCC at Durham University in September 2005.

liberty, on the one hand, and counterterrorism and security, on the other. What will be explored is the balance between what we consider to be some of the fundamental values of human rights as universally applicable, alongside the right of all countries to make their own laws, and regulate the freedom of individuals within those laws.

These are huge questions which are the everyday currency of political exchange between all countries, and the subject of constant discussion in multilateral fora such as the UN, the EU or the GCC meetings. The importance of such questions has also grown in recent years. However, the dialogue did not begin with 9/11, nor with war in Iraq, nor with the 2004 G8 Sea Island Summit. The importance of reform was recognized by the Arab members of the UN in the series of papers on development in the region. Indeed, the form of government, consultation and the relationship of religious and secular authority was a subject for debate within the countries of the region as far back as the 1830s when Sheikh Rifa'a al Tahtawi wrote his book on post-revolutionary France.

Western democracies must approach these issues, not only with sensitivity, but with some sense of humility. No one has cornered the market in wisdom, nor in the depth and expertise of debate. There is a history of debate in the region on the forms of government and there have been huge changes throughout the twentieth century, some of which are the legacy of European intervention: the French in Syria and Lebanon, the Germans in fostering nationalization in nascent Baath parties and the British throughout much of the region.

Changes, developments and reforms are gathering momentum; they are significant and many, though not all, are welcome. But they are likely to succeed and be sustained only if they are Arab-inspired, Arab-led and Arab-nurtured – and furthermore they must also be perceived as such. There are major political changes in the wider region, but there are other dynamics at work including enormous economic pressure and deepening sectarianism which fuel real uncertainty about where political change is leading.

The significance of the Iraqi elections in January 2005, the drawing up of the Iraqi constitution and the referendum upon it, the death of Yasser Arafat and the Palestinian elections, the Syrian withdrawal from Lebanon and the presidential multi-candidate elections in Egypt all mark out a change – but so far a *transitional* change; the ultimate destination cannot be taken for granted.

In the Gulf itself change may be more cautious, but it is clear. The most obvious example is Saudi Arabia's first municipal elections in 40 years between February and April 2005 under the suffrage of all men over the age of 21. In Saudi terms it was a huge step. Prince Saud told a conference in London in April 2005 that he hoped and believed women would be able to vote in future elections, although he was far more reticent on the question of women standing for office.

Many commentators have speculated on how Saudi political life may change with the passing of King Fahd and the succession of King Abdullah. The indications are that the former Crown Prince is open to discussion about Saudi development economically, in relation to women, communications, even machinery of government; but within the system in which he must work. Saudi Arabia may be the most absolute of monarchies, and one of the most economically powerful countries in the region and beyond, but like all governments, the Saudi government is a coalition, not just within a family – but within other powerful elements of the state, the security forces, the religious elite. In one sense, there is an opportunity for the powers of King Abdullah to be freed up; as compared to his ability to act as Crown Prince, obliged to consult with a separate King's diwan before decisions were taken. However, he has to be acutely conscious of the fact that he is not the absolute monarch of the conventional textbooks, but the leader of a group of powerful princes, each backed by competing groups and interests.

The question has been asked about whether King Abdullah is a reformer. He has taken some brave initiatives – the proposal of the two-state solution to solve the Israel–Palestine conflict, offering Arab support for the state of Israel in return for the creation of a Palestinian state, a proposal supported by President Bush in Crawford in June 1998. February 2004's Counter-Terrorism Conference in Riyadh was another Abdullah initiative, confronting more openly than ever before Saudi Arabia's own, home-grown terrorist problem. Perhaps more significantly, the organization of the Islamic Conference Summit on Islamic Thought in Mecca in December 2005 to promote moderate Islam was a real opportunity to observe how the King deals with this most sensitive of subjects.

Saudi Arabia is not the only country in the Gulf to have experienced a recent change of leadership. The United Arab Emirates may not have all the hallmarks of absolute monarchy, but it does have very far-reaching presidential powers. President Sheikh Zayed, a wily and clever politician with a real gift for telling a good story, was succeeded by his son Sheikh Khalifa. The late Sheikh had welded the emirates together as a powerful political, and military, power in the region. He also invested the huge oil wealth of Abu Dhabi in education, training and the environment. The emirates vary considerably. Dubai, fast becoming a real hub of economic growth in the region, has a very different feel from more conservative, less showy Abu Dhabi. But politically they operate on a very similar basis: no electorate, no local elections, no elections for the unicameral Federal National Council whose forty members are appointed by the seven Emirs to serve a two-year term. The President and Vice-President of the UAE are elected by the smallest of electorates – the seven Emirs.

The Emirates are therefore inarguably less democratic than Saudi Arabia, yet the UAE feels and is a more liberal society: there is more personal freedom, no religious police, greater liberty for women, although not in the Sheikh's own court, and, of course, most notably in Dubai, there is the wholesale embracing of the tourist industry and all that this implies.

Oman, Bahrain, Kuwait and Qatar of course are all monarchies, based on the hereditary principle. In all four countries the Prime Minister is appointed by the monarch, as are all ministers, except in Kuwait, where the Prime Minister appoints and the monarch approves the appointment. Bahrain and Oman have a bicameral system of *shura* or *majlis* with a mixture of the monarch's appointees and elected members, on a universal franchise of those over 20 in Bahrain and 21 in Oman.

Kuwait and Qatar have a unicameral national assembly. Under the Qatari constitution two-thirds will be elected by popular franchise of those over 18 and one-third appointed by the Emir; in Kuwait all 50 members of the National Assembly are elected by men over the age of 21 – and women were granted the vote in May 2005, the same year that saw the appointment of the first woman minister in Kuwait. Elections are forthcoming in Bahrain and Oman, and in Kuwait in 2007.

In all the Gulf kingdoms, with the exception of the UAE, there is some form of elective representation – but there is a sense of momentum towards more representative participation and consultation. There has of course long been the tradition of consultation in the Gulf, but what has changed is that rather than the monarch consulting tribal leaders and family members, the people are now deciding who should be their representatives in that consultation. However, this is not democracy. These assemblies do not make the law, as they do in Western democracies generally; nor do they form the elected body from which the government is formed, as is the case in the UK. That said, they are influential upon government, and the monarchs and their ministers do listen to their views in forming policy.

The fact is that indigenous moves to political reform, particularly the moves in the Gulf states, predate the developments in Iraq, the Palestinian elections and President Mubarak's changes in Egypt. What is important is that the push from the West, whether in the form of G8 initiatives, or from elsewhere, does not undermine the indigenous efforts of the reformers on the ground. It is vital to the success of these developments that they are not claimed to be the result of Western pressure. Such a claim lays reformers open to accusations of bowing to Western pressure from the traditional elements in their societies who want neither reform nor engagement with the West. Such a situation is particularly acute in Saudi Arabia, where Saudi liberals are under discernibly more pressure.

Wider Influences – Economic, Sectarian and the Emergence of the Arab Nation State

Other regional dynamics must not be overlooked in the haste to view events through a reform prism. First the economies of the Gulf. They are broadening and diversifying, but the primary influence is still the oil market and how that develops. Secondly, there is sectarianism – particularly Sunni and Shia – which is rising. Both minorities and majorities who had previously been excluded from politics are now far more assertive and very ready to exploit participatory politics to advance their demands. Finally, there is also the entrenchment of the Arab nation state. Few now contest the modern state boundaries – not even the pan-Arabists or Islamists. On the whole, oppositionists are trying to change a state's policy, not overthrow it – although some of the terrorist rhetoric is clearly far more extreme. These three elements, economics, sectarianism and the emergence of the Arab nation state, are all key components in the development of political reform in the region.

The fact is that the region as a whole is under huge economic pressure. Despite oil wealth, the countries of the region simply cannot sustain the growth they need for the next 20 or 30 years; the rate of modernization is falling behind the rest of the world; and alarmingly, unemployment is high amongst a rapidly growing and youthful population. Indeed the World Bank has estimated that 100 million new jobs will be needed by the year 2020, just to sustain the already very high unemployment rate.

Coupled with the frustration some of the population feel over the slow progress on democratic reform and good governance, this economic stagnation leads to increased migration away from the region of those who might lead genuine reform. It also leads, in some at least, to a sense of alienation and strengthens the appeal of radical fundamentalism. However, the Gulf leaders and their advisers are able to recognize these dangers, as are the other reformers in the region. The Arab League statement in May 2005 on development and modernization demonstrated a regional recognition that change was necessary and that economic reform was a key component in that change.

Saudi Arabia

As the most powerful, in every sense, country in the Gulf it is Saudi Arabia which is *crucial* in this respect. Saudi Arabia has 25% of the world's proven oil reserves, vast reserves of gas (at least the fourth largest in the world) with further discoveries every year coupled with huge reserves of ore and minerals. In addition, it has huge power as a swing producer that can immediately increase oil production. Oil accounts for 90% of Saudi GDP and the country's trade surplus will reach a staggering US$64 billion in 2005, fuelling GDP growth of nearly 8%. The private sector is growing at 5% and there is a 48% rise in the stock market and the construction industry.

However, there is a big consideration to be taken into account. The Saudi economy still needs substantial reform and diversification to cope with its very young population – 60% are under 20. The official unemployment level is 12% but it is commonly believed to be between 20 and 30%. Foreign workers — mostly from the developing world – make up around 88% of the private sector workforce. Despite the policy of 'Saudization', many young Saudis are simply not employable because of higher wage costs, high focus on religion in education and their cultural attitudes.

Internally, investment is needed in all parts of the economy. Diversification is driving the government's reform programme. New laws that are either being formulated or awaiting royal approval concentrate on increasing legal transparency, levelling the playing field between foreign and Saudi firms, labour mobility and capital markets and insurance laws. There is also an ambitious privatization programme covering telecoms, water, mining, power, railways and other utilities. The government recently halved corporation tax from 40% to 20%.

Externally, Saudi Arabia is also moving to opening its economy. It signed a trade agreement with the EU in 2003. It has signed 27 bilateral trade agreements as part of its moves towards World Trade Organization (WTO) accession. Progress may be slow on issues like dual pricing, TRIPs (Trade Related Aspects of Intellectual Property Rights) and insurance, but to try to accelerate progress the UK has been actively involved in explaining the implications of WTO membership to the Saudi business community, and in acting as a conduit for Saudi concerns with other members of the WTO community.

Saudi Arabia must open up economically if it is to sustain its huge youthful population into the first 30 years of the 21st century. And in opening up economically, Saudi Arabia has to consider not only the development of the obvious internal economic mechanisms, but the other dimensions of economic growth and sustainability – education, training, the role of women and the growth of the institutions of civil society.

The UAE

The UAE provides an interesting parallel and contrast. It is very rich, remarkably diverse and forward looking. It holds 9% of the proven oil reserves worldwide, and is committed to increasing output to 3.6 million barrels per day by the end of 2006. Of the reserves, 90% are in one Emirate – Abu Dhabi. It has huge resources of natural gas which together with the oil sector accounted for 32.5% of the value of UAE economic activity in 2004.

But what the UAE has managed to achieve – and this is what is truly significant – is diversification. Last year there was a 9.4% increase in non-oil activity. Oil accounts for only 20% of its GDP, much less than other Gulf states, demonstrating the success of its diversification policy, particularly towards tourism, which accounts for 25% of GDP in Dubai. It is developing manufacturing and financial services and GDP was forecast to grow by 7% in 2005. In huge contrast to Saudi Arabia, unemployment is only 2% despite an annual population growth of 7%. Abu Dhabi is investing into industrialization and business parks – growing this section of the economy by a staggering 10% in 2003. And Dubai of course has become the trading hub of the Gulf, establishing free trade zones and an entrepreneurial spirit exemplifed by extravagant projects and very aggressive competition.

It is perhaps one of the many apparent contradictions of the Gulf that the UAE, arguably the most open economically of the economies and the most liberal, at least as far as foreign visitors are concerned, should also have the least developed *democratic* institutions.

Oman, Kuwait, Bahrain and Qatar

Oman, Kuwait, Bahrain and Qatar are, of course, all heavily dependent on oil and gas. Kuwait, Bahrain and Qatar are all enjoying economic growth of impressive proportions – 8% in Kuwait, 7.7% in Bahrain and a staggering 15% in Qatar. Oman, in many ways a very different country from its neighbours, sustains growth at between 1% and 2% a year. Kuwait, like Saudi Arabia, faces real issues of future employment for young people with 90% of the population reliant upon the state for employment or other financial support and 15,000 graduates entering the job market each year.

Bahrain has enjoyed more success at diversification – the new Formula 1 race track is emblematic of the determination of the King and Crown Prince in this respect, but it too has many of the underlying problems of high dependence on oil revenues (70% of government income), and a fast-growing young population and serious unemployment.

Qatar, of course, has become a byword for economic success. With a GDP per capita of over US$36,000 it is one of the richest countries in the world. There is an ambitious programme of reform and development, and private sector activity grew by 10% in 2003. Oman is also developing its manufacturing and telecommunications sectors. The development of tourism and banking have also received a great deal of attention. The government under Sultan Qaboos has an economic development target with the aim of economic diversification to reduce oil's domination of the economy until it accounts for less than 20% of GDP and to encourage private sector investment.

Just as the political development of the Gulf region is very varied, so is the economic picture. All these countries are, by any standards, very rich; much richer than most of the other countries in the region, both in terms of absolute wealth and in terms of per capita income. But the very resources that have made them rich – oil and gas – have also caused significant problems. These industries simply do not provide enough jobs for their populations, particularly as newer technologies are less labour intensive, and the populations continue to grow at what would be considered to be extraordinarily high levels in the West.

These factors, an often highly educated, relatively rich population of young people without work or political power in the midst of a region with international problems on the scale of Iraq, Israel/Palestine and increasingly Iran, coupled with the growth of sectarianism and aggressive fundamentalism are the recipe for a very potent political cocktail.

Stability in the region will depend on a range of factors. The ability and willingness of governments to address the need for diversification in their economies will be a major factor in creating and sustaining that stability, but it will not be the only crucial issue.

Sectarianism is an extremely important issue. Whether it develops into aggressive religious fundamentalism, or is expressed largely in anti-Western sentiments or in fiercely divisive antipathy between Sunni and Shia, such sectarianism has been increasing, throughout the region as a whole and to some extent within the Gulf itself. The most obvious example of sectarianism is in Iraq where the removal of Sunni majority domination of the political process, whilst empowering the previously largely excluded Shia majority, is causing huge problems in the drawing up of the constitution and in the continuing violence. This violence is concentrated largely in the four Sunni provinces where 85% of the incidents occur – Baghdad, Ninewa, Aqabar and Saladin. The Shia-dominated Iranian authorities are watching events with more than a passing interest. Their cause will be served by a Shia-dominated government in Iraq, but not by the break-up of that country if sectarianism runs its course, nor by a secular-dominated Shia government whose authority rests on a demonstrably popular mandate.

Syria's concerns are obvious too. Having seen the breakdown of the other great Baathist Sunni regime in the region, Syria's concerns have all too obviously been manifest by the way in which terrorists and arms have passed through their borders into Iraq.

In short both Syria and Iran, from very different perspectives, have reason to look hard at sectarianism within their own borders, and to assure the international community that they can demonstrate good neighbourliness to Iraq, by securing their borders against insurgent activity.

The importance of Wahhabism as an element in the Sunni holy war is a matter of dispute amongst Muslim scholars and others, but there is little doubt that many Sunnis themselves believe that it was Islamic jihad waged by the guerrilla fighters in Afghanistan which defeated the Soviet Union, not any Western-generated ideas of democracy and reform. For many of them, defeating the Soviet Union was a mere prelude to defeating a degenerate and soft-nosed USA.

Bernard Lewis recently took this argument further by suggesting that in a genuinely free election, fundamentalists would have substantial advantages over moderates and reformers. The language of democracy, he claims, is mostly strange to Muslims, but the language of fundamentalism is very familiar, evoking long-held Islamic values both to criticize the existing secular authoritarian order, and to offer a real alternative. To spread this message, the fundamentalists use the effective network that communicates through the powerful and authoritative voice of the mosques.

In the balance between democracy and religious fundamentalism, democracy has a further huge disadvantage. Democracy by its very nature must allow fundamentalists freedom of action and freedom of speech. The fundamentalists, by contrast, suffer from no such ideologically-based inhibitions. Democracy must allow fundamentalists to argue their case whilst fundamentalists must endeavour to suppress that democratic argument. This ideological battle is no longer a purely regional problem, it is arguably being conducted throughout Europe. The situation is clearer in the United States, of course, where commentators openly acknowledge 'good guys' and 'bad guys' with a moral certainty which is less than convincing to most Europeans.

One of the interesting ways to assess the attitudes of the region is to look at their responses to the UK's efforts to curb terrorism, as exemplified by the Prime Minister's announcements following the London bombings. There have been two recurring themes often running alongside each other. One is that there has been growing hostility to the Muslim community in the UK, and that Muslims are likely to suffer from any new laws to combat terrorism. The other is that for far too long the UK has been soft on radicals, who have abused the asylum system to promote instability back in their home countries.

The next question to consider is whether the countries of the Gulf have themselves tried to regulate religious messages, such as those coming from the mosques. On balance, it would seem the answer is yes. In Kuwait there is strict regulation and monitoring of the mosques by the Ministry of Islamic Affairs which sets tight guidelines on what imams are allowed to discuss in their sermons. Similarly, there is tight control in Oman, where the Ministry of Religious Affairs appoints all imams who must train and pass examinations at the Islamic University attached to the Grand Mosque. In Qatar the mosques are controlled by the Emir through a government department and imams are civil servants.

Saudi is also authoritarian – all mosques are under the control of the Ministry for Islamic Affairs which pays the imams' salaries – but a separate government committee defines the qualifications of imams and there is the feared Committee for the Prevention of Vice and Promotion of Virtue or religious police.

It is perhaps an interesting reflection that in the Gulf, as in most countries of the region, imams must be licensed or regulated in some form or another – just as Church of England clergy, rabbis, non-conformist and Catholic clergy in the UK are also regulated. However, thus far imams in the UK are not.

One of the manifestations of this subtle change is in attitudes towards women. Women are an issue, not only in the Gulf, but throughout the Arab world. From the wearing of hejab or abbaya, education, family law, rights of property and rights to work women have become a real focus. However, the situation is not uniform across the region. Palestinian women, with or without a hejab, are often the breadwinners in their families. They are also very likely to be members of a non-governmental organization. The women are politically aware, economically active and highly articulate.

The same is true, but in subtly different ways, in Egypt, where Mrs Mubarak's tireless work has resulted in primary education programmes in village schools for girl children at one end of the spectrum, and the appointment of women judges at the other. The clause in the Iraqi constitution for women to make up a target figure of 25% of all elected assemblies of the future is an extraordinary departure for the region, and of course there are now women government ministers in countries as different as Morocco, Syria and Kuwait.

I am writing this as a former minister, and this has given me a particular experience. As a woman I maintained contact not only with my ministerial counterparts – overwhelmingly male in number – but also with the wives and families of many people I met. My experiences vary from the all-women private audiences in Saudi Arabia and Abu Dhabi to being the first woman to address the Jeddah economic forum. Some points were common in all these encounters. Women are hugely influential, not only upon their husbands, but possibly more so, upon their sons. They are well informed, hold very strong views and are not afraid of expressing them forcefully in private. They are also every bit as sensitive to the huge dilemmas of security and liberty, of the grief and horror of suicide bombings and of the future of their children as women anywhere are. They also have a sense of the inevitability of change. But overwhelmingly they are clear that change must be from within their own culture, and be fashioned by themselves at their own pace. It must not be imposed from outside, however good the intentions are and however urgent the proposals of change may be.

In this respect, as in so many others, the region as a whole will impact on the Gulf increasingly. The Arab business women conferences reflect the concerns of their male counterparts. The outcome of the huge changes in Iraq, whatever one thinks of the conflict which began these changes, will be hugely influential; the presidential elections in Egypt; the strengthening voices of human rights and civil liberty in Morocco and Tunisia; the efforts of Libya to normalize its relationships in the region and with the West; the withdrawal of Syria (at least in part) from Lebanon; and the powerful voices of Lebanese patriots in the streets of Beirut – all these have their part to play.

However, the most important issue concerns developments in the Israeli–Palestinian conflict. This is the most explosive, visceral and all-consuming issue for Arabs, and all are passionate about it. In my experience the Israeli–Palestine issue is far more significant than any other single political subject – and certainly more important than Iraq.

How the West, and particularly the United States and the European Union, handle their relationships with Palestine and Israel crucially will be seen as evidence of the sincerity of our commitment to everything a two-state solution symbolizes – fairness, no double standards, a commitment to Palestinian security, as well as Israeli safety – but above all that most precious of values to an Arab – justice.

Both Israelis and Palestinians have signalled significant and potentially long-lasting shifts in their traditional positions towards each other. But coupled with the cautious optimism we would all like to feel, we know that the underlying grievances are as deep-rooted as ever. Israel believes the Palestinians must make more effort to deal with terrorism, Hamas, Islamic Jihad and others; and the Palestinians see the continued building of the security barrier, particularly together with plans for continued growth on the West Bank, as undercutting the Roadmap's commitment to a viable and contiguous state of Palestine. And frankly both are reasonable criticisms of each other's positions.

This chapter has attempted to deal with the Gulf agenda on political progress, economic reform, sectarianism, Arab nationalism, religion, women and impact of the rest of the region, components which are interlinked and to some extent dependent on each other. Terrorism, and the Arab responses to what is happening not only in their own region but outside the region too, have also been touched upon.

In conclusion, the commitment to maintain and deepen dialogue and practical help to the region must be real and sustained. However, it is for each country to find its own way forward and help must be directed in a way which is consistent with the needs of the individual countries concerned.

The government of the UK has focused on ways to promote democracy in the region, improve education systems and tackle the barriers to investment. It has also endeavoured to engage others, NGOs and business in dialogue, in expanding civil society and business involvement across all these issues. There is the Democracy Assistance Dialogue under way between governments and political institutions on political processes, elections and women's participation. Meanwhile, on civil society dialogue, Qatar and Bahrain are in the forefront, supporting work on transparency and corruption, the rule of law, human rights and women in employment.

Education has been another vital area, with Charles Clarke, the former British Education Secretary, holding very successful meetings in London in 2004 to discuss *practical* ways in which literacy, adult education, skills for employment and the effective use of IT can be improved. Literacy experts met in Algiers and Cairo in April and September 2005, while Jordan too hosted education ministers in May.

On investment and finance, the Arab Business Council and the G8 are supporting an Investment Task Force linked closely to the OECD and

UNDP Governance and Investment programme. The UK is supporting a micro-finance initiative, a Private Enterprise Partnership and a Network of Funds to coordinate funding in the region. Entrepreneurship is being fostered by Morocco and Bahrain, to support diversification, create new jobs and stimulate innovation. And the UK is pressing ahead with the Forum for the Future dialogue between the EU and the region in November 2005.

Problems in the Gulf and the region as a whole are truly formidable, but there is also an unprecedented range of opportunities available to help make a real improvement in the lives of hundreds of thousands of people in the region, and thereby improve peace, security, prosperity and justice. Commitment to this goal is essential not only for a peaceful future in the region, but also for a peaceful future for the rest of the world too.

3

Patterns of Democratic Deficit: Is it Islam?

Bahgat Korany

In the historiography of the prosperous research industry on democracy and democratization, Huntington's 1991 analysis stands out. This classic study analyses the process in terms of three waves. The third wave focuses on the 1970s with regime change in Portugal, Spain, Greece and democratic emergence/continuation in Latin America, Asia and Eastern Europe.

The 1990s witnessed the end of the Cold War and what could be termed the fourth wave with the transformation into 'emergent democracies' of the 27 ex-communist states in Eastern Europe and Central Asia. Are the 22 countries of the Arab Middle East part of this fourth wave of democratization or do they have to wait for a fifth wave, or even longer? Though the attention of the established conceptual literature is beginning to change after the 2003 invasion of Iraq, this literature is still handicapped by its usual benign neglect of the region.[1] As our survey noted in 1995, neither O'Donnell, Schmitter and Whitehead's influential comparative study of democratization, nor Diamond, Linz and Lipset's analysis of the transition process, included any country from the Arab Middle East. Surveys of research areas and courses in most North American universities revealed the same benign neglect or contentment with over-generalization.[2]

This benign neglect contrasted with interest in the subject in 'native' literature. As early as 1984, the Beirut-based Centre for Arab Unity Studies published the *Crisis of Democracy in the Arab World*.[3] Similarly, established periodicals like *al-Siyassa al-Dawliyya* (Cairo) or *al-Mustaqbal al-Arabi* (Beirut) have increasingly included articles on the process of transition in the region. Moreover, since its inception in 1986, the 20 volumes of Al-Ahram's *Arab Strategic Yearbook* have devoted on average 40 pages per volume to the topic. Recently established think tanks, like the Cairo-based Center for Future and Strategic Studies, are joining in with in-depth workshops and debates.

Despite diversity of 'native' views and analyses, none of them affirms that Arab democratization is solid and healthy.[4] In fact, according to data-analysis of 19 Arab countries over the 30-year period 1973–2003, some regimes are regressing as far as democratization is concerned.[5] This finding is important for the conceptual literature. It shows that the democratic transition process is far from linear, it can indeed regress and even break down. If the 'transition paradigm' is to be truly representative of various aspects of empirical reality, it has to integrate non-linear aspects of democratization.

So the tracing of ups and downs in the democratization process shows that the Middle East political landscape is not stagnant. With debates about *shuracracy* or consultation and the practice of *ta'aduddiyya* or pluralism, the domestic landscape is best characterized as one of movement but not yet substantial progress. Thus, whether in terms of the situation on the ground, or native analysis or foreign-collected data, one basic point stands out: Arab Middle East democratization is a poor relation.[6] This democratic deficit should not, however, be a reason for non-treatment or conceptual avoidance. For if we do not explain 'Arab exceptionalism' or analyse the slow pace of Arab transition, is not our knowledge of the assets and liabilities of the transition process deficient? Moreover, given the crucial aspect of this region (e.g. world energy, birthplace of three major religions, 'Mecca' for 1.2 billion Muslims), if we do not invest in its in-depth analysis how can we decode its regional/global interactions or indeed explain the actual lagging of the democratization process or contribute to its success?

Given this nascent conceptualization about Arab democratization, or the lack thereof, this chapter will start with a look at what takes place on the ground. It will single out two patterns in the process and attempt some general conclusions. The focus will be on two big countries of the Arab Middle East that represent, at present, two contrasting patterns of transition. Whereas Iraq incarnates the externally processed transition par excellence, Egypt embodies the domestically induced one, with obvious variations in between, whether we think of Kuwait, Lebanon, Bahrain, Algeria, Morocco or even the Sudan or Syria.

After comparing Iraq's and Egypt's contrasting patterns, the chapter will proceed to try to explain why the two cases are different, considering potential reasons for the common democratic deficit despite different inducements and pressures. As we know, the special responsibility of 'Islam' and its potential impact on the process have usually been held responsible, directly or indirectly. This allusion to Islam's responsibility increased after the 9/11 attacks against New York and Washington. Consequently, the chapter will focus on discussion of the Islamic issue. It will analyse conceptual debates about the role of Islam, and present the different findings of survey research about the potential correlation between Islam and democratization or lack thereof. Both analysis and data show that Islam has been over-generalized whereas in reality it is very varied; its various interpretations/practices are only one among other factors, and some of these other factors could have a more direct impact on the transition process. Consequently, the chapter ends by suggesting four other factors influencing the Arab Middle East's democratic deficit and dynamics.

Comparing Patterns of the Democratic Deficit

Iraq

Dealing with this country involved the difficulty of distilling from the flood of mass media coverage since Iraq's 1990 invasion of Kuwait that which is relevant to our research problem: the objective/process of building a 'new democratic Iraq'. It is equally important at the outset to divide the present Iraqi context into two distinct phases: the elimination of the Saddam regime and the construction in its place of a new one.

The first phase was rather easily achieved, for the regime did not have much popular basis and counted on repression to maintain its 'republic of fear'. The system's anatomy was personalized around Saddam, was family and clan-based with the President's sons, Udai and Qusai, controlling economic resources and the security networks, and Saddam's other family and clan members, the Tikritis, stabilizing the system's control. Neither the Baath party nor the National Assembly had any real say over family, clan and clientalist relations. To get rid of such a regime was not costly for the invading forces.[7]

But this pattern of easy takeover was not repeated in the second phase. On the contrary, the easiness of the first phase became misleading as a pattern because it distracted planners from the huge stumbling blocks on the road to building the 'new democratic Iraq'. Another reason for the difficulties facing this second phase was a misapplication of the lessons of history, especially concerning the building of democracy in Germany and Japan following the defeat of these two countries in the

Second World War. For in the case of Iraq's invasion, US unilateralism did not have the moral–legal legitimation that the Second World War invading forces enjoyed. More importantly, Iraq's invasion revealed the complexity of the Iraqi social fabric, ethnic relations and political networks, a complexity that the US did not plan for, as the memoirs of Paul Bremer make clear.

As a result of the various misperceptions, the US agenda in Iraq had to change its priorities, in practice if not in theory. Though democratic transition is still the objective, the immediate daily reality is the lack of any modicum of security. At present, Iraq's arena is almost the renowned Hobbesian 'war of all against all', as is borne out by the statistics.

By May 2006, more than 2400 US military had been killed, and about 250,000 Iraqi combatants. In just the first five months of 2006, 6000 Iraqis were slaughtered, a carnage of 1200 per month or 40 per day on average. It seems that this average will probably get worse rather than better in the immediate future. Moreover, this average does not, of course, include the number of injured: e.g. from 19 March 2003 through to 29 January 2006, there were 16,548 injured in the US military alone,[8] with reports putting the number of Iraqis injured above 100,000 for the same period. With kidnapping of foreigners approaching 300, and almost 15,000 Iraqis in US custody,[9] law and order are still hard to maintain. The estimated strength of the insurgency nationwide ranges from 15,000 to 20,000, with foreign fighters from various countries estimated at between 700 and 2000. This has led to the internationalization of the fighting. With the average number of weekly attacks approaching 600,[10] and with oil installations and personnel increasingly targeted, the deterioration of the economic infrastructure and daily life is inevitable. Thus, the pre-war crude oil production of 2.5 million barrels per day had fallen to 1.78 million and the 2.5 million barrels per day for export had fallen to 1.17 million by January 2006.[11] Unemployment reached 40%, and total debt, even after debt reduction, was 137.2% of GDP.[12] As a result, surveys among Iraqis show their first priorities to be the need to rebuild infrastructures (80% of those surveyed), followed by the demand for economic development and job creation (67%).[13] Even more telling was the need expressed for law and order by the insistence on the establishment of a strong *central* government – 68.62% of those surveyed expressed a desire for this option (even in Shia areas the figure was 66.2%).[14] Iraq might be opening up technologically with the increase in the number of telephone and internet subscribers (from pre-war 833,000 to 4,590,398 in August 2005)[15]. But with many Baathist leaders still at large and political parties registered for the December 2005 elections reaching 300, this is a society in flux with unsettled political dynamics rather than one making an orderly transition to a 'new democratic Iraq'. A British Ministry of Defence survey of Iraqi citizens in August 2005 showed that 67% felt less secure because of the occupation.[16] And though 58% of the eligible population voted in the 2005 elections, the results showed, much more than anything, the ethnicization and factionalization of Iraq rather than its spirit of common citizenship.

Egypt

The story of Egypt's transition is in many respects a contrast to Iraq. As President Sadat explained in regard to his 1976 liberalization/democratization initiative:

> When I became convinced of the necessity of debating different opinions publicly, I suggested to the people the establishment of forums within the existing unique political organization: the Arab Socialist Union. I asked some trustworthy and influential well-known personalities to discuss the forum concept and supervise the process of democratic dialogue. The dialogue was active also in the People's Assembly, directed by Mahmud Abu-Wafia [Sadat's brother-in-law].
>
> The consensus that emerged indicated the necessity of establishing three such forums: one each for the Right, the Left, and the Center. Nothing is unusual about such a tripartite division, since it is a universal practice that encompasses all different political views. Elections for the forums started in 1976. I followed the election campaign very closely and I was surprised. The campaign's conduct overlooked the existence of the Arab Socialist Union and adopted instead a truly multiparty style. Whereas the Right and the Left each got some seats, it was the Center which acquired a landslide victory.
>
> On the basis of this experience, many decisions were taken. I said to myself: why do we not call things by their real names? I thus went to the inaugural session of the People's Assembly, as is my habit. I declared the abolition of the forum concept and the establishment instead of the multiparty system.[17]

Though useful as an insight into the decision process for democratization, this is an unbelievably simplistic and deceptively straightforward account of the transition process and should not be taken at face value. It leaves out of the process its necessarily political aspects, that is, its complexity.[18]

Sadat's assassination in October 1981 during a public military parade notwithstanding, regular power transfer brought Vice-President Hosni Mubarak to head the country. During Mubarak's reign of a quarter of a century, a multiparty system of sorts formally continued, with four presidential elections and six parliamentary ones, the last of which took place in the winter of 2005. Election results show the dominance of the governing National Democratic Party, the NDP, the continuing decline of the official opposition parties and the rise of the 'forbidden/illegal' Muslim Brotherhood, as well as the Independents.[19]

The last elections in 2005 are significant in emphasizing and even magnifying some of the problems of Egypt's transition process. On the surface, the results did not show many surprises, except the greatest number of MPs from the Muslim Brotherhood ever elected: totalling 88 out of a total of 432 MPs, i.e. 20%. The governing National Democratic Party continued its dominance with 311 MPs. But the NDP got this majority after many of those candidates elected as Independents – as much as 50% of its majority – joined its ranks. In other words, as many as 50% of NDP MPs did not win because they carried the party's ticket. In many cases, they actually won because they were outside the NDP. This fact shows the fragility of the governing party, despite the governmental and media support it enjoyed during the election campaign.

But political party fragility is not limited to the governing NDP. Of the more than seventeen political parties registered in Egypt, only three won any seats in the National Assembly. Moreover, the number of their representatives was really small: six for the Wafd, the first political party ever constituted in Egypt and usually the most visible in the political process; two for the Progressive Unionist Rally and only one for Ghad (the 'Future', whose head came second after Mubarak in the first multi-candidate presidential elections in October 2005). Thus the great number of Independents that assured the NDP majority as well as the mere nine seats (or 3%) for the three principal opposition parties after almost thirty years of formal party politics show indeed the absence of any grass-root political parties.

The electoral process was also fragile; only 26% of those eligible to vote (not the whole population) actually bothered to vote. Moreover, the process was marked by violence, thuggery, vote-buying, non-secret ballots, and occasionally rigged election results. As a consequence, many are sceptical about the actual democratic representativeness of the new National Assembly. A few legal suits contesting results in many constituencies are still before the courts. A public row is also raging between the government and the judges who witnessed many election irregularities. They accuse the government of encroaching on their independence. Moreover, the Assembly's work will be even more marked by political polarization between the governing NDP and the Muslim Brotherhood, officially illegal as a political party. Politically, the 25 MPs that stayed as declaredly Independent could arbitrate the process, but they do not share much among themselves and hence do not constitute a unified political front or even coalition.[20]

If the political landscape continues as it is, no political party – except the governing NDP – will have the 5% of the popular vote or the 250 MPs required to have a candidate in the coming presidential elections. Consequently, the 2005 constitutional amendment of article 76 from one candidate to multi-candidate presidential elections becomes no more than cosmetic and pure formality. Moreover, some analysts are expecting an increasing 'religiosity' of the political process. In addition to the presence of the Muslim Brotherhood as the main opposition, the increasing use of religion in political slogans and parliamentary debates will be forced on the governing party itself with the aim of preventing the Muslim Brotherhood from capitalizing on Islam's mobilizing power.

This brings us to the discussion of 'why' the slowness, if not failure, of democratic transition in the Arab Middle East.

The Islam/Democracy Debate

Any discussion about the slowness or failure of Arab democratic transition must deal with the role of 'Islam', as Islam is a prominent common element among these countries. Moreover, its centrality in the democratization debate had been emphasized even before the 9/11 terrorist attacks. But it should be said at the outset that the discussion of this issue has been hazy and even inconsistent. Notice for instance Huntington's position:

> Islam has not been hospitable to democracy . . . because in Islam, no distinction exists between religion and politics or between the spiritual and the secular, and political participation was an alien concept.[21]

Seven years later, Huntington reversed the issue and became less categorical:

> Islamic doctrine . . . contains elements that may be both congenial and uncongenial to democracy . . . . The real question is which elements in Islam . . . are favourable to democracy and how and under what circumstances these can supersede the undemocratic aspects.[22]

At best, then, the correlation between Islam and democracy is inconclusive. Part of this inconclusiveness is the diversity of Islamic interpretation itself and the *differentiated* political conduct within the 1.2 billion Muslims. Across the centuries, Muslim sects and their scholars have provided varied interpretations of many rules of *worldly* conduct. On political issues "religious scholars provided both a rationalization of authoritarian politics and an ideological and practical source of dissent".[23] In fact, contemporary debates in Islamic thought have "both endorsed this heritage and challenged it, interpreting Islamic scriptures in a democratic manner".[24] For instance, whereas traditionalist Islamists consider democracy anti/un-Islamic, modernist Islamists consider it Islamic/Islamizable and pluralist secularist Muslims consider it necessary.[25]

This diversity within the ranks of Muslims is reflected in two main issues of civil society and politics:

1. In relation to the status of women, Islam's impact is both positive and negative. Initially, Islam abolished a number of patriarchal and tribal practices. However, in contemporary societies Islamic scholars have provided a rationale for 'state feminism' but also more strict rules leading to regressive practices.[26]

2. Despite their common Islamic culture, political systems of Muslim countries show great diversity. They range from Pakistan under military dictatorship, to theocratic and dynastic Saudi Arabia where the 'Koran is our constitution', to Iran's revolutionary republic. This regime diversity is coupled with diverse Muslim' attitudes towards democratic institutions and norms.[27]

Recent empirical surveys of the attitudes of 31,386 literate Muslims in 32 Muslim countries in the Middle East, North Africa, Asia and also some Muslim minorities in the US and Europe confirm the diversity of Muslim attitudes. In the words of M. A. Fattah:

> Muslims' values are shaped by personal experiences, including religious influences, so it is natural that democracy in Muslim countries would be influenced by religion. This study demonstrates that Islam is one of many environmental factors shaping attitudes about democracy and that its salience, while relatively strong, varies from society to society and individual to individual.[28]

Fattah's findings confirm earlier surveys where Kamal el-Menoufi concluded that Islam – precisely because of the great diversity in its practice – is a neutral factor.[29]

Despite this diversity, there is substantial agreement among Muslims surveyed on the negative role of incumbent rulers and their Western supporters in 'corrupting' Islam and obstructing democracy. Various Islamic movements quote specifically 'official Islam' and its *ulama* as promoting non-democratic rules and behaviour:

> Muslims have a high degree of dissatisfaction with ruling elites. In twenty-four out of thirty-two countries where Muslims live, respondents desired a pro-democratic rule rather than the ruling incumbent. Of respondents from the remaining eight countries, only those from two were clearly pro-incumbent, and those from the remaining six were unsure . . .
>
> The importance of religion in Muslims' daily lives is evidenced by the weight they attach to the teachings of the *ulama*. Respondents in twenty-six countries surveyed, pay more heed to *ulama* than to either public intellectuals or government officials. To the extent that state-sponsored *ulama* are essentially government officials, there is distrust, but in this case Muslims actively seek out independent *ulama* for their opinions on major social and political issues.[30]

Neo-Islamists and Democracy

These independent Islamic scholars could have a different analysis concerning the relationship of Islam and democracy. In fact, a new brand of Islamists, the neo-Islamists, go as far as negating an organic incompatibility between Islam and liberal democracy.

[69]

Unlike fundamentalists and also contrary to a stereotypical conception of the relationship between Islam and democracy, this neo-Islamist brand is less dichotomous, less black and white, and emphasizes common ground. Although still considering Islam as the solution, neo-Islamists are far from the view that democracy represents unbelief and Western bigotry.

Among those neo-Islamists bent on renewal and adaptation of Islamic thought and political practice are some influential Azharite sheiks (e.g., Yusif el-Qaradawi),[31] prominent essayists (e.g. Fahmi Huwaidi),[32] well-respected judges (e.g. Tariq al-Bishri),[33] university professors and ex-ministers (e.g. Ahmad Kamal Abu al Magd),[34] and prolific authors (e.g. Muhammad 'Emara,[35] who has published more than 54 books and hundreds of articles).[36]

What united the authoritative thinkers of varied backgrounds and professions was that, although their starting point is Islam, they distance themselves from standard fundamentalists, especially the radical and violent ones.[37] Unlike the standard fundamentalists – even those of the traditional Muslim Brotherhood – the neo-Islamists have the ubiquity of change and the inescapable presence of the (dominant) other at the top of their agenda. The main issue for them is how to cope with these problems now and in the future. Rather than being obsessed with the past, they tend to be future-oriented and practical rather than purely doctrinaire. Consequently, they are much less literal in their interpretation of sacred texts. They insist on the role of reason, of *ijtihad* (independent judgement) in dealing with the burning issues facing Muslims nowadays. Foremost among these issues is the type of political system desired and the role of Muslims in it.

Another important premise tending to bring them together is their refusal to view modernity and authenticity as incompatible. As in the possible combination of democracy and Islam, a third, intermediary road is feasible, combining renewal with faith. The prime criterion in the interpretation of texts and basic principles is the interest of the people, their *maslaha*. In insisting on these premises, they do not hesitate to criticize influential but rigid fundamentalists, whether revolutionary (e.g. Sayyid Qutb) or doctrinaire (e.g. Mawdudi).

In their elaboration of the (compatible) relationship between Islam and democracy, neo-Islamists' starting point is the inescapable presence of diversity among Muslims since Islam's early days. They cite the Quran extensively to prove it.[38] Indeed, diversity has even been codified in

Muslim history as sects, and in the early Abbasid period in the eighth and ninth centuries among the Sunnis alone, there were 13 sects.[39] From this factual observation they establish the analogy between sects in jurisprudence and parties in politics.[40] Thus they reject the fundamentalists' one-party rule of Hezbollah (God's Party), and the exclusion of other parties dubbed Hizb al-Shaytan (party of Satan).[41] They explicitly advocate the establishment of multipartyism.[42]

Some go even further to imply that multipartyism can be beneficial for progress because it ensures avoidance of the ruler's tyranny.[43] Multipartyism could even be considered an integral part of Islam. Since Islam upholds complete equality among believers, diversity of opinion and thought could consequently be codified through the establishment of political parties. These parties would then negotiate their differences. The important thing is to avoid dissidence because the unity of the umma is supreme, as are the pillars of Islam. No negotiations or compromises can exist regarding these two aspects. Other than these two provisions, the presence of diversity and the respect for equality among Muslims make democracy mandatory as a means of settling differences.

The neo-Islamists accept that the word democracy does not exist in the Arabic language and that it is used by Muslims in its foreign form. But they brush this fact aside as of little importance or too formalistic (the history of Islam, they state, shows acceptance of some foreign terms and practices of foreign civilizations). What the neo-Islamists consider important is not the foreign origin of the term democracy but its negative associations that are enshrined in the Muslims' collective psychology. For the masses, democracy is indeed associated with the colonizing West and its attempts to dehumanize Muslims, to take away their identity and authenticity. These negative associations have been exploited – either through ignorance or bad faith – in electioneering campaigns to put candidates favouring democracy on the defensive by accusing them of being anti-Islamic.[44] But in reality there is no inherent incompatibility between Islam and democracy. Seven tenets of the Islamic system show as much.

1. Final decision-making prerogatives belong to the umma (community), which is the ultimate sovereign.
2. The umma is a responsible entity; that is, it is in charge of its destiny.
3. Freedom is a universal, inalienable right, and nobody is to be forced

to act against his or her will even in order to adopt Islam – as the Quran states (e.g., the Cow, Surat 256; the Cave, Surat 29; Yunus or Jonah, Surat 99). From freedom of choice follows freedom of opinion, as long as it does not negate the primacy of religion or question its basic principles.

4. All believers are basically equal.
5. The presence of the Other is legitimate and should be respected (al-Hujurat, or the Chambers, Surat 13; al-Rum, Surat 22; Hud, Sura 118,119).
6. Injustice, even by Muslims against non-Muslims, is forbidden as unethical and should be resisted (al-Shura, Surat 42; Pilgrimage, surat 39, Women, Surat 148).
7. Law and legality are supreme in the community, and the legitimacy of authority is a function of its respect of Islam's legal system (*shariah*).

Since there is no epistemological or built-in incompatibility between the basic principles of Islam and those of democracy, the best system for Muslims is the one based on *shura* (consultation). For the ruler, *shura* is compulsory, as is accountability.[45]

Two basic points should be reiterated from this cursory analysis of some of the basic readings of neo-Islamists. First, the relationship between Islam and democracy is not one of mutual exclusiveness but rather of adaptation and accommodation because at the level of basic principles of tolerance and respect for freedom of choice they do converge. Second, Islam does impose limits beyond which accommodation and adaptation cannot go: respect for the basic pillars of religion and obedience to *shariah*. It is the function of *ijtihad* (independent scholarship) and the work of reason to show where accommodation and compromises can or cannot be established. *Ijtihad* then allows practice to top (rigid) doctrinal interpretation and thus helps Islamic flexibility and compromises in response to evolving daily practices.

Moreover, not only at the doctrinal level but also at the individual one, surveys found more support for democracy among Muslims as a function of their high level of education, their gender (women are more pro-democracy), their practice of political participation through voting, their direct experience with democracy (living in a democratic country) and their opposition to authoritarian incumbent rulers.[46]

If Not Islam, Then What?

Given then this diversity and adaptability of Islam and Muslims' behavioural patterns, research should now concentrate on specificities and empirical situations in order to promote field-based generalizations. We should also continue to investigate the influence of other relevant factors. A few prime candidates are:

The rentier state

Given the high profile of oil and its socio-economic impact, this factor competes with Islam in its characterization of Middle East states.[47] Whether these states are direct or indirect rentier states, oil producers or labour exporters, capital investors or aid-receivers, none escapes the impact of rentierism. For instance, the rentier state's spending patterns – from co-opting opposition forces to 'securing' military/security forces – weaken the political space for potential civil society activists. By being a *bakshish* state, this rentier state has reversed the historical democratic rationale from 'no taxation without representation' to 'no representation without taxation'.

Robustness of authoritarianism and 'absence' of viable alternatives

Whereas research on the impact of civil society and opposition forces should continue, equal attention should be devoted to the incumbent rulers' use of various instruments to decapitate this opposition. These instruments range from co-option to plain political repression. After an initial period of easy 'pre-emptive' democratization measures, the incumbent rulers find it costly in terms of power concessions to deepen the transition process. Given the fragmentation or lack of credibility of most opposition forces and the low level of popular mobilization for democratic demands, the incumbent rulers find it easier and less costly to suppress any potential threats against the regime and prevent 'chaos and disorder'.

Fear of uncertainty

The weakness of grass-root and institutionalized opposition make the existing government the 'guarantor' of political stability and the 'only alternative' to political and even societal breakdown. It is important to emphasize the two sides of the equation: governmental repression but also weakness and lack of credibility of opposition political parties. In fact many of these parties suffer from undemocratic aspects similar to those of the incumbent regime: lack of transparency, lack of elite circulation, intolerance of dissidents, low membership, patronage and clientalism, structural organizational defects and modest know-how of marshalling popular mobilization. They are thus easily co-opted/eliminated by the existing regime.

In such a context of perceived non-governmental void, the alternative to the incumbent regime is a worse political regime or plain chaos. For instance, secularists and liberals often fear the rise of Islamists; Islamists fear plain secularists' clampdown, communal minorities fear different forms of majoritarianism. The regime, its security elites and doctrinal allies capitalize on this fear of uncertainty about the alternative or 'jumping into the unknown' to exaggerate the catastrophic and impending impact of change. Note this reflection on Egypt's 2005 parliamentary elections by Ambassador E. D. Walker, former ambassador to Egypt, former Assistant Secretary of State for Near Eastern Affairs, and former President of the Middle East Institute:

> The most striking element of the election was the victory of the Moslem Brotherhood. I am quite sure that the government knew that a number of the Brotherhood's candidates would succeed . . . [I]t works to the advantage of President Hosni Mubarak to show to his constituencies and to the United States that the alternative might not be so attractive if he is out of power. I think that there is a certain amount of complicity in allowing the Muslim Brotherhood to campaign so visibly and identify itself as a group running candidates.[48]

The sayings of authoritative Islamic scholars (e.g. Ibn Taymeyya 1263–1328) are (ab)used to affirm the position that basic political and religious duties cannot be fulfilled "except through power and authority of a leader". Given the (manipulated) political void, the present leader is to be preferred to the abyss of the unknown.

External factors

The analysis of external factors has been unduly neglected.[49] Many incumbent rulers capitalize on the presence of an external threat (e.g. Israel) to bolster a 'national security state' with a dominant role for military and security forces. In this context, the role of dissidents and the possibility of breakdown of law and order are depicted as the actions of a 'fifth column' or a Trojan horse aiming to undermine the security of the homeland, for the profit of the enemy. In this context, any form of political dissent is depicted as a 'threat' to national security.

Moreover, the conduct of open elections is depicted as an open door allowing 'ill-intentioned demagogues' and 'phoney democrats' to abuse the democratic process (e.g. Islamists in the 1991 Algerian elections, Hamas in the 2005 Palestinian elections, the Muslim Brotherhood in the 2005 Egyptian elections). Their 'alliance' with 'rogue' states (e.g. Iran) could herald the potential rise of an international 'undemocratic' alliance to (ab)use the ballot box to carry out a democratic miscarriage.

In the post-9/11 context, this is a weighty argument for Western governments and their civil societies to guarantee their support for incumbent regimes. Indeed, such argument dampens condemnation of political repression by world democratic forces and could attenuate their insistence on punitive measures against repressive regimes.

Conclusion

The comparison of different transition patterns, externally pressured or domestically induced, shows the prevalence of the democratic deficit. But its causes cannot be reduced to one single factor, Islam or otherwise.

Since the issue of democratization has moved from academic circles to top the international agenda, its analysis in the Middle East has to resist the pressuring logic of daily political events or succumb to media dictat. It has to avoid substituting the pitfalls of an 'instant research industry' for the previous benign neglect. Given the strategic and socio-economic importance of the Middle East, a well-planned research programme about its democratization process, or lack thereof, has to avoid the trap of over-generalizations, in favour of empirical analysis of specific patterns and their characteristics. Such a research programme should trace the ups and downs of the democratization process, its varied pace, its limited successes or great failures and the potential causality of these patterns. This well-planned research process is mandatory both for the decoding of Middle East dynamics as well as for truly understanding the diversified patterns of a universal democratization process.

NOTES

1 Marsha P. Posusney and Michele Angrist (eds.), *Authoritarianism in the Middle East* (Boulder and London: Lynne Rienner, 2006), p. 2.
2 Rex Brynen, Bahgat Korany and Paul Noble (eds.), *Political Liberalization and Democratization in the Middle East, Vol. 1 – Theoretical Perspectives* (Boulder and London: Lynne Rienner, 1995), p. 5.
3 For details, see Bahgat Korany, Rex Brynen, Paul Noble (eds.), *Political Liberalization and Democratization in the Middle East, Vol. 2 – Comparative Experiences* (Boulder and London: Lynne Rienner, 1998), pp. 1–10.
4 On the findings and analyses of ten case studies, see ibid., especially last chapter pp. 267–278.
5 Eva Bellin, 'Coercive Institutions and Coercive Leaders', in Posusney and Angrist (eds.), *Authoritarianism in the Middle East*, pp. 21–42.
6 Bahgat Korany, 'Arab Democratization: A Poor Cousin?', in *Political Science and Politics* 27/3 (September 1994), pp. 511–513.
7 Jason Brownlee, 'Political Crisis and Restabilization', in Posusney and Angrist (eds.), *Authoritarianism in the Middle East*, pp. 43–62.
8 *Iraq Index*, 30 January 2006 (Washington, D.C.: The Brookings Institution), pp. 14–16.
9 Ibid.
10 Ibid., pp. 17–20.
11 Ibid., p. 28.
12 Ibid., pp. 29–31.
13 Ibid., p. 37.
14 Ibid., p. 41.
15 Ibid., p. 33.
16 Ibid., p. 39.
17 *Mayo Newspaper* (official organ of the governmental National Democratic Party), 4 May 1981.
18 For details about this complex process and its evolution, see Bahgat Korany, 'Restricted Democratization from Above: Egypt', in Bahgat Korany, Rex Brynen, Paul Noble (eds.), *Political Liberalization*, Vol. 2, pp. 39–70.
19 See the table in ibid., p. 52.
20 International Center for Future and Strategic Studies, Workshop on 'The 2005 Parliamentary Elections', Cairo, January 2006.
21 Samuel Huntington, 'Will more Countries become Democratic?', in *Political Science Quarterly* 11/2 (Summer 1984), p. 208.
22 Samuel Huntington, 'Democracy's Third Wave', in *Journal of Democracy* 2/3 (September 1991), p. 11.
23 Nazih N. Ayubi, 'Islam and Democracy', in David Potter et al. (eds.), *Democratization* (Cambridge: The Polity Press, 1997), pp. 345–366.
24 Ibid.
25 Moataz A. Fattah, *Democratic Values in the Muslim World* (Boulder and London: Lynne Rienner, 2006), pp. 26–30.
26 Ayubi, 'Islam and Democracy'.

27 Fattah, *Democratic Values*, p. 89 for the presentation of this Islamic diversity in a diagrammatic form.
28 Ibid., p. 4.
29 A personal discussion with Dr Kamal el-Menoufi, Dean (1998–2005) of the Faculty of Economics and Political Science, Cairo University.
30 Fattah, *Democratic Values*, pp. 85–86.
31 Yusuf al-Qaradawi, *On the Jurisprudence of the State in Islam* (Cairo: Dar al-Shuruq, 1997) (in Arabic).
32 Fahmi Huwaidi, *Islam and Democracy* (Cairo: Al-Ahram, Center for Translation and Publication, 1993) (in Arabic).
33 Tariq al-Bishri, *The Contemporary Legal Situation Between Shari'a and Positivist Law* (Cairo: Dar al-Shuruq, 1996); al-Bishri, *What is Modernity?* (Cairo: Dar al-Shuruq, 1996); and al-Bishri, *The General Traits of Islamic Political Thought in Contemporary History* (Cairo: Dar al-Shuruq, 1996) (in Arabic).
34 Ahmad Kamal Abu al Magd, *The Dialogue of Confrontation* (Cairo: Dar al-Shuruq, 1988); Abu al-Magd, *A Contemporary Islamic Vision* (Cairo: Dar al-Shuruq, 1993) (in Arabic).
35 Muhammad 'Emara; see especially, *Islam and the Philosophy of Rule* (Beirut: Arab Foundation for Study, 1977) (in Arabic); *Islam and the Bases of Rule* (Beirut: Arab Foundation for Study, 1972) (in Arabic); *Schools of Islamic Thought* (Cairo: Dar al-Mustaqbal al-'Arabi, 1983); *The Fall of Secular Extremism* (Cairo: Dar al-Shuruq, 1995) (in Arabic).
36 There are many others, for example, Muhammad Salim al-'Awa, *On the Political System of the Islamic State* (Cairo: Al-Maktab al-masri al-hadith, 1975); Khalid Muhammad Khalid, *The State in Islam* (Cairo: Dar Thabet, 1981); and Khalid, *Memoirs: My Story with Life* (Cairo: Dar akhbar al-yom, 1993).
37 For a tour d'horizon, Gilles Kepel, *Le Prophete et Pharaon: Les mouvements islamistes dans l'Egypte, contemporaine* (Paris: La Decouverte, 1984); and for a much more recent analysis, Hala Mustafa, *Political Islam in Egypt: From Reform to Violent Movements* (Cairo: Al-Ahram Center for Political and Strategic Studies, 1992); and especially the most thorough and recent survey, Nabil 'Abd al-Fattah and Diya Rashdan (eds.), *A Report on the State of Religion in Egypt* (Cairo: Al-Ahram Center for Political and Strategic Studies, 1996) (in Arabic).
38 Abu al-Magd, *Dialogue*, pp. 6–13.
39 Huwaidi, *Islam and Democracy*, pp. 23, 43, 45, 50.
40 Emara, *Schools of Islamic Thought*.
41 Al-Qaradawi, *On the Jurisprudence*.
42 Huwaidi, *Islam and Democracy*, pp. 64–70.
43 Ibid., pp. 78–85, 160–163; and al-Qaradawi, *On the Jurisprudence*, pp. 47–160.
44 Al-'Awa, *On the Political System*, p. 84.
45 Huwaidi, *Islam and Democracy*, pp. 97–102.
46 Fattah, *Democratic Values*, p. 128.
47 For a framework characterizing the dominant component of the region, see Baghat Korany, 'The Middle East After the Cold War: Torn between Geo-Politics and Geo-Economics', in Louise Fawcett (ed.), *International Relations of The Middle East* (Oxford: Oxford University Press, 2005), pp. 59–76.
48 Edward Walker et al., 'The Future of Egypt', A Panel Discussion, *Middle East*

Review of International Affairs (MERIA), Vol. 10, No. 2 (June 2006) (electronic version).

49 See for instance F. Gregory Gause III, 'Regional Influences on Experiments in Political Participation in the Arab World' and Gabriel Ben-Dor, 'Prospects of Democratization in the Arab World: Global Diffusion, Regional Demonstration, and Domestic Imperatives', both in Rex Brynen, Baghat Korany, Paul Noble (eds.), *Political Liberalization*, Vol. 1, pp. 283–306 and 307–332 respectively.

PART 2

REFORM IN THE ARABIAN PENINSULA

4

Political Reform in Bahrain: The Turning Tide

Neil Quilliam

Bahrain's reform process differs from other processes taking place in the Gulf Arab states. Whereas reforms in the other GCC states have been driven by a combination of external factors and the rulers' desires to re-market their countries images, the Bahraini experience has been driven by domestic factors alone. Bahrain's demographics, which favour the Shia community, has pitted the Sunni-led regime against a majority 70% Shia population. The Shia community's leaders argue that they have been marginalized from the formal power structures and continue to face institutional discrimination. This sense of injustice has driven the Shia community and other civil society groups to demonstrate for change. Throughout the 1990s, the emirate was caught up in violent struggle between opposition groups and the state security apparatus.[1]

Upon the ascension of Sheikh Hamad bin Isa Al Khalifa to the throne in 1999, he launched a process of political reforms. This chapter argues that whilst Bahrain's reform process is limited in scope, it has nevertheless raised public expectations and, therefore, reached a point of no return. If King Hamad were to reverse the reforms, Bahrain would experience substantive and sustained social unrest that would undermine the existing social contract between state and society.

It is incorrect to describe Bahrain's political experience as democratization. Although there may appear to be institutions that accord with a functioning democracy, they do not enjoy the same authority shared by other parliaments and judiciaries in developed countries. Moreover, King Hamad is a constitutional monarch in name, but an absolute ruler in practice. By definition, constitutional monarchs refrain from engaging in daily political life and preside over institutions vested with clearly defined powers that cannot be subverted by a higher authority. In Bahrain's case, Hamad is clearly in command, as he directs government business and governs parliament's agenda.

This chapter also argues that Hamad's intentions have never been to democratize Bahrain's political system, but to consolidate the ruling Al Khalifa family's position within the emirate. Conversely, Bahrain's civil society has sought to wrest some authority from the state and invest it in society. In other words, Bahrain's reform process, which was instituted in 2002, is characterized by the archetypal struggle between state and society. Although it started as a top-down process, and the ruling family has successfully contained most nascent opposition parties/societies, civil society groups continue to press for more concrete reforms.

Reforms

Sheikh Hamad Al Khalifa assumed power upon his father's death in 1999. Upon his ascent to power, Sheikh Hamad introduced political reforms such as the reduction of restrictions on freedom of expression and association, the removal of travel restrictions on dissidents, the abolition of state security laws, and the extension of full citizenship rights to women. Many political prisoners were released through a series of amnesties; furthermore all exiles were allowed to return.[2] In response, the public supported Sheikh Hamad's reform blueprint, namely, the National Action Charter, with an overwhelming 98.4% approval at a plebiscite held in February 2001. The National Action Charter promised to instate political reforms, including amendment of the 1973 Constitution that would lead the way to an elected parliament as the sole legislative organ in the state. Such reforms raised the expectations of the public that the King would eventually reinstate the parliament, which had been dissolved in 1975.[3] Nonetheless, these hopes soon dissipated with constitutional changes instituted in 2002, whereby Sheikh Hamad proclaimed himself King of Bahrain, and announced that Bahrain was a 'modern, democratic and constitutional monarchy'.[4]

Political Reform

Sheikh Hamad's ascension to power in March 1999 led to a new dialogue between the state and opposition. Bahrain was caught up in a farcical situation during Sheikh Hamad's first few months of office, as the Bahrain Freedom Movement (BFM) – based in London – called for the suspension of protests as a sign of goodwill and the government released

300 jailed political activists the following May. As part of the political theatre, the state security court dismissed these gestures and sentenced a leading opposition figure, Sheikh al-Jamri, to 10 years imprisonment, with a fine of US$13,300 and another fine designed to recover damages caused during the unrest. Within 24 hours, however, Sheikh Hamad dismissed the charges and ordered the release of Sheikh al-Jamri.[5]

The process of political reform had gained momentum by September 2000, as Sheikh Hamad appointed new members to the Consultative Council, which included four women. In his address to the Council, in its opening session, Sheikh Hamad called for a new national 'dialogue' over the constitution. The tenets of good governance were beginning to re-emerge, and in December 2000, a committee was appointed to assist in drafting a National Action Charter.

The National Action Charter allowed for the restructuring of the political system with a constitutional monarchy, an elected parliament and an appointed advisory council. As part of the reform process, the government announced that legislative powers would be restricted to the elected body. As a means of inclusion, Sheikh Hamad called for a public referendum on the content of the Charter, and some 217,000 Bahrainis, male and female over the age of 21, endorsed the Charter with an approval rate of 98.4% of the electorate between 14–15 February 2001. In accordance with the new political environment, Sheikh Hamad pardoned all political prisoners. As a result, local opposition leaders endorsed the Charter and urged their supporters to approve the Charter. The next parliamentary election was to be held in 2004, although the opposition requested that the date be brought forward.[6]

Another significant step in the political reform process was undertaken in February 2001 when the state security law was abolished. This marked a structural turning point in state–society relations. Accompanying this decision was the move to create a human rights commission within the Consultative Council. It was created to investigate human rights abuses; furthermore, Amnesty International was also permitted to visit Bahrain for the first time in 1999.[7]

Constitutional Amendments

Under the new constitution, the King extended his authority considerably. He declared himself as the 'protector of religion and home-land', a 'symbol of national unity'. He concentrated authority in the hands of the head of state, who was also the supreme commander of the defence forces and head of the executive, legislative and judicial branches of government. The king was to have power to appoint and dismiss ministers, acting ministers, ambassadors, heads of public institutions, judges and members of the Consultative Council. He also had extensive legislative power as he was entitled to "amend the Constitution and propose laws, and he is the authority for their ratification". Furthermore, the King empowered himself to restrict the National Assembly's own legislative mandate. According to the controversial constitutional amendments, the National Assembly comprised two 40-member chambers: a Chamber of Deputies elected directly by the public through a universal suffrage; and a Consultative Council to be appointed by the King. This effectively ensured that the king had veto power over any legislation.[8]

Recognizing their weakness and impotence, most opposition leaders expressed their disappointment and hoped that the King would listen to their demands. Dissidents criticized the King and accused him of abrogating his promise to institute democracy.[9] Constitutional amendments were perceived to have exceeded what was approved in the plebiscite. Nonetheless, criticisms were 'non-confrontational' and opposition leaders did not take to the streets. The regime, on the other hand, dropped references to 'participation' and 'national reconciliation', and reforms appeared to be perceived by the regime as royal favours (*makrama*).[10]

Subsequently, elections were held for the lower house of a new bicameral legislature on 24 October 2002. These were the first elections to be held in Bahrain since 1973. Although political parties are not permitted, political societies have been allowed some political activity. These societies could be divided into Islamist associations such as: Al Wifaq (The Islamic National Accord Society – Shia), al-Asalah Society (Salafi Sunni), al-Menbar (Sunni offshoot of the Muslim Brotherhood), Arab–Islamic Wasat Society (Centrist Islamist running on an anti-sectarian platform), Islamic National Accord (Shia), National Islamic Forum;[11] and secular ones, which include: National Action Charter Society (liberal), Democratic Progressive Forum (leftist pro-democracy), National Democratic Action Society (left-wing nationalist), National Democratic Gathering Society and al-Methaq (liberal).[12]

Denouncing the reforms undertaken by the King, especially, the role of the new upper house, four political opposition organizations (which are mainly Shia), namely, The Islamic National Accord Society (Al Wifaq), the National Democratic Action Society (NDA), the Arab Nationalist Democratic Society, and the Islamic Action Society, boycotted the elections.[13] The absence of the main political opposition societies, and the turnout of 53.5%, allowed for the formation of a Sunni-dominated parliament (with 28 out of 40 deputies).[14]

Economic Context
The economic scene has enabled Sheikh Hamad to carry out his policies without substantial resistance from the public. Although Bahrain is a small oil producer – with proven oil reserves of 125 million barrels, all concentrated in one field, Awali[15] – compared to its neighbouring Gulf Arab states, it has managed to benefit from oil price increases, which have stimulated economic growth. Oil prices have risen since Sheikh Hamad's assumption to power in 1999 and Bahrain's revenues from oil have increased by over 80%.[16]

Thus, the royal family and political elites supported his policies. The King managed to cultivate the support of the ruling elite by entrenching the patrimonial system. He appointed trusted members to the ruling family council in senior positions in government and public institutions. Patronage offered to members of the ruling family (almost 3,000) included raising their allocated monthly stipends; undertaking new housing projects in Rifaʿa, the Al Khalifa exclusive residence town; providing housing grants of more than BD172m (US$450m) extended to local elites; in addition to writing off up to a third of every housing loan owed to the state housing bank. Around 30,000 families, nearly 40% of Bahraini citizen households, gained from these royal favours.[17]

In spite of the prosperity of the economy signified by a high GDP growth, which reached 5.4% and 5.3% in 2004 and 2005 respectively,[18] the economy remains vulnerable as it is dependent on oil which forms around 70% of budget revenues,[19] especially as Bahrain serves as "an important service hub for the much larger surrounding oil economies". This vulnerability is further entrenched through Bahrain's hydrocarbon sector which forms the basis of its two major industries, namely refining and an aluminium smelter.[20]

Pressure on the authorities is increasing to promote measures that diversify sources of income away from oil, which is witnessing falling output. The government has planned a major reform to labour laws to help keep Bahrain competitive. The government is joining with private investors to inject large amounts of money into major housing and tourism developments such as the Lulu island resort to help diversify income streams. Allocations for infrastructure spending are high: US$2.76 billion for projects over the next two years, in a move designed to attract further foreign investment.[21]

Bahrain also boasts a burgeoning financial sector. Bahrain's financial centre, despite competition from Qatar and Dubai for banking and financial business, is the biggest in the Gulf. Bahrain has managed to establish itself as a main global Islamic financial centre. Bahrain has enjoyed an annual growth in the Islamic fund sector of 32.2% between 2000 and 2005. Currently, the kingdom hosts 78 authorized funds, compared with 37 at the end of 2002. Thus, Bahrain has around 34% of the world's total Islamic funds, whose annual growth globally is estimated to range between 15–20%, and is the largest host in the Gulf region. It is projected that the volume of Islamic funds in Bahrain will grow between 30 and 40% by the year 2010.[22]

Eager to sustain economic growth and diversify its economic activities, Bahrain was keen to sign a controversial bilateral free trade agreement (FTA) with the United States. The agreement

> which was passed by the US House of Representatives in December 2005 and must now pass to the Senate for approval – has angered Saudi Arabia, adding to economic strains on Manama as Saudi Aramco has cut back on its oil grant allocations and share of the offshore joint Abu Safah field. But it points to a willingness to change the institutional framework to allow Bahrain to take advantage of globalization. This is a theme particularly promoted by Crown Prince Salman Bin Hamad Al-Khalifa, whose chosen instrument for promoting a business agenda is the Bahrain Development Board.[23]

Constitutional Crisis

In March 2004, four opposition groups – Al Wifaq Society, the National Democratic Action Society, the Nationalist Assembly and the Islamic Action Society – sought to collect enough signatures to urge the King to annul the 2002 constitutional amendments. The amendments awarded the appointed Shura Council the same legislative powers as the elected Council of Representatives. The Shura's 40 members were appointed by the King. The opposition had opposed the new system claiming it resulted in a weak parliament.

The Bahraini Royal Court advised the opposition groups against organizing the petition, and stressed that only the parliament and the King had the right to propose changes to the constitution.[24] Nonetheless, the opposition groups started to collect signatures. Subsequently, 19 party members were arrested and charged with advocating changes to Bahrain's political system by illegal means, encouraging hatred of the state and distributing false news and rumours. The arrests marked a setback to the reform process, as they were the first political arrests made during King Hamad's reign.[25]

There is a discernible tension amongst the ruling family between liberalizing the political environment, as a precursor to attracting much needed inward investment, and maintaining a firm grip on power. Human rights, for instance, once advocated by King Hamad, have come to be reviewed with a little more suspicion. The Bahrain Centre for Human Rights received a stern warning from Assistant Undersecretary for Social Affairs Sheikha Hind bint Salman Al Khalifa that it could lose its licence if it continued to engage in political activities. The Centre was advised against violating articles 18 and 50 of the Association Laws, which ban civic society organizations from engaging in political activities. The Centre had clearly contravened government interests when it involved itself with 15 of the detainees arrested for collecting signatures for the petition for constitutional changes.[26]

Another indication of the tensions between reformers and conservatives came when the proposal to legalize political parties was rejected by the Legislative and Legal Affairs Committee in the Bahraini Parliament. The committee voted down the proposed bill "because it favoured a gradual practice of politics" in the kingdom. The creation of political parties, the committee argued, would endanger the newly launched democratic experiment in Bahrain.[27]

The repeated requests of the opposition and the regime's resilience have led to rising tensions which have culminated in the demonstrations that have become a feature of political life in Bahrain.

Demonstrations

The government lifted a ban on political demonstrations in February 2002. Since then, rallies sometimes involving thousands of people have become commonplace in Manama. The majority of gatherings have been peaceful but have the capacity of turning violent. A demonstration in front of the US embassy in April 2002 to protest against Israeli–Palestinian violence descended into a riot, resulting in a protestor being killed by the police.[28]

There have been several incidents of young men going on the rampage in the area of Exhibition Road, assaulting passers-by and damaging cars. The area is frequented by a large number of mainly Arab tourists. The most serious incident occurred on New Year's Eve in 2003 when several dozen young men were arrested for rioting after a football match.[29]

The attacks appear to be part of a nascent campaign led by Shia youths against officials. It is likely to be symptomatic of growing discontent among the Shia community over the slow pace of political change. Although ruler Sheikh Hamad bin Isa Al Khalifa has introduced a number of political and economic reforms, the community continues to feel marginalized from the political process and suffers from institutional discrimination. Furthermore, the Shia population is sensitive to developments in Iraq and to Sunni-led insurgent attacks upon their co-religionists. Although Bahrain has known sectarian unrest, which peaked in the mid-1990s, it has abated since 1999. This unrest was largely confined to Shia villages west of Manama and on Sitra Island, though arson and bomb attacks occurred in public places in central Manama.

The US-led Iraq War in March 2003 seems to have fuelled demonstrations in Bahrain. Although the demonstrations are linked to the war, they are more symptomatic of a building frustration within Bahraini society. In October 2003, for example, riot police were called in to quell a disturbance at a concert staged in the city centre by Lebanese singer Nancy Ajram when 200 protesters claimed her songs were 'immoral'.[30] Furthermore, in March 2004, several restaurants and houses suspected of selling alcohol were vandalized by groups of disenchanted youth.[31]

Clashes between Shia protesters and the police in May 2004 in Manama led to Sheikh Mohammed bin Khalifa Al Khalifa's dismissal, even though he had been Bahrain's Minister of Interior since 1974. Around 5000 protesters carried banners of Shia religious leader Grand

Ayatollah Ali al-Sistani, and shouted "Death to America". One banner carried by some demonstrators read "America must leave our holy shrines ... This is a red line they cannot cross. They are playing with fire." Despite the fact that the march had been given the go-ahead by the authorities, the police tried to block them at the halfway mark, saying the protest did not have interior ministry approval. The police action came two days after the King held a rare meeting with dissident leaders and ordered the release of the political prisoners accused of illegally trying to change the Bahraini political system.

On 19 May, King Hamad ordered the release of the prisoners following a meeting at the Royal Court with the leaders of nine political groups, including the four main opposition groups.[32] The King urged the politicians to embrace civilized and peaceful dialogue. He acknowledged citizens' right to express their anger and protest against aggression in Palestine and violation of 'sacred shrines' in Iraq. Giving backing to legal, peaceful protests, the King said, according to the Bahrain News Agency, "We share the anger of our people over the oppression and aggression taking place in Palestine and in the holy shrines (in Iraq). People had a right to peaceful protests." Subsequently, King Hamad ordered an official investigation into clashes between police and the protesters.[33]

Although protesters were demonstrating against the US military presence in Iraq's Holy Shia cities, the confrontation illustrated the underlying tensions present within Bahraini society; and it raised fears of a return to the sectarian violence that afflicted the Gulf state between 1995 and 1998. By dismissing his hardline interior minister, King Hamad sought to appease Bahrain's Shia community.

The series of violent clashes between police and demonstrators, which saw 20 Bahrainis wounded, including Jawad Firuz, a Shia opposition activist and member of Manama city council, was symptomatic of the creeping frustration felt by the Shia community towards Bahrain's political system. Moreover, it was not the first time that the Shia community has expressed dissatisfaction with King Hamad's political reform process.[34] This process, which has included a return to parliamentary politics, the release of political prisoners and the inclusion of Shia ministers in the government, has not satisfied Bahrain's majority Shia community. Their discontent with the governing system has, as we have seen, manifested itself in a number of ways, including the petition calling for constitutional reforms, the attacking of Asian homes suspected of selling alcohol, demonstrations against Nancy Ajram and groundswell resistance to hosting the Formula One racing event.

There are clear signs that Bahrain's political reform process is moving too slowly for the Shia community, which has articulated its concerns in the form of petition, protest and vandalism. The King, on the other hand, has demonstrated his unwillingness to contemplate constitutional change, as this would affect the ruling family's grip on power. Therefore, King Hamad has resorted to a more traditional method of co-opting opponents and bestowing patronage upon them. The dismissal of the interior minister, the commissioning of an investigation into the demonstration, and the release of the new political prisoners, were designed to appease the opposition without committing the government to a fundamental compromise. It was a quick fix solution. Hence,

> an endless round of demonstrations continues, the latest over the sentencing of several individuals for their participation in December 2005 riots at Bahrain airport over the arrest of Shiite cleric Khalid Hamed Mansour Sanad, as he returned from Iran. Protesters continue to complain that the government deliberately tries to aggravate demonstrators through their heavy-handed response. Some 200 family and non-governmental organization members turned up at the airport to stage a sit-in protest, but some were later arrested. Protesters were put on trial. Found innocent of charges of using violence, they were convicted of staging an illegal meeting and sentenced to jail terms of up to two years; the Appeal Court has commuted this to 12 months. Sanad was subsequently released and left the country. Peaceful and violent protests have rumbled on, and the security forces have been accused of beating some detainees, whose families and supporters have continued to organize peaceful public protests (which are now commonplace, and are broadly tolerated by the authorities).[35]

Limitations of Reforms

As the regime has failed to respond to their demands, the opposition has adopted confrontational strategies, such as holding limited demonstrations by the unemployed, victims of torture and women's rights activists. Such activism has become the way to voice discontent with the reform process advocated by the King. The opposition utilized two main contentious issues in mobilizing support for their campaign against the regime, namely human rights abuses and political naturalization of stateless bedouins.

The King's contempt for public opinion was manifested in the royal decree that institutionalized human rights violation by granting impunity to officials who had been involved in human rights abuses prior to February 2001. This deprived alleged victims from legal compensation and left their torturers at large. The King refused to listen to local and international human rights watchdogs and revoke the decree.[36]

Bahrain has granted citizenship to around 10,000 bedouins, who despite residing in Bahrain for generations had been stateless and subject to 'systematic discrimination'. Although this was a consensual decision, opposition groups claim the government has manipulated this policy to change the composition of the Sunni/Shia population in favour of the former. The opposition's efforts were apparently successful in exerting pressure on the elected members of the parliament to push the issue on the agenda of the parliament. Hence, although a parliamentary commission denied these allegations, they are still widely believed by the public.[37]

Other forces joined the opposition and in April 2004 a diverse group of critics launched a petition calling for constitutional reform. The police reacted violently by jailing 17 of the demonstrators; however, King Hamad pardoned the petitioners and called for dialogue with the opposition. Subsequently, in May 2004, when police then abused some Shia clerics who were demonstrating against American aggression against holy shrines in Iraq, the King promptly fired his own uncle, who had been interior minister since 1974 and replaced him with Major General Sheikh Rashid bin 'Abdullah bin Ahmad Al Khalifa. The King's popularity rose again.

The regime's repressive policies culminated in the arrest of Abd al-Hadi al-Khawaja, the former executive director of the banned Bahrain Centre for Human Rights (BCHR) and the disbandment of the BCHR, after his blame of the Prime Minister, Sheikh Khalifa Al Khalifa, for the country's current economic problems and past human rights abuses.[38] Al-Khawaja's arrest, in September 2004, triggered more demonstrations. This exerted pressure on the government to release al-Khawaja following a royal pardon in November 2004. Nevertheless, demonstrations continued; in March 2005, around 80,000 protesters (including women) took to the streets of Sitra, the third largest island located south of Manama which is a predominantly poor Shia community, in response to Al Wifaq's call to urge for constitutional reforms in defiance of a government ban on the demonstration.[39]

Successive demonstrations ensued during March–June 2005 demanding democratic reforms. A peaceful march, instigated by the Shia-led opposition, followed unsuccessful talks with the government on constitutional reforms to empower the parliament's elected assembly, which currently stands on an equal footing with a state-appointed chamber.

In March 2005, the government drafted an anti-terrorism law, where terrorism is defined broadly as "any threat or use of force to disable the provisions of the constitution or the laws, to disrupt public order, to expose to danger the safety and security of the kingdom and to harm the national unity or the security of the international community". Furthermore, Article 6 of the draft law proposes the death penalty for "whoever creates, establishes, organizes or manages, in violation of the provisions of the law, an association, body, organization, group, gang or a branch thereof".[40]

Furthermore, in July 2005, the parliament issued a new law of association, which was endorsed by the King. The law stipulates that political societies can be formed only as long as they are not based on class, profession, sect, or geographical principles. A new provision raised the minimum age to join a society from 18 to 21.[41] The law also "bans foreign donations to societies and requires government permission for contacts with parties in other countries". Significantly, the law "has forced the opposition to act – societies that failed to register by early November 2005 ceased to be recognized as political groups".[42]

The new law, therefore, represented a setback to civil and political liberties in Bahrain. Thus, it was decried by the opposition and they appealed to the King not to ratify the law which would 'restrict their operations' after the law had been passed by the parliament and the Consultative Council. In particular, political associations were concerned about raising the minimum age of joining a society, as large numbers of their constituencies were under 18, so the number of their supporters would drop.[43] Paradoxically,

In mid-February, the Foreign Affairs Ministry announced plans to establish a new human rights body that will pursue accountability for alleged torture cases. How this will co-operate with the National Committee for Martyrs and Victims of Torture, established in 2002, is unclear. The NCMVT was set up to campaign for recognition of those tortured and to cancel King Hamad's Decree No 56 of October 2002, which effectively bans any legal action against any civilian or military official accused of involvement in human rights violations before February 2001.[44]

The four main opposition groups' decision to participate in the 2006 election is an important turning point in the reform process. The King effectively persuaded them to endorse and operate within the 'legitimate' political system and seek change from 'within'. The societies that boycotted the previous elections and then decided to engage "have lost the street-level support of populist activists who now see the Islamic Haq movement as the real and uncompromising opposition".[45] Al Wifaq's decision to take part in the elections verges on the historic. Its absence from the process would likely have derailed the political process altogether and led the country to another period of social unrest and violence. Nevertheless, its decision to engage meant that whilst it endorsed the system, it sought to change it from within. The decision, however, has divided Al Wifaq's leadership and supporters, and the likelihood of extra-constitutional attacks against the symbols of state will increase, if progress towards empowering the lower chamber of parliament continues to stall.

Thus, the political reform process has been manipulated by the regime to curtail liberties. Not only has the regime maintained its tight grip over power, economic and political resources, but it has also failed to address fundamental societal issues, namely sectarian tensions, unemployment and corruption.

Sectarian Tensions

Tensions between the disadvantaged Shia Muslim majority (70%) and the minority Sunni Muslim elite have always been a feature of politics in Bahrain. The Sunni minority has traditionally formed Bahrain's political and economic elite: the ruling Al Khalifa dynasty is Sunni, as are many leading merchant families. The Shia majority, burdened with high unemployment and systematic discrimination in employment (they occupy 18% of jobs in the public sector), housing and services, has long bridled at Sunni dominance of the state administration and the local economy.[46]

Villages located outside Manama are inhabited mainly by Shias. The deteriorating housing conditions of these villages have been vividly described in an International Crisis Group (ICG) report which stated that these houses accommodated "as many as ten or more family members in three-room mud hovels. In some instances, families shared space inside their homes with livestock, creating wretched conditions and clear health risks. There are over 40,000 families waiting for government-promised subsidized housing." Impatient for change, between 1994 and 1998 Shia activists staged arson attacks on shops, schools, banks and hotels. The introduction of wide-ranging political reforms since 1999 has eased, but not eliminated, sectarian tensions.[47]

Women's rights issues have further complicated sectarian tensions as rights advocates have campaigned to take issues which are significant to women out of religious or family courts and submit them to civil courts. However, this has been resisted by Shia religious figures, who see this initiative as an attempt to reduce "the community's power and influence".

Unemployment
Despite its promising economic performance, highlighted above, economic problems plague the kingdom, especially unemployment and poverty. A study commissioned by the Crown Prince ('Reforming Bahrain's Labour Market') in 2004 projected that unemployment would reach 35% by 2013, where 70% of those employed will be occupying jobs below their skill level and, more importantly, falling short of their expectations.[48]

One can conclude that Bahrain's political reforms have been partially driven by its economic dilemma. Bahrain sought to enhance its image as a prerequisite to signing a FTA with the US that opened the US market to Bahraini exports. However, given the fact that expatriate labour constitutes more than 60% of the population in Bahrain, it is unlikely that a FTA would help create jobs, as expatriates form the pool of skilled labour for employers, especially for jobs that Bahrainis are unwilling to take.

According to official statistics, Bahrain's total population stood at 650,604 in 2001, of whom more than 60% (405,667) were Bahraini nationals.[49] The rest of the population were expatriate workers (mostly from Asia), who constituted nearly 60% of the economically active population.[50] Although high by international standards, the figure is low compared to other Gulf Arab states, where nationals usually amount to a minority.

There are 16,000 unemployed persons in Bahrain, according to government estimates. Yet there are some 270,000 expatriate workers in the economy. There is, therefore, a skills gap, not an employment gap. There are plenty of jobs, but Bahrainis are not getting them first – and not because they do not need them. Many Bahrainis have not benefited greatly from the country's development, and average incomes are as low as BD180 (US$481) a month. With an already bloated public sector unable to absorb new entrants in the job market, Bahrain has committed itself to encouraging the private sector to be the engine of economic and employment growth.

The private sector, however, tends to prefer expatriate employees over local, either because they are cheaper, or more appropriately qualified, while they also have fewer rights than nationals, making it easier to sack them and harder for them to switch employer if they are unhappy.

Previously, government policy focused on the nationalization of the workforce by quota. Quota policies, requiring that companies employ an increasing number of nationals as a percentage of their workforce, are common throughout the Gulf, but have been shown to be seriously inadequate in addressing the underlying causes of unemployment and underemployment among nationals. The government's new proposals promise to shake up the labour market entirely, removing unhelpful national employment quotas, instituting anti-discriminatory labour regulations, and introducing fees for expatriate staff to equalize the costs of hiring local and foreign workers.

After initial scepticism, many in the private sector have since come round to the proposals on closer reading. Businesses were concerned that the sudden introduction of fees would drive up costs overnight and put them out of business. The bill that was put to parliament, however, calls for a gradual implementation of reforms to allow the private sector to adjust to fees, and minimize any negative impact on the economy. In the beginning, the entry fee for expatriate workers will be BD100 (US$267), the same as the current cost of a work permit. Subsequent monthly fees will begin at around BD10 and be increased over a period of several years.

The end of the quota system, which should be phased out in 2009, will actually give companies far more flexibility to hire the skilled expatriate labour they need. In addition, the introduction of standard regulations on the hiring and firing of both national and foreign employees will enable businesses to increase the productivity of their staff in a more competitive environment. As a result, if the government's parallel education reforms are not effective at preparing the local workforce for the jobs on offer, the private sector should not suffer.

The law, once it has passed through the Shura and been signed by the King, will establish an independent Labour Market Regulatory Authority (LMRA) to collect and monitor data on the labour market, meaning that future policy can be adapted to the changing environment. In addition, a Labour Fund will be established, overseen by a board from the private sector, into which revenues from the new fees will be poured. This fund will be used to ease the transition, through such schemes as helping companies train and develop Bahraini staff or buying new machinery and equipment to reduce reliance on unskilled labour.[51]

Corruption

Although Bahrain ranked favourably amongst Arab countries in the Transparency International Corruption Perceptions Index, with a rank of 36 out of 158 countries in 2005,[52] corruption is a source of grievance for the public. The elected parliament, in turn, is under pressure to act responsibly and independently by challenging the government. This was evident in a televised row in January 2004 between members of the Chamber of Deputies and the government. They were discussing the findings of an eight-month enquiry into administrative and financial irregularities at the General Organization for Social Insurance and the Pension Fund Commission, the organizations which handle all public and private sector pensions respectively. These irregularities allegedly lost them "hundreds of millions of dinars".

Deputies pushed to cross-examine three ministers individually. Although they were not members of the ruling family, some of the officials implicated in the affair belonged to the ruling family. It was also thought that a criminal investigation could implicate the Prime Minister himself. Thus, the speaker of the parliament, Khalifa al-Dhahrani, reminded the deputies that similar confrontations had led to the dissolution of the parliament in 1975, and he asked them to restrain themselves to avoid delivering the same fate to the National Assembly for another 28 years. This warning sparked protests and King Hamad promptly issued a statement commending the government and deputies "for their cooperation and the quality of their debates" which represented "a victory for democracy" in the kingdom. The Prime Minister also declared that "directives have been issued to government officials urging them to cooperate fully with parliament".

Eventually, the three ministers were summoned to the Council, where investigations were held for three weeks after which the ministers managed to preserve their posts.

> By invoking article 145 of the Council's own by-laws, which stipulates that ministers cannot be held accountable for actions performed when they held portfolios other than their current ones, the government managed to limit questioning of the Minister of State. It also invoked article 45 of the July 2002 royal decree, which effectively exempted the Minister of Finance from scrutiny. The Minister of Labor, appointed in November 2003, was deemed too new to the job to be held accountable. The episode reflected poorly on the government as a whole, however, as the commission's report revealed that losses incurred by the pension funds resulted from bad investment decisions, mismanagement, and corruption.[53]

This episode revealed the impotence of the National Assembly to hold the government accountable and that democratic reform which entailed instating a lower house was a façade. This was highlighted when, in February 2006, some deputies "accused the government of non-cooperation, saying its rejection of five of six motions they had presented was the latest sign of its unwillingness to cooperate".[54]

Conclusion

This chapter has argued that reforms were introduced to help the ruling family, which has become synonymous with the state, and to reassert and consolidate its authority after facing six years of domestic turmoil. In other words, King Hamad used the reform process to re-orient state–society relations, but there was no intention to divest the state of its authority.

The combination of economic crisis and social discontent compelled him to entertain political reforms. His succession in 1999 was an optimum moment to institute change, as it signified the beginning of new era. Although his uncle, Sheikh Khalifa bin Salman Al Khalifa, the hardline Prime Minister retained his position, Hamad appeared committed to reform and was able to appeal to Bahrain's political and social discontents. Moreover, his early moves showed that reconciliation between the opposition and the regime was possible and the likelihood of meaningful reforms was probable.

However, the regime's success has been delimited by its failure to address the dilemmas of society, namely, marginalization of the opposition; sectarian discrimination between the majority Shia and dominant Sunni minority; corruption; mounting unemployment; high rates of poverty; and a rising cost of living.

So far, the regime has continually resorted to repression in order to maintain order.[55] However, this tactic is proving less successful as the regime has had to respond to public pressure by castigating the actions of its security forces. It should be noted that although the majority Shia population is unhappy with the current state of affairs and would like to see more reforms and a substantial improvement in their conditions, they support the Al Khalifa ruling family. They merely look for more participation and accountability and responsiveness of the government.

It is important to understand that Bahrain's reform process will not follow a linear path. As with most reform processes, its momentum will be aided by pressures from civil society groups and other actors, and constrained by the limited vision of the country's leadership. The tension between state and society will shape the overall process. Moreover, external influences likely from Saudi Arabia and the US may affect the pace of change.

There has been little international pressure placed upon the Bahraini government to accelerate or deepen the reform process. On the contrary, Saudi Arabia, its large neighbour, has watched events with some concern and counselled against empowering society at the expense of the state. It shares a particular concern over the politicization of its own Shia community, which is primarily located in the oil-rich Eastern Province. Shia activism in the Eastern Province during the 1980s, partially inspired by the Iranian Revolution in 1979, led to an ongoing confrontation between the Saudi Shias and the security forces.

The US, which has sought to promote democracy in the Arab region, has placed little pressure on the Bahraini government. It would seem to be the most likely recipient of such pressure, as Bahraini civil society is active and has made some progress that requires consolidation. In fact, some of Bahrain's civil society groups have called upon the US to intervene more forcibly, but to little avail.

The process has reached a critical stage. Hamad's attempt to manage expectations has failed. The high expectations that followed the success of the referendum have dissipated, and the more conservative members of the ruling family have managed to slow the pace of change. Subsequently, the struggle between state and society has now moved into a new phase. It is likely to intensify over the next two years; the opposition groups will try to influence the process either through legitimate means – for example, participating in national elections – or by a return to violent measures. In keeping with his top-down approach to reform, Hamad has more or less compelled the four main opposition groups to engage in the official process by threatening to close illegal political societies. The decision to legalize political associations offered opposition groups the chance to represent their constituents and mobilize their efforts within a legal framework. However, the political associations' law under which they must now operate has placed a number of constraints on their activities.

Since starting the process, the regime has sought to co-opt the opposition into the governing system, whilst containing their influence. Nonetheless, the four main opposition groups (now legitimate associations), which enjoy widespread support, are intent on enforcing changes to the system. The Bahraini government does not enjoy the same natural resources as its neighbours, so it is unable to 'buy-off' its opposition; moreover, the Shia community's sense of political and economic marginalization has ensured that it will pursue change over the long term.

NOTES

1 See Falah al-Mdaires, 'Shi'ism and Political Protest in Bahrain', *DOMES: Digest of Middle East Studies*, Vol. 11, No. 1, Spring 2002, pp. 20–44; J. E. Peterson, 'Bahrain's First Reforms under Amir Hamad', *Asian Affairs*, Vol. 33, Part 2, June 2002, pp. 216–227; Naomi Sakr, 'Reflections on the Manama Spring: Research

Questions Arising from the Promise of Political Liberalization in Bahrain', *British Journal of Middle East Studies*, Vol. 28, No. 2, November 2001, pp. 229–231.

2   Abd al-Hadi Khalaf, 'Political Reform in Bahrain: End of a Road', *Middle East International* at http://meionline.com/features/194.shtml, 19 February 2004.

3   Brian Evans, 'Moving Backwards in Bahrain', *Middle East International* at http://meionline.com/features/378.shtml, 7 July 2005.

4   'King Hamad: Bahrain to Become a Modern Constitutional Democracy', http://www.arabicnews.com/ansub/Daily/Day/020215/2002021534.html, 15 February 2002.

5   http://news.bbc.co.uk/1/hi/world/middle_east/389382.stm.

6   Gulf Centre for Strategic Studies, 'Parliamentary Elections and the Future of Democracy in Bahrain', *Bahrain Brief* at http://www.bahrainbrief.com.bh/english/dec2002-issue.htm, Vol. 3, No. 11, December 2002.

7   *Bahrain, Country Profile* (London: EIU, 2001).

8   Khalaf, 'Political Reform in Bahrain'.

9   The London-based Bahrain Freedom Movement spoke of "a constitutional putsch even more alarming than the 1975 dissolution of parliament".

10 Khalaf, 'Political Reform in Bahrain'.

11 The Shia Islamic Action Society was suspended in September 2005 and it was required by the government to cease all activities after a 'crowded festival' was organized to honour those imprisoned for their involvement in an alleged 1981 coup. However, it soon resumed its activities. See *Wikipedia*, http://en.wikipedia.org/wiki/Islamic_Action_Party.

12 Gulf Centre for Strategic Studies, 'Bahrain's Political Societies Profiled', *Bahrain Brief* at http://www.bahrainbrief.com.bh/english/april2002-issue1.htm, Vol. 3, No. 4, April 2002.

13 'Bahrain: Four Political Societies Boycott Elections', http://www.arabicnews.com/ansub/Daily/Day/020904/2002090418.html, 9 April 2002.

14 Gulf Centre for Strategic Studies, 'Parliamentary Elections and the Future of Democracy in Bahrain', *Bahrain Brief* at http://www.bahrainbrief.com.bh/english/dec2002-issue.htm, Vol. 3, No. 11, December 2002.

15 In addition to oil reserves in Alwai Oilfield, Bahrain might have undiscovered oil reserves in the Gulf of Bahrain, see Energy Information Administration, http://www.eia.doe.gov/emeu/cabs/Bahrain/Oil.html.

16 Khalaf, 'Political Reform in Bahrain'.

17 Ibid.

18 Energy Information Administration, http://www.eia.doe.gov/emeu/cabs/Bahrain/Background.html.

19 'Steady Growth Expected in Non-oil Revenues with Current Strategy', *Bahrain Tribune*, posted at Middle East and North Africa Financial Network, http://www.menafn.com/qn_news_story_s.asp?StoryId=76476.

20 Energy Information Administration, http://www.eia.doe.gov/emeu/cabs/Bahrain/Background.html.

21 'Risk Management Report: Bahrain', *Gulf States Newsletter*, Issue 777, 10 March 2006.

22 Oxford Business Group Briefings, 'Bahrain: Sukuks on the Rise', 10 May 2006.

23 'Risk Management Report: Bahrain'.

24 'Bahrain Warns the Opposition against Demanding Constitutional Amendments',

http://www.arabicnews.com/ansub/Daily/Day/040427/2004042710.html, 27 April 2004.

25 http://news.bbc.co.uk/2/hi/middle_east/3691647.stm.

26 Bahrain Centre for Human Rights, http://www.bchr.net/sections/index. php?action=view&newsid=127.

27 'Political Party Reforms', *Arab Reform Bulletin*, http://www.carnegieendowment. org/publications/index.cfm?fa=view&id=1589, Vol. 2, No. 7, July 2004.

28 'Bahrainis Held a Peaceful March towards the US Embassy', http://www. arabicnews.com/ansub/Daily/Day/020518/2002051815.html, 18 May 2002.

29 Uli Schmetzer, 'Iraq Standoff Raising Anti-U.S. Fever: Protesters Turn Up Heat on Gulf States', *Chicago Tribune*, 4 January 2003, posted at http://www.ccmep. org/2003%20Articles/010403_Iraq_standoff_raising_anti-us_Fever.htm.

30 Al-Jazeera, 'Bahrain Protest at Provocative Show', http://english.aljazeera. net/NR/exeres/1C7E7A67-C1EF-437F-A9B1-0319B974FE6C.htm, Tuesday 28 October 2003.

31 US State Department, *Country Reports on Human Rights Practices: Bahrain*, 28 February 2005, http://www.state.gov/g/drl/rls/hrrpt/2004/41719.htm.

32 'Bahrain: Petition Detainees Released', http://www.arabicnews.com/ansub/ Daily/Day/040520/2004052012.html, 20 May 2004.

33 Ali Al-Qadumi, Shila Abulhasan, and Ali Muradi, 'Bahrain IM Sacked over Attack on Protest against Holy Sites Sacrilege', http://www.jafariyanews.com/ 2k4_news/may/23_bahrainprotest.htm, 23 May 2004.

34 Al-Jazeera, 'Anti-US Protests Shake Bahrain', http://english.aljazeera. net/NR/exeres/5BB5398A-365A-414D-BD2D-19FEFB93918F.htm, Sunday 23 May 2004.

35 'Fraught Mood in Bahrain, Caught between Compromise and Continued Opposition', *Gulf States Newsletter*, Issue 780, 28 April 2006.

36 'Rights Group Calls for Reform in Bahrain', *Daily Star* at http://www.dailystar. com.lb/article.asp?edition_id=10&categ_id=2&article_id=16385, 1 July 2005.

37 Khalaf, 'Political Reform in Bahrain'.

38 Nora Boustany, 'In Bahrain, Doubts about Reform', *Washington Post*, http:// www.washingtonpost.com/wp-dyn/content/article/2005/06/23/ AR2005062301895.html?nav=rss_opinion/columns, 24 June 2005.

39 Mazen Mahdi, 'Bahrain Warns Opposition after Pro-Reform Rally', *Arab News* at http://www.arabnews.com/?page=4&section=0&article=61126&d=27&m=3&y= 2005, 27 March 2005.

40 Evans, 'Moving Backwards in Bahrain'.

41 'Bahraini Groups Criticises New Political Law', *Middle East International* at http:// www.middle-east-online.com/english/?id=14076=14076&format=0, 21 July 2005.

42 'Risk Management Report: Bahrain', *Gulf States Newsletter*, Issue 777, 10 March 2006.

43 Habib Toumi, 'Bahrain Says New Law Will Help "Sensible" Growth of Societies', *Gulf News*, 17 August 2005.

44 'Fraught Mood in Bahrain'.

45 Ibid.

46 Boustany, 'In Bahrain, Doubts about Reform'.

47 International Crisis Group, 'Bahrain's Sectarian Challenge', *Middle East Report*, No. 40, 6 May 2005.

48 Evans, 'Moving Backwards in Bahrain'.
49 http://www.bahrain.gov.bh/census/htm2/603.htm.
50 http://www.bahrain.gov.bh/census/htm1/a6.htm.
51 Oxford Business Group Briefing, 'Bahrain: Labour Reform', 23 April 2006.
52 Although Bahrain ranked better in 2004, 34 out of 145 countries, its score remained the same 5.8 out of 10, where 10 is the least corrupt according to perceptions of business people and country analysts. http://www.transparency.org/policy_research/surveys_indices/cpi/.
53 Abd al-Hadi Khalaf, 'Bahrain's Parliament: The Quest for a Role', *Arab Reform Bulletin* at http://www.carnegieendowment.org/publications/index.cfm?fa=view&id=1536, Vol. 2, No. 5, May 2004.
54 'Fraught Mood in Bahrain'.
55 The Paris-based Reporters sans Frontières issued its Worldwide Press Freedom Index ranked Bahrain a dismal 143rd out of 167 countries in 2004, which signifies a sharp deterioration in its rank as 67 in 2002. Evans, 'Moving Backwards in Bahrain'.

5

Deconstructing Before Building: Perspectives on Democracy in Qatar

Ahmed Abdelkareem Saif

The events of 9/11 and the US invasion of Iraq plus a combination of other factors have created a new sense of momentum impelling the countries of the Arabian Peninsula towards an era of profound economic and political change. Democratization is rapidly becoming the US policy of choice to meet the challenge of anti-Americanism and radicalization in these countries. The US administration believes that only democracy can undermine the conditions that engender political radicalism.[1] In spite of some prominent detractors,[2] the Bush administration has adopted the view that democracy is not only feasible but also necessary in the Arabian Peninsula and the Muslim world at large.

The United States, however, may get a sort of democracy in these countries but this may have unforeseen consequences for regional security and stability, similar to what is happening in Iraq. This chapter questions the democracy in Qatar, in particular, and the countries of the Arabian Peninsula more generally. It will be argued that patching up existing systems will not work and that partial reforms will only lead to escalating violence. In order to ignite a process for authentic democracy, the old political and cultural infrastructure should be deconstructed. Only then can genuine reform be implemented. Such deconstruction is a must to ensure the avoidance of façade democracy, disorder and chaos.

The Arabian Peninsula in the American Democratic Perspective

American policymakers have long grappled with the so-called 'democracy dilemma' in the Arab world: how should the United States promote political liberalization without threatening the core of US interests in the Middle East? These interests include maintaining Israel's security, ensuring reliable access to and a reasonable price for petroleum reserves

[103]

in the Gulf, preventing terrorism and the spread of weapons of mass destruction, and supporting US investments. Yet supporting genuine democratic change may not only provoke tension with Arab regimes whose cooperation is essential to the achievement of US interests, it also risks bringing to power groups that would actively reject an American agenda.[3]

Because of this democracy dilemma, the US administration recognizes that limited political reform could help to maintain the stability of the region. Expanding participation in politics and decision making could decrease opposition to unpopular regimes and thereby contribute to the long-term viability of key, moderate Arab regimes friendly to the US.

Muqtader Khan argues that the United States faces two contradictory imperatives: on the one hand, the fight against terrorism that compels Washington to seek closer ties with autocracies throughout the Middle East. On the other hand, the US increasingly believes that it is precisely the lack of democracy in many of these countries that helps and breeds Islamic extremism.[4] Democracy in the Middle East will clearly mean that states in the region will be less willing to comply with US interests at the cost of their own national interests. Solving this uncomfortable dualism is central not only to the future of the war on terrorism but also to the future and shape of the Arabian Peninsula and the Middle East.[5]

Qatari Political Liberalization in Regional Perspective

In spite of its small geographic size, Qatar is emerging as a relatively major player in the Gulf, to some extent at the expense of Saudi Arabia. Much of Qatar's policy can be understood as an attempt to remove or decrease the perceived overbearing Saudi dominance. Since His Highness Sheikh Hamad bin Khalifa al-Thani came to power, he has challenged Saudi hegemony in three areas: firstly, by cementing close relations with the US, contradictory to the Saudi perception that prefers a covert obedience to the US while at the same time maintaining a traditional Islamic public discourse that is resistant to the West; secondly, by establishing limited relations with Israel; and thirdly, by implementing calculated political liberalization, including the founding of the controversial Al Jazeera satellite channel.[6]

This can all be seen in the Qatari challenges to Saudi Arabia that manifested themselves within GCC debates and perhaps even in border clashes, where Qatar resisted frequent Saudi attempts to expand Saudi Arabia's borders at the expense of the smaller Gulf sheikhdoms. Moreover, it is possible that Qatar sees the balance of power within the GCC countries shifting gradually away from Saudi Arabia. The demise of Saddam Hussein means that Qatar no longer needs to look for Saudi protection or has to carefully consider oversensitive Saudi domestic politics, let alone wrestle with the uncertain destiny of the Saudi monarchy.

If Iraq overcomes its current multiple divisions and develops in the direction of a stable pro-Western, American bastion, we may see a group of small pro-Western Gulf monarchies with liberalizing tendencies, arrayed against a hesitant Saudi Arabia, a country that is dependent on the US but is unwilling to publicly declare it, and a country in desperate need of political and economic reform, but moving very slowly towards it and sometimes appearing to move in the opposite direction. A stable Iraq, if achieved, would, in essence, replace Saudi Arabia as 'point man' for American influence in the region.[7] By proceeding with reforms Qatar might also play a key regional role if Saudi Arabia reached a deadlock in the reform process due to domestic socio-political contradictions.

To understand Qatar's endeavour we must question how the decision makers in Qatar perceive the threats they face, and we must look at the institutional, social, political and ideological conditions that tend to intensify or reduce such threats. Qatar is a homogeneous tribally-based society where most inhabitants are descended from central Arabia and embrace Wahhabi Islamic jurisprudence which is the same as that of Saudi Arabia. Unlike Saudi Arabia, however, the small size of population in an area enhanced by oil wealth enabled the regime in Qatar to move swiftly towards liberalizing politics and adopt more universal values without incurring great resistance. Such advancement is beneficial to the regime in Qatar in three ways: firstly, it allows itself to distance itself from Western allegations that Wahhabism breeds violence via its rigid interpretation of Islamic tenets; secondly, it allows the regime in Qatar to escape the influence of Saudi hegemony. The demise of Saddam's regime in Iraq, an escalation of American criticism of Saudi Arabia and the regime's uncertainty, hostile American attitudes against Iran, and the direct US military presence in the region make the American umbrella the most convenient one for the regime in Qatar. Accordingly, Qatar has to harmonize its policies and image with the American ones. Finally, after witnessing two coup attempts[8] instigated by Saudi Arabia in 1996 and 2005, it is beneficial to the ruler of Qatar to rejuvenate his legitimacy through institutionalizing the system of government and establishing a new base of support through democratic institutions that surmounts the old Saudi-style base of legitimacy enjoyed by his predecessor.

Nevertheless, democracy is not a ready-made product that can be imported and implemented straightaway. Over the past two decades, the Middle East has witnessed a 'transition' away from – and then back towards – authoritarianism.[9] It is now clear that liberalized autocracy has proven far more durable than once imagined.[10] Brumberg argues that Middle East regimes are becoming less, rather than more, autocratic in response to what they see as the social, economic, political, and geostrategic challenges facing their regimes.[11] Such political eclecticism has the benefit of making the Arab rulers more durable, and Qatar, therefore, may persist as a liberalized autocracy rather than a full democratic polity.[12]

Democratic Measures in a Stagnant Pool

Since seizing power in 1995, the regime in Qatar has taken numerous steps to promote economic and political liberalization, which are probably modest in comparison with what is needed, but undoubtedly remarkable and even progressive, as well as occasionally controversial and unexpected compared to what exists in other Arabian countries, as will be seen below.

The media

An unprecedented step was taken by the Emir in 1996 when he abolished the Ministry of Information, thus indicating the abolition of government censorship of the press and reflecting his serious intentions towards reform. Freedom of the media represents one of the most striking examples of the new era of freedoms in Qatar and is most obviously represented in Al Jazeera, which is now the most famous and controversial satellite TV channel in the region. This station began its programmes in 1996 as an independent TV channel owned by private capital. It is now testing the limits of media openness to an extent never seen or heard before in any Arab country.

The station has introduced daring and provocative programmes and news bulletins unknown before in the Arab world. These include direct broadcasting from 'hot spots' around the world and criticism of Arab rulers and governments and their internal and external policies. On several occasions, Al Jazeera has caused real diplomatic crises between Qatar and other Arab countries, such as Saudi Arabia, Kuwait, Bahrain, Egypt and Jordan, who responded in some cases by verbal or media attacks on Qatar and by closing the station's offices in their countries. Al Jazeera enjoys the unlimited protection of the Qatari government because it accepts one de facto limitation on its freedom: it does not criticize the Qatari government in any way, but it has also been involved in a mysterious undeclared alliance in its scope and aims with the Muslim Brotherhood.[13]

The obvious impact of Al Jazeera is manifested in the manifest effect it has had on the regional media. It forces media in other Arab countries to open up and to relax applied restrictions and censorship in order to cope with the new standards laid down by Al Jazeera. This can clearly be seen in the increasing number of outspoken TV channels based in Dubai and sponsored by various countries.

CMC elections

In 1998, the Emir decided to hold the first-ever general elections for membership to the Central Municipal Council (CMC). All Qatari men and women over the age of 18 would be eligible to vote and run as candidates for the 29-member Council, an advisory body attached to the Ministry of Municipal Affairs and Agriculture that oversees the work of the nine municipalities in the country. By 17 October 1998, the deadline for registration of candidacy for the CMC election, there were 280 candidates, including 8 women. The number of women who registered as voters was high, some 45% of the eligible population. This is a percentage that compares favourably with similar numbers in many developing countries. The 8 women who registered as candidates for the Council showed the diverse range of political participation in Qatar. On 8 March 1999, however, many candidates dropped out, bringing the number of those running for election to 227, including 6 women. Women cast their ballots in places separate from men. Voting participation was extraordinarily high, with a turnout of about 95% of registered voters in Doha and 75% in the rest of the country. The election results produced great frustration, since none of the female candidates won a seat in the CMC, which indicated that Qatar remained a traditional society that was uneasy about placing women in high positions, even in local politics. Nonetheless, one of the most significant aspects of the new phenomenon of the involvement of women in elections and the public-policy process was the changing attitudes of the families and relatives of the women involved.

Moreover, government ministers and other public officials took the initiative and began to replace, where possible, appointed bodies by elected ones in the councils attached to their ministries. The first significant election to demonstrate the new spirit was that of the powerful Board of the Qatar Chamber of Commerce. The elections for that Board took place in April 1998, when some 3700 Qatari businessmen voted in a secret ballot to elect the 17 members of the Board. Until that date, members had been appointed by the Emir, based on a recommendation by the Minister of Finance and Economy.

The ideas of democracy even flourished in schools and institutions of higher education. In December 1998, the Deputy Assistant Minister of Education and Higher Education issued a statement announcing that "in accordance with the orientation of the Emir" the ministry would apply the democratic process to all aspects and at all levels of the ministry. Until then, few people in Qatar dreamed of involving students in any kind of representative bodies for fear that such activities could thrust young people into politics.

With the rise of the democratic tide, Qataris also began to discover some of the 'problems' associated with elections, notably election fraud and ballot rigging. In November 1998, the first case of electoral fraud was registered when the Ministry of Finance and Economy cancelled the elections to the board of al-Muntazah Consumer Association after it was discovered that the number of ballots cast was higher than the number of voters by some 100 votes. The ministry then called for new elections.[14]

Educational reform

The government of Qatar launched a comprehensive initiative to reform the educational system under the title "education for a new phase", with the objective to cope with successive developments in this field at the international level. The new system aims to found new commissions to assume the mission of development and reform under the supervision of the Higher Council for Education, which is chaired by Qatar's Crown

Prince Sheikh Tamim Bin Hamad al-Thani. This initiative, which started in May 2001, is considered the cornerstone of efforts towards reform in Qatar, which considers education to be crucial if progress is to be made.

Qatar has also fostered its educational partnership with Western counterparts by establishing the Qatar Foundation in 1995. It comprises of a group of Western institutions[15] which support the development of quality human resources through centres of excellence in education, research and technology. Such an initiative is seen as important for engaging the Western world and the Islamic–Arab world through higher education and its cultural component. The Foundation aims to foster understanding among different cultures as it crosses international borders, and to spread universal Western values.

The Middle East Partnership Initiative (MEPI)

To stress its commitment to the democratization of the region, the United States announced a new partnership in December 2002 to focus on encouraging development in three areas critical to progress in the Arab nations: economic, educational and political reform. The Middle East Economic Partnership (MEPI) aims to expand political participation, support civil society and fortify the rule of law. The MEPI has now established two regional offices in Doha and Abu Dhabi and tries to facilitate democratic norms by supporting non-governmental initiatives. The MEPI has, however, been widely criticized in the region: firstly by regional state officials, who argue that it constitutes a direct intervention in the state's domestic affairs, and secondly by observers from the region who dispute the sincerity of the United States' initiation of democratic change in the light of the modest funds devoted to the MEPI.[16]

Democracy forums

Reform at a regional level requires countries of a certain region to derive support and receive inspiration from each other. In this respect, one 'model' country can play an important role in stimulating the region as a whole. The political leadership in Qatar is emerging as a progressive force in the Arab world that can serve as such a model. Qatar is trying to set the standard for other neighbours to follow with regard to democracy, reform in Islam, education, economics and the rights of women. Therefore, since 2003 Qatar hosted a series of conferences on the topic of reform in the Middle East. The first conference was in 2003 and focused on educating Arabs about elections and the participation of women in politics. Another conference in 2004 dealt with human rights in educational curricula. This was followed in 2005 by another conference focused on issues relating to development, strengthening economic growth and fostering peace in the region.

Related to this, Qatar has worked keenly to organize the annual Doha Forum on Democracy and Free Trade, which has met every year since 2000. These conferences have brought together participants from all around the world representing officials, decision makers, heads of trading companies, diplomats, academics and intellectuals in order to discuss critical issues for the international community within the framework of a common desire to move the democratic process forward, to develop citizens' participation in establishing free trade legislations and to remove frontiers and obstacles to a more equitable globalization, and consequently a better future. Throughout its six previous sessions, this forum has emphasized the values of peace, tolerance, security and freedom while prohibiting all kinds of violence. Through this annual forum, Qatar aspires to be a crossroads for intellectual contributions to the progress of the region.

The constitution

In a referendum conducted in April 2003, 96% of voters approved the 150-article constitution. The roster of electorates showed only 71,400 eligible to vote among 150,000 nationals out of a population of 650,000, mostly expatriate workers. The constitution cleared the way for the separation of executive, legislative and judiciary branches and stipulated that no changes could be made to the document for the first 10 years it was in effect. It allowed 30 members of parliament to be elected and reserved power to the Emir to appoint the remaining 15 members. Legislative elections were scheduled to take place in 2006, but they have been delayed to an unspecified date[17]. Though not convincing, the government announced this delay was to give more time for people to get acquainted with the democratic process, thus ensuring an effective parliament.

The constitution, however, established a 4-year term for the 45-member parliament, in which women would be eligible to run for office. The semi-elected parliament would have the right to draw up legislation, question cabinet ministers, review and vote on the government's budget proposals and debate decisions taken by the cabinet ministers – all of whom would still be appointed by the Emir, who remained the head of state. The Emir retained the right to veto legislation, but was also required to reconsider any vetoed bills that were resubmitted by the legislature within three months. The Emir could also dissolve the parliament, but under the constitution was obligated to call for new elections within six months.

In addition, the constitution explicitly guaranteed the rights of freedom of expression and freedom to form societies, but not political parties, and stressed the right of women to vote and hold elected office. The document called for an independent judiciary based on Islamic law. While Article I explicitly stated that the *shariah* is the 'main source of legislation', there was apparently room for applying liberal interpretation in the law. The constitution, however, allowed all religions to practise their faiths. Interestingly enough, the constitution also outlawed any offensive war by the state. Nonetheless, the constitution continued to guarantee the primacy of the ruling family and did not constitute an authentic full democracy in terms of peaceful alteration of power or the institution of a constitutional monarchy.

By comparison and based upon constitutional and institutional developments, the GCC countries are divided into three categories: those which have adopted a Western-oriented style, which comprises Kuwait and Bahrain; those with a hybrid or mixed style, swinging between traditional and quasi-Western style, which includes Qatar and Oman; and those with a traditional style, such as Saudi Arabia and the UAE. On a constitutional spectrum, where one end represents Western democracy and the other end represents traditional absolutism, we find that the GCC countries Bahrain, Kuwait, Qatar, Oman, the UAE and Saudi Arabia are scattered from democracy to absolutism on the following scale:

TABLE 1
Degree of Democratization among the GCC Countries

Democracy	Bahrain	Kuwait	Qatar	Oman	The UAE	Saudi Arabia	**Absolutism**[18]

Source: Ahmed A. Saif, *Constitutionalism in the GCC States* (Dubai: Gulf Research Centre, Research Paper 4, 2004), p. 29.

Qatar has both civil and *shariah* courts, but only *shariah* courts have jurisdiction in criminal matters and there are ad hoc security courts, but such cases have been rare.[19] Qatar's Ministry of Civil Service Affairs and Housing promulgated new regulations in May 2005 for non-governmental societies and professional associations that streamline the operating requirements for associations, but forbid affiliation with groups outside Qatar and restrict membership of organizations to Qatari nationals over 18 years. The societies are not allowed to deal with political issues and all their activities, including fundraising, are monitored by the ministry. In May 2005, Qatar also outlined a catalogue of human rights abuses that include prolonged detentions, mistreatment of foreign workers and the use of children as jockeys in camel races.

The role of women

Some of the most dramatic progress for women in the Arab world has been realized in Qatar – a country committed to the full participation of women in public life. In February 2004, Qatar was selected to host the first of a series of regional women's leadership conferences sponsored by the US State Department in cooperation with the Elections Committee of the Supreme Council for Family Affairs of Qatar. The conference provided interactive training, and taught skills for successful electoral and advocacy campaigns in preparation for parliamentary elections.

The new transition for Qatari women has been greatly facilitated by the support of Princess (*Sheikha*) Mozza al-Misnid, the wife of the new Emir. She has a university degree and speaks three foreign languages: English, French and Spanish. Contrary to her counterparts in other GCC countries, she is very active in public life. She was appointed as the head of the Supreme Council for Family Affairs, and often gives speeches on public occasions. In December 1998, she led a two-hour, all-female march through the streets of Doha in support of a local charity, the first event of its kind, not only in Qatar but in the whole region.

The new democratic orientation in Qatar is giving Qatari women rights they have never enjoyed before. Women in Qatar have already achieved a number of high-level government positions, such as deputy assistant minister. They are allowed to travel and study abroad by themselves, although they are segregated in Qatar at all levels of education including the university. Nonetheless, allowing women to vote, to be candidates, and to hold public office in the new Municipal Council and the forthcoming parliament, has opened unprecedented new horizons for Qatari women in fields that were heretofore the sole prerogative of men.

Despite this, however, the traditional cultural environment still does not help to promote the representation of women in elected bodies, as shown above in the CMC elections. It is widely believed, however, that as the democratic process is incremental, with a developing educational system and increasing exposure to the external democratic world, Qatar's society will gradually accept and support a greater role for women in public life.

Why All these Measures are Meaningless

In spite of the remarkable democratic steps taken by Qatari government, it is hard to claim that they are conducive to an authentic democracy for the following reasons:

Absolute independence

The state in Qatar, as in the rest of the GCC countries, lives in two contradictory situations. It is highly dependent on the external world, which makes it vulnerable and susceptible to outsiders, but at the same time it is privileged with absolute domestic independence. Mohamed Ghubash explains this phenomenon saying that the financial revenues of the state in the Gulf are absolutely independent from the cycle of national economy because they depend heavily on oil that is explored, produced, refined and marketed by foreign companies; thus, the citizens have no bargaining power vis-à-vis the state, as thoroughly discussed by the well-known theory of 'rent'.[20] The state also has an absolute independence from the workforce by depending to a large extent on expatriates. Consequently, citizens have no power to organize themselves in syndicates and unions or to exert enough pressure on the government through strikes.[21] Finally, the state also has an absolute independence from its citizens at the level of defence and security by depending on external powers for protection. Consequently, the state appears extremely powerful against its citizens and weak against the external world.[22] In such a context, it is unlikely that the powerful, omnipresent state would recede and promote democracy either in the absence or presence of powerless civil and political institutions.

Imbalanced distribution of power

Although the promulgated constitution represented a milestone in Qatar's political life, the distribution of power still favours the palace in a way that places the pace and direction of reform in the hands of the Emir. The constitution states that the rule is hereditary in the al-Thani family, and the Emir holds political and military powers in addition to legislative and judiciary prerogatives. The executive has leverage over other authorities and the Emir and his office are unaccountable before any other authority. The distribution of power is immensely unbalanced and, because of that, reforms will remain gifts granted by the ruler who, logic dictates, is unlikely to foster an authentic democracy.

Testing genuine democracy in Qatar

As noted by Marina Ottaway "significant" reform does not mean perfect reform. The challenge is to distinguish between partial steps that are significant, because they start altering the distribution of power and the character of the political system, and those that are merely window dressings.[23]

Ottaway argues that one way to approach the difficult problem of differentiating between significant and cosmetic reform is the concept of a paradigm shift. Transition from an authoritarian to a democratic system requires a political paradigm shift, an abandoning by those controlling the government, but often also by their opponents, of old assumptions about the fundamental organization of the polity, the relation between the government and the citizens, and thus the source, distribution and exercise of political power. Without such a paradigm change, a country can still show some progress toward a less repressive political system without making real progress toward democracy. The wave of post-Cold War political transitions provides numerous examples of political reforms without paradigm change, leading to the rise of semi-authoritarian regimes.[24] The concern here regarding democracy in Qatar is that, without having real and active political and civil bodies, there cannot be any shift and it is more likely that the regime is transforming into a semi-authoritarian one.

Old wine in new bottles

Since the 1970s, many techniques have been used to manipulate society and to distract the energy of youth away from involvement in the politics of the GCC states. Among these tools is the use of the massive oil revenues to offer the people tax-free services, such as education, healthcare, tax-free income, subsidized utilities etc., known in the region as the welfare state.

Also, increased public expenditures have been directed particularly towards sports and clubs so that sports absorb youthful momentum in the region and became the first topic of concern in youth gatherings. However, since 2000 and up to the present day, these regimes have discovered a new effective technique to keep people away from politics: the stock market. While there can be no doubting the economic usefulness of the stock exchange and shares to the national economy and to the people, these financial markets have played an unexpected political role in shifting the attention of the people away from politics towards gaining money.[25] Now share fever is sweeping the whole region, making people politically indifferent while completely deluged in the shares market.

The ability of the state to manipulate this tool has been enhanced by the sharp increase in oil prices and the huge surplus that has been made in recent years, which fuels the share market through public expenditure and keeps shares attractive for people who hope to make easy money in unrealistic and extraordinary regional stock markets. This tool may work in the short to medium term but will not work in the long run, because the market, by virtue of its nature, has tools to readjust itself and a crash is very possible, which will bring with it harsh political and social outcomes.

Engineering democracy

As noted by Francis Fukuyama, democracy cannot come about in any society unless there is a strong domestic demand by local actors, such as the elites and the political and civil societies.[26] Thus, it does not matter what the external actors do to promote democratic transition if there is no real domestic mobility. The constitutional and institutional arrangements per se do not guarantee democracy will survive without enhancement from the underlying conditions. As Robert Dahl points out, if the underlying conditions are highly favourable, democracy is likely to succeed regardless of the type of constitution and institutions, and if these conditions are highly unfavourable no arrangements will save democracy.[27] The Qatari underlying conditions are mixed: some are favourable and others are not. In this case, Dahl argues that democracy is chancy; therefore, a well-drafted constitution and well-designed institutions probably help democracy to survive.[28]

Qatar is undergoing an unbalanced modernization. Despite its shortcomings, the political elite are far more progressive when compared with social and economic components. If social attitudes, values and behaviours and economic output production[29] are considered on the one hand, and political leadership on the other, the latter is shown to be far ahead. With the increase in discrepancies between these factors, crises of identity, legitimacy and participation may occur that would weaken the political system. However, although the new institutions of the political system may function, they do not necessarily work as intended. The introduction of new institutions will certainly alter existing power structures over time, but not necessarily in the way that was imagined.

Therefore, in addition to the help of the United States and other Western countries in promoting democracy in Qatar, there is a need to set the stage for favourable conditions for democracy and push the underlying mechanisms that bring the country to democracy so that it becomes more likely and sustainable. The first way to approach this problem is to investigate the conditions that facilitate democratic transition. Francis Fukuyama points out that there are basically four conditions. The first has to do with the level of development. Rich countries have an easier time sustaining democracy than poor ones. Second is culture. Culturally diversified societies more easily transform to democracy than others. The third has to do with neighbouring countries. The more democratizing neighbours there are, the more possible the trickle effect and democratic diffusion. The final condition has to do with the prevalent ideas in a society that may or may not help in democratic transformation.[30] Despite the importance of these conditions, they are still not enough to guarantee a sustainable democracy.

Historical evidence suggests negative results when meeting these conditions while maintaining the old construction. An authoritarian regime can introduce selective reforms that end with a distorted democracy and nevertheless survive. In some cases these reforms fail because of a lack of faith, as was the case with Sadat of Egypt and the policy of openness in the 1970s, and sometimes because of the hypocrisy of the main democratic powers in their dealings with and support of authoritarian regimes, such as in the cases of Saudi Arabia before 9/11 and Iraq under Saddam Hussein in the 1980s. But probably the most important reason for the failure of democratization is domestic resistance to genuine democracy in different forms. This may be justified through a need to maintain peculiarity that includes religion and traditions; or may occur because of misunderstanding and misperception that lead to a rejection of Western political thoughts; or may result from conspiracy theories that portray democracy as a Trojan horse that seeks the demise of Islamic civilization; or may happen simply because of a conflict of interests and the desire of the old guard to maintain the status quo.

Thus, I would argue that to achieve a successful and sustainable democracy we should not be patching up and building on an old political and social set-up, but first we should deconstruct the roots of authoritarianism before introducing democracy. In the following sections I will tackle some of these roots and discuss the need to uproot them. I will then examine the viability of the concept of deconstructing before building.

Deconstructing rigid and obsolete values

There is a great deal of confusion and overlapping between religion and tradition in the Arabian Peninsula. Over time people have codified religious tenets to match their customs in a slow and unconscious process; consequently they become more reluctant to change their values, believing that this would equate to a change to the religion itself. Amongst disputed values, for example, are democracy in which sovereignty rests in the people not in God; and women's rights in the public space, where leadership and the power of jurisdiction are privileges that historically have been confined solely to men. This religious understanding is still endemic in the societies of the Arabian Peninsula and is mixed up with tribal norms enhanced by strict Islamic jurisprudence, such as Wahhabism, as in Qatar.

As far as the incompatibility between Islam and democracy is concerned, recent surveys conducted by Pippa Norris of Harvard University and Ron Inglehart of the University of Michigan,[31] and published by the Pew Research Center, have revealed that Muslims overwhelmingly prefer democracy to any other form of government,[32] but though this preference may be visible in the more civil, tolerant and diversified Muslim societies, it is surely not so in Qatar and other countries of the Arabian Peninsula, nor likely to be, at least for the near future. Paradoxically, there is nothing in the essence of Islam that is fundamentally opposed to democracy, justice, freedom, fairness, equality or tolerance. Therefore, misunderstanding democracy has to be clarified and incorrect prevailing values deconstructed before implementing pluralistic values of democracy.[33]

Deconstructing social structure

Changing social structure away from a tribally-based society is a prerequisite for the flourishing of a civil society that embraces democracy and permits groups to aggregate around interests rather than around values. This, however, requires altering the mode of production that heavily depends on an oil-based economy and the mode of consumption that depends equally on consuming only imported materials. Altering these modes will enable the emergence of an endogenous bourgeoisie, which will change the structure of the traditional tribally-based society into a more civil society. Social components in Qatar are not as well defined as one might perceive. Division overlaps both vertically through ethnic and ancestral differences and, horizontally, through an individual's occupation – mainly in the state sectors – and the assets they hold – mostly directly or indirectly from the alliance with the state. These vertical and horizontal overlappings cement each other and reproduce themselves. Moreover, civil consciousness is still weak in terms of organized aggregation and the struggle for collective interests because of the lack of a real domestic base of production and the hegemonic role of the state over sources of wealth that enables it to create its own elites.[34]

In the pre-capitalist[35] Qatar society, one finds firstly that modes of production are very closely intertwined with modes of coercion, and secondly, that modes of circulation and distribution are as important, if not more so, than modes of production. One outcome of the articulated nature of modes of production is that aspects of horizontal stratification such as class and the elite are intertwined with aspects of vertical differentiation such as tribes, sect and ethnic differences.[36] Therefore, changing social structure starts with changing the mode of production by diversifying the economy, allowing more room for the private sector in the national economy on the one hand, and changing the modes of consumption and distribution by changing the role of the state and its relation to society on the other.

Deconstructing power concentration

In the more common approach, democratization is seen as a three-phase process: a period of liberalization, followed by a transition represented by the holding of competitive multiparty elections, followed finally by a prolonged period of democratic consolidation. The problem with this conceptualization of the process of democratization is that many countries experience only the first two phases.[37]

Generally speaking, the dominant assumption in the region is that only incumbent regimes have the power to launch a meaningful reform process without risking destabilization. This assumption is widely embraced by the people in the region and by Western countries. People who live in authoritarian countries have little experience with grass roots organization and are used to seeing the government as the source of all problems as well as all solutions. Those who do not share this perception are more likely to be recalcitrant and advocate violent and radical change rather than incremental reform. In addition, the focus on change from the top is also the result of political expediency for many Western powers. Change from the top would safeguard the interests of foreign countries that are interested in stability and that advocate democracy, not as a means to bring about sweeping change, which can be dangerous, but as a means to create mildly reformist regimes deemed to be more flexible and thus more stable than authoritarian ones.

However, political change that alters the distribution of power rarely comes solely at the initiative of the government. Reform is usually a response to pressures within the society that affect the balance of power in a country, make change imperative and put real pressure on the government to reform.[38] Democratic reforms are thus those that affect, or at least have the potential to affect, the distribution of power and make power subject to a popular mandate. They must contribute to limiting the power of the executive, allowing the emergence of other centres of power and introducing an element of pluralism. At the present time there is an extraordinary concentration of power in the hands of the Emir of Qatar, similar to his counterparts in other entities in the Arabian Peninsula. This is the fundamental problem of democracy in the entire region. Meaningful reform, by necessity, requires a remarkable shift in power distribution.[39]

Deconstructing the mechanisms of reproducing the same elite

From various elections that have taken place across the region, it is clear that those elements allied in one way or another to the government have had the lion's share in the representative assemblies, municipal and local councils and even in the chambers of commerce. This indicates the corporatist nature of the state that reproduces its elites. Therefore, it is essential to break up this cycle. The easiest available mechanism, although it is not the best, is to temporarily adopt the system of quotas for various political, civil, regional, gender and ethnic groups to be represented at national and local levels. This will end the monopoly of reproducing the same political elite in the system and will open the process of elite rotation and lead to new coalitions and bargaining that would broaden the process of representation.[40]

Ballot box or controlling state funds

The conventional assumption is that democracy is manifested by having elections. Nonetheless, elections do not make a democracy, as seen across the region with much ballot rigging and government intervention. The most brutal regimes often seek to legitimize their rule through manipulated elections. Hence, for elections to be a true reflection of the will of the people, they must be embedded in societies with strong civil institutions and a diffusion and devolution of power. Decentralization of power and fair and just elections thus necessitate the decentralization of power and the stopping of illegal access to state funds.

In this aspect Qatar has no special commissions or institutions charged with eliminating corruption. It also lacks an independent auditing body outside the executive and there is no regional or local watchdog organization that operates in the country. Though the government launched a major initiative to combat corruption in government procurement in 2003, this was not enough, as such a supervisory organ has to be outside the executive.

Transparency International's 2005 Corruption Perception Index ranks Qatar fourth among Arab countries and 32nd out of 159 countries worldwide with a score of 5.9 on a scale from 1 to 10, where 10 represents no corruption, as shown in Table 2.

TABLE 2
Transparency International Corruption Perception Index 2005

Country	Country Rank	Regional Rank	2005 CPI Score
Oman	28	1	6.3
United Arab Emirates	30	3	6.2
Qatar	32	4	5.9
Bahrain	36	5	5.8
Kuwait	45	7	4.7
Saudi Arabia	70	8	3.4
Yemen	103	12	2.7

Source: Composed from: http://www.transparency.org/news_room/latest_news/press_releases/cpi_2005_18_10_05.

The point worth noting here is that it is imperative to monitor a state's revenues and expenditures in a transparent and accountable system before having elections, to avoid misusing the state's power and wealth and to provide equal opportunities to all competitive parties.

The Prospects for Democracy in Qatar

There are both external and internal barriers to democratization in Qatar. The internal barriers have to be deconstructed as explained above and the external ones are to a great extent dependent on US policy in the region. The most important components of US policy regarding democracy in Qatar are as follows.

Changes in US policy

US policy that promotes democracy has to transform its approach from a negative to a positive image in the eyes of the people in the region. If pro-democracy forces in Qatar, and in the region at large, get on board with the new US policy, assuming that the United States is able to convince them of its sincere intentions, then the inertia will shift in favour of democracy. The biggest challenge that the US administration faces is distrust and lack of credibility in the region. Political and civil activists in the region look at the behaviour of the US administration in the region as a calibration of events, and act accordingly. Thus, the US needs to build a partnership for change, trust and respect with political and civil elements. People in the region are keen to change but are afraid the American initiatives are aimed simply at eliminating immediate terrorist threats and rearranging the region in a way that enhances US capabilities in the competition with other major international powers. Also a significant portion of the population in the Arabian Peninsula believes that the so-called 'war on terror' is not only a war on Islam but also an unjust effort to destroy the Muslim world in order to advance the interests of Israel and fundamentalist Christians, both of whom enjoy extraordinary influence on the White House.[41]

Political leaders and civil society activists need to grasp and act on a novel development: it is probably the first time that the declared American agenda matches that of the Arab people in the region. The promotion of democracy and economic reforms in the region provides an unprecedented opportunity for people to rally around the shared political goal that they all perceive as legitimate, urgent and practicable. There is a discernible shift but it is not yet enough – reforms have been significant but not yet decisive.

Success in Iraq

In spite of the fact that the GCC countries have benefited from ousting Saddam Hussein, the new dynamics have created a number of long-term challenges to the GCC states. Many of these challenges may exacerbate the long-standing problems that each GCC state faces, to differing degrees, such as foreign affairs, military weakness, domestic politics and social-economic affairs.[42]

The impact of such possible futuristic outcomes might even be worse than that of past impacts because of the ability of Arab satellite news networks and the internet to deliver uncensored news rapidly and the close ethnic, tribal and religious linkages between the Gulf Arabs and Iraqis. Both possible scenarios for Iraq are problematic for the GCC countries, if they maintain the status quo unreformed. A democratic Iraq would be a more compelling client for the United States in the Gulf than the monarchies of the GCC, as well as a very potent symbol for Shia and other groups pushing for change in Arab Gulf societies. More dangerously, if the current anarchic Iraq persists, it would cast a spell of instability over the entire region.

In sum, then, the governments of the GCC states and their peoples have an enormous amount at stake in the development process in Iraq and the need to reform their own societies generally. Though no GCC state is threatened by an invasion or economic collapse in the near or medium term, Gulf Arabs must begin to reform their societies and develop new collective, integrated institutions with their allies to guarantee a secure and prosperous future.

Destiny of Saudi Arabia

The other important factor in determining the pace and direction of reform in Qatar is the destiny of the House of al-Saʿud. The Saudi government also has to reform the kingdom's political, social and economic institutions, address sectarian and provincial grievances, and confront the groups in Saudi society committed to political violence at home and abroad.[43] Confronting terrorist organizations is not easy because an important portion of Saudi society, including military elements and religious elites, share the objectives and the world view of these organizations. This is exacerbated, as Anthony Cordesman argues, by the fact that the Saudi state does not have the intelligence assets, perspective or the will necessary to meet these challenges.[44] The situation may worsen because of reluctance to speed up genuine reforms, particularly if continued high oil prices enable the government to buttress the society with high public expenditures.

A part of the Saudi monarchy might be willing, but unable, to reform, which will eventually exacerbate the situation and lead to an intra-division that would threaten oil supply. This could force the US to allow the disintegration of the Saudi state from within, but to ensure the stability and prosperity of any newly carved-out state in the oil-rich eastern province of the current Saudi state. This scenario is possible and, if it happened, it might push democracy ahead in the Gulf sheikhdoms by freeing them from the traditional, dominating Saudi role. In this case, more harmony would be seen among the GCC countries.[45]

Developments in other GCC states

It is more likely than not that as more GCC countries adopt some sort of democratic measures, this will affect neighbouring countries, which will begin to imitate the process. This may start a trickle effect that diffuses the impact into neighbouring regions, encouraging people to demand more, which will force other regimes to make more concessions. The diffusion effect is already quite clear as was seen on 30 November 2005 when two women were elected to the Jeddah Chamber of Commerce. These were the first elections in Saudi Arabia that allowed women to vote and run for office. The UAE also have had for the first time, in December 2005, a semi-elected house of representatives with two female members.

Conclusion

Democratization is measured in years, decades and generations. As then-National Security Adviser (later Secretary of State) Condoleezza Rice noted, "The United States knows we must be patient and humble. Change is often difficult and progress is often slow."[46] Richard Haass also noted that democratization is a process fundamentally driven by a country's citizens: if any foreign government tries to impose democracy on a country, the result will be neither democratic nor durable.[47] This chapter has shown that in addition to the catalytic role that might be played by the US and other European countries in the promotion of democracy, it is also crucial to have favourable domestic conditions for the democratic process, and to start a systematic change. The main argument here, however, is that democracy is viable in Qatar but that to set the stage it is imperative not that new democratic institutions are built and more democratic measures are gradually introduced, but, more importantly, that the old set-up is eliminated or radically changed before a new one is built.

NOTES

1   See Thomas Carothers, 'Promoting Democracy and Fighting Terror', *Foreign Affairs* (January 2003), p. 84.
2   See Lewis, 'Islam and Liberal Democracy: A Historical Overview', *Journal of Democracy*, Vol. 7, No. 2 (1996), p. 57.
3   These concerns however can be mitigated if moderate Islamists seized power, since moderate political Islam, such as the Muslim Brotherhood in Egypt and Qatar, Islamic Work Front in Jordan and the official religious establishments in both Saudi Arabia and Pakistan, have shown a high level of pragmatism and for a long time have enthusiastically cooperated with the US. The example of the Islamic government in Turkey is a good case that refutes such fears.
4   Muqtader Khan, 'Prospects for Muslim Democracy: the Role of U.S. Policy', http://www.ijtihad.org.
5   Paula Dobriansky, 'The Core of US Foreign Policy', *Foreign Affairs*, Vol. 82, No. 3 (May/June 2003), p. 142.

6   Grey E. Burkhart and Susan Older, *The Information Revolution in the Middle East and North Africa*, National Defense Research Institute and RAND, 2003, p. 18.

7   Ibid.

8   The first coup attempt took place in 1996 to reinstate the previous ruler and the second happened in 2005 to oust the incumbent ruler. Interestingly, both were instigated by Saudi Arabia, as declared by Qatar, and mainly involved influential official figures from the same tribe 'Bani Murrah', which resulted in about 6000 citizens being stripped of their citizenship and expelled to outside the country's borders with Saudi Arabia in June 2005. This clearly illustrates continuing Saudi efforts to bring Qatar back under its traditional hegemony for security reasons.

9   Adam Przeworski, 'The Games of Transition', in Scott Mainwaring et al. (eds.), *Issues in Democratic Consolidation: The New South American Democracies in Comparative Perspective* (Notre Dame: Notre Dame University Press, 1992), p. 109.

10 Carothers, 'The End of the Transition Paradigm', *Journal of Democracy*, Vol. 13 (January 2002), p. 9.

11 Daniel Brumberg, 'Democratization in the Arab World? The Trap of Liberalized Autocracy', *Journal of Democracy*, Vol. 13, No. 4 (October 2002), p. 59.

12 Thomas Carothers defines the "gray zone" as one in which regimes are "neither dictatorial nor clearly headed toward democracy", see Carothers, 'The End', p. 9.

13 Al Jazeera provides an open and accessible platform for the Muslim Brotherhood. Many of its key staff, including the director, affiliate to the Muslim Brotherhood. This is controversial and contradictory to Al Jazeera's liberal orientation and thus poses many questions.

14 Saif, *Constitutionalism in the GCC States* (Dubai: Gulf Research Centre, 2004), pp. 26–27.

15 http://www.post-gazette.com/. Among the established institutions are: Carnegie Mellon, Weill Cornell, Virginia Commonwealth University and Texas A&M University.

16 The Administration committed $29 million for pilot education, economic and political reform projects in 2002. In the fiscal year 2003, it funded $100 million in programmes, and worked to award $89.5 million with fiscal year 2004 funds. In the Administration's fiscal year 2005 budget, Congress provided the MEPI with $74.4 million. http://mepi.state.gov/c10130.htm.

17 Initially elections for the first partially elected parliament were supposed to take place in 2006, but they were delayed to allow adequate time for preparations. At the time of writing this chapter in June 2007 the government has not yet assigned a date for such elections as stated in the 2003 constitution.

18 Saif, *Constitutionalism*, p. 29.

19 Saif, *Constitutionalism*, pp. 26–27. For more details on Qatar's judiciary system see also Saif, *Arab Gulf Judicial Structures* (Dubai: Gulf Research Centre, 2004), pp. 22–31.

20 Ghubash, 'The Gulf State: An Authority More than Absolute and Society Less than Crippled', in Ali Al-Kuwari et al., 'Towards a Radical Reform in the GCC Countries', Unpublished Manuscript, Development Forum, 25th Meeting, Doha, 2004, pp. 14–32.

21 Ibid.

22 Ibid.

23 Ottaway, 'Evaluating Middle East Reform: How Do We Know When It is Significant?', Carnegie Papers, *Middle East Series*, No. 56, February 2005, pp. 3–5.
24 Ibid., p. 6.
25 This issue however needs more attention and the author is working on further studies.
26 Fukuyama, 'Do We Really Know How to Promote Democracy?', Speech in New York Democracy Forum, 24 May 2005.
27 Dahl, *On Democracy* (New Haven and London: Yale University Press, 1998), p. 128.
28 Ibid.
29 Oil and gas here should not be counted, as they are produced outside the real national economy. For further discussion on this topic see Hazem Beblawi and Giacomo Luciani (eds.), *The Rentier State* (Kent: Croom Helm, 1987).
30 Fukuyama, 'Do We Really Know How to Promote Democracy?'
31 Siraj Mufti, 'Muslims Love Democracy', *Muslim Democrat*, Vol. 4, No. 2 (July 2002), p. 1. Also see The Pew Research Center at: http://people-press.org/reports/display.php3?ReportID=185.
32 Khan, 'Prospects for Muslim Democracy'.
33 The first Islamic state, established by the Prophet of Islam, was based on a social contract called the Constitution of Medina. The state of Medina was a multi-cultural and multi-religious federation. The constitution of Medina established equality with identical rights and duties between Muslim and non-Muslim citizens. Communities with different religious orientations enjoyed religious autonomy. The constitution of Medina established a pluralistic state, a community of communities. For a more systematic and detailed discussion of the compatibility of Islam and Democracy see John Esposito and John Voll, *Islam and Democracy* (Oxford: Oxford University Press, 1996) and Noah Feldman, *After Jihad: America and the Struggle for Islamic Democracy* (New York: Farrar, Strauss and Giroux, 2003). Also see the chapter 'Reflections on Islam and Democracy', in Muqtedar Khan (ed.), *American Muslims: Bridging Faith and Freedom* (Bettsville, MD: Amana Publications, 2002).
34 Nazih Ayubi, *Overstating the Arab State: Politics and Society in the Middle East* (London and New York: I.B. Tauris, 1995), p. 174.
35 Qatar, as other countries in the Arabian Peninsula, is neither capitalist nor socialist, but a dependent state that is greatly affected by trends and policies prevailing in the West.
36 Ayubi, *Overstating the Arab State*, p. 175. More arguments and analyses on this topic will be found in James A. Bill, 'Class Analysis and the Dialects of Modernization in the Middle East', *IJMES*, Vol. 3 (1992), pp. 417–434; S. Ibrahim, *The New Arab Social Order: A Study of the Social Impact of Oil Wealth* (Colorado: Westview Press, 1928); Khaldoun Al-Naqeeb, 'Changing Patterns of Social Stratification in the Middle East: Kuwait 1950–70 as a Case Study' (PhD Dissertation, University of Texas, Austin, 1976); Al-Naqeeb, *The State and Society in the Gulf and Arabia: A New Perspective* (Beirut: Centre for Arabic Union Studies, 1987); and Mahmoud Abd al-Fadil, *The Classes Formation in the Arab World* (Beirut: Centre for Arabic Union Studies, 1988).
37 Ottaway, 'Evaluating Middle East Reform', p. 7.
38 Ibid., pp. 7–8.

39 Ibid., p. 12.
40 I should say this idea is still embryonic and needs more research to pinpoint the most suitable mechanism to avoid the process of reproducing the same political elite.
41 See Khalil Shikaki, 'This is a War on Islam', *The Guardian*, 11 September 2002.
42 Sean Foley, 'The Gulf Arabs and the New Iraq: The Most to Gain and the Most to Lose?', *MERIA*, Vol. 7, No. 2 (June 2003).
43 'Saudi Shi'a Clamor for End to Discrimination after Saddam's Fall', Agence France Presse, 23 April 2003 (Lexis/Nexis, 1 May 2003).
44 Anthony Cordesman, 'Saudi Security and the War on Terrorism: Internal Security Operations, Law Enforcements, Internal Threats and the Need for Change' (Washington, D.C.: Center for Strategic and International Studies, 2002). http://csis.org/burke/saudi21/SaudiWaronTerr.pdf.
45 In such a situation, the GCC would be dissolved in favour of a new collective organization.
46 Condoleezza Rice, Lecture, New York, 1 October 2002.
47 Richard N. Haass, 'Toward Greater Democracy in the Muslim World', *The Washington Quarterly*, Vol. 26, No. 3 (Summer 2003), pp. 137–148.

6

Oman's Approach to Development

His Excellency Sayyid Badr bin Sa'ud Al-Busaidi

The modernization of Oman is a historical process that has been underway for as long as the very idea of modernization has existed. It is not a sequence of events that will lead to some inevitable goal, nor does it have necessary outcomes, which, once achieved, will lead to the proclamation that Oman has been 'modernized'. Instead there is a process of development, in which the traditions of Oman's culture keep evolving, in accordance with their own principles, towards a future that, by definition, cannot be accurately predicted.

This is as true of the development of Omani democracy as it is of every other aspect of the process. Sometimes the process of modernization is discussed as though it were a kind of race, in which the 'less-than-modern' have to catch up with the modern, after which, presumably, they can become post-modern.

Oman is not chasing some grand illusion of uniform modernity. There is no single model of what it is to be modern, which every nation and people must aspire to. Instead there is a whole range of modernities into which different traditions and cultures can develop.

Oman is, therefore, not on course for some predetermined state of modernity. Instead, we are moving, in a gradual and organic way, through a process of development of our own institutions, our own traditions, our own ways of doing things – socially, politically and economically. Our vision is driven by an understanding of our past.

By attending to some basic historical principles, we can create a uniquely Omani future. This means that our democratic institutions may not necessarily look quite like democratic institutions from elsewhere in the world. Instead they are evolving as traditional Omani institutions. The discussion so far has been rather philosophical, and should move to concrete examples of the particular achievements of Omani modernity.

It is widely recognized that our development has been extraordinarily rapid since 1970. This phase in our history tends to be viewed as a time of sudden change and of course the discovery of oil in the 1960s led to an economic transformation that was unprecedented.

But however remarkable the social changes made possible by oil revenue, the periods before and after 1970 enjoy deep underlying historical continuity. It is too simple to see 1970 as a moment of abrupt change and to identify Oman after 1970 as modern while describing pre-1970 Oman as 'medieval'.

In reality the 'new', 'modern' Oman has its roots deep in Omani history. For instance, the Basic Statute of the State of 1996 is rightly identified as Oman's modern constitution. It provides for a distinctively modern set of human rights, and lays the foundations for state institutions of a modern character, including an elected legislature. The Basic Statute might even be described as exceptionally modern since it establishes the free market as a basic economic principle of the state. Such a commitment is not usually found in constitutional documents. However, even in this modern commitment we find something of the past, for free trade and the spirit of enterprise have long been integral to the prosperity of the Omani nation. From the mid-18th to the mid-19th century Oman's maritime trade gave it economic interests all around the Indian Ocean. Just as this most modern of Oman's constitutional provisions turns out to have its roots in the past, so do its provisions for political institutions.

From the time when Oman first began to distinguish itself as a nation, it did so because of a commitment to a distinctive political culture, one in which consent, consultation and accountability were essential elements of political leadership. The practice of this consultation and accountability – which we call *shura* – has continued across centuries of Omani life. It functions as a key principle of government at national, regional and local levels. Its incorporation in the Basic Statute, and in contemporary political institutions such as the *Majlis al-Shura* and the *Majlis al-Dowla*, represents a formal codification of long-standing custom and practice. In other words, it is a modernization of existing social and cultural norms.

In the political arena, then, development and modernization in Oman have roots. They are native growths, and while they are open to the grafting-on of other ideas, they are not simply transplants, brought from one culture and transferred to another. Their success depends upon the fact that they are indigenous species. Over the last 30 years we have been able to proceed gradually through a series of ever-expanding institutions of political participation, up to and including a parliament elected by universal adult suffrage. We have been able to do this because we have always had a political culture in which the principles of consultation and accountability have been fully understood and widely practised.

Of course we must not underestimate the scale of the change that has taken place in Oman since 1970. There are periods in the history of all nations in which change is more rapid than anything experienced before, and it is undoubtedly the case that this period has been one of Oman's most remarkable periods of change.

I have lived through it personally and have experienced, along with my whole generation, the extraordinary nature of the transformation that our country has experienced. Many aspects of Omani life have thrived through the remarkable foresight and vision of His Majesty Sultan Qaboos bin Sa'id Al 'Bu Sa'id. Good examples of this are Oman's education provision, its welfare services and its road network. The next section will concentrate on the health sector, however.

The World Health Organization (WHO) now ranks Oman's health service as the best in the world in terms of access, and in the top five on other key measures, such as cost-effectiveness. This is all the more remarkable because in 1970 Oman had nothing but a couple of small clinics. Today the Omani health service works because it is based on providing primary healthcare to citizens in every village of the country. This also includes basic preventive medicine. It has been developed from the ground up. It is supported by local networks of health volunteers, who have enjoyed remarkable success in educating their fellow citizens and developing a culture of collective health awareness. This is backed up by the accessibility of basic treatments in small local centres. These local centres are linked to a nationwide network of local and regional hospitals, in a structure of devolved responsibility. Policy and priorities are set in accordance with local needs. The principles underpinning this development are recognizably democratic principles, even if they arose out of practical problem-solving rather than a specific programme of democratization. Local people were asked what they needed and then helped to do it for themselves.

The bottom line is that Oman has succeeded in eradicating smallpox, tuberculosis and malaria. It has also introduced a policy of birth spacing that is vital to the sustainability of its economic and social development. Health is seen as part of a package of grass-roots policies, which also include local governance, education and women's rights. Such a package is not something that can be addressed by means of a technological fix imposed from above.

Among the challenges for the further development of the health sector are the increasing cost of pharmaceuticals and the inevitable demand for more and better high-tech equipment. However, the basic structure is sound because it is built upon the secure foundations of villages and local communities, and because citizens have been involved directly in its development. Because of these measures, the service is answerable to the specific day-to-day needs of our people, rather than to external conceptions of what a 21st-century health service might look like. This basic idea governs Oman's entire modernization and development project.

Oman is building gradually upon structures and principles that have shaped its society for a very long time. It is not moving towards an imagined goal called 'modernity', but is living the experience of modernity through the transformation of Omani society to meet the needs of the contemporary world. It is doing so in a way that is attuned to the aspirations of our people, adapting and transforming Oman's own social and cultural inheritance and blending in ideas and practices that may enhance the process. Oman does want to be modern, because Oman *is* modern. However, modernity will be pursued in an Omani way.

7

Economic Governance and Reform in Saudi Arabia

Rodney Wilson

It is instructive to compare the economic management of the post-millennium oil revenue boom with that of the 1970s to see what lessons have been learnt from that earlier experience. Economic reform is usually associated with a change in strategic direction as well as in the mechanisms through which the economy is governed, but in the case of Saudi Arabia, a traditional society, yet a young country, there has never been the time for either economic policy or systems of economic governance to become embedded. The Kingdom, because of its oil resources, has always been part of the global economy, and this is likely to continue given that it has one quarter of world oil reserves.

The effectiveness of governance is evaluated here in terms of macroeconomic performance, which has been broadly favourable compared to other oil-exporting states such as Algeria, Libya, Nigeria or Iran. It is easy to criticize Saudi Arabia's economic management, but the Kingdom has been better served by its governance system than many of its neighbours. Economic reform has been limited, but there has been a tendency to say if the economy is not broken, why fix it! What reforms there have been in recent years have mainly involved the financial system rather than the wider economy, and these are regarded as successful as the Kingdom's banking sector is modern and sophisticated in comparison to many other Arab countries, and most of the employees are local citizens.

Some see the authorities as excessively complacent however, especially given the scale of unemployment amongst Saudi Arabian citizens, although the extent of this unemployment is contested. Others worry that the second oil revenue boom is a convenient excuse to postpone economic reform as it reduces the need to face up to economic realities and make difficult choices. This can be argued in the case of taxation and government spending where the additional revenue from oil has given the authorities more room for manoeuvre, and has put decisions over new taxes on hold. The government does appear to be prioritizing employment creation for local citizens however, although it is by no means clear that the optimal strategy is to simply replace foreign workers with Saudis, as this may undermine competitiveness and actually destroy jobs. This is especially the case as the economy becomes more open to global markets, and as the issue of the Kingdom's competitive position in Asia looms larger as these economies advance.

An Open Economy!

The concept of economic openness demands closer scrutiny in the context of the changing role of the state in Saudi Arabia. From its early years the Kingdom was open in the sense that exports were highly significant for the domestic economy, which continues to be the case. By the 1970s, however, with the nationalization of Aramco, the Arabian American Oil Company, and with the Kingdom playing the key role in OPEC, the supplier's cartel, the Oil Ministry was intervening to affect both international oil pricing and the level of Saudi Arabia's exports. In other words there was an attempt, never wholly successful, to reduce the vulnerability of the domestic economy to oil price fluctuations in world markets.[1] This policy continues, and it is unlikely that in the near or even distant future the Oil Ministry will permit international oil companies to invest in Aramco, or open up the Kingdom's oil fields to foreign producers.

Policies on economic openness do not reflect political ideology in the Kingdom, as in many countries where socialism or nationalism has prompted governments to play a major interventionist role in economic activity. Rather, they reflect the power structures of the Kingdom, including the thinking and aspirations of business-minded princes from the House of Saud, and the need to secure support from the merchant classes, from whom extremely wealthy business families have emerged. One important question is the extent to which these business families need support from and the protection of the state, or in other words government patronage, which is often seen as one of the defining characteristics of a rentier state. The premise here is that state patronage is still important, but that the relationship between the business community and the state is increasingly characterized by interdependence, as the government needs the private sector to create the jobs for local citizens to prevent more widespread popular discontent.

This has made the government more prepared to listen to the demands of the business community, who are well represented both within the House of Saud itself, where some of the princes have been correctly called Royal Entrepreneurs,[2] and in the wider business community who are disproportionately represented in the *majlis al-shura*, the Kingdom's appointed consultative assembly. Ironically, greater democracy and a move towards a partially elected *majlis al-shura* might reduce business representation, and undermine the more technocratic members of the assembly, by strengthening the position of the religious conservatives and the assembly members they openly support. This was apparent from the municipal elections in 2005, highlighting that there is a potential conflict between democratization and liberalization in Saudi Arabia as elsewhere at present in the Islamic world. This may change, as the religious leaders themselves become more business orientated, signs of which are already apparent amongst those *shariah* scholars serving on the boards of Islamic banks, and conventional institutions providing *shariah*-compliant financial products.[3]

The Consequences of WTO Entry

Saudi Arabia was finally admitted to the World Trade Organization (WTO) in December 2005 after over 12 years of negotiation to gain accession.[4] It was the last Gulf Cooperation Council member to be admitted, an unusual situation given that since 2003 all these countries have the same common external tariff of 5%, and have largely aligned their trade positions. For countries to be admitted to the WTO they require the support of all their major trading partners, and in Saudi Arabia's case the major stumbling blocks were the attitudes of the United States and the European Union. In the case of the former, the Bush administration's views were undoubtedly clouded by the events of 9/11, plus the United States disliked Saudi Arabia's position in OPEC, which the Americans perceive as a body rationing oil exports in a manner contrary to free trade. Furthermore, Washington viewed Saudi Arabia's boycott of goods exported from Israel as discriminatory. In the end, however, Washington was prepared to back down on these issues, as it knew it was unrealistic for the Saudi Arabian government to give ground on such fundamental matters given popular opinion in the Kingdom.

Instead the difficulties with the negotiations with the United States came down to Saudi Arabia's restrictions on foreign banks and insurance companies gaining access to the Kingdom, and subsidies to agriculture, especially wheat. Saudi Arabia backed down on these issues agreeing to abolish export subsidies on grains, although subsidies on foodstuffs sold domestically remain. The Kingdom also agreed to open its financial sector in a phased manner, with the permitted share of foreign ownership in local banks raised from 40% to 60% and foreign insurance companies allowed to own 60% of local companies.[5]

For the European Union, the main issue was the Kingdom's policy on feedstock prices for the petrochemical industry that were perceived to give Saudi Arabia an unfair competitive advantage over European producers. In the end, a compromise was reached with the Kingdom promising to review its feedstock pricing policy in return for a phasing out of the European Union 11.5% tariff on its petrochemical exports. Saudi Arabia successfully argued that as there is no international gas market price, it would be unreasonable to expect it to eliminate its natural advantages in gas by artificially raising prices to local industries.

Entry into the WTO has been broadly welcomed by the business community in Saudi Arabia, although some concerns have been expressed that the opening up of the services sector, including financial services, could threaten jobs in banking that have been successfully transferred to local citizens. Such fears are misplaced however, as the requirement to hire local citizens will be applied to foreign banks authorized to operate in the Kingdom, and as most will be involved in investment rather than retail banking, this could open up lucrative employment opportunities for Saudi Arabian citizens. The losers are more likely to be the offshore banks operating from Bahrain, as once the Saudi Arabian banking system is opened up the rationale for doing business from Bahrain is undermined.

Other claims, such as that Saudi Arabia would be forced to open up its market to alcohol and pork products, were clearly absurd. The more justifiable concerns are from small retail businesses that fear that large companies will enter the market and threaten their sales. However many international retailers are already represented in the Kingdom's shopping malls through agreements they have reached with local distributors. WTO entry will not make much difference to the international branded goods being sold, and in any case, these are often focused on a more affluent market segment, whereas the smaller retailers are largely catering for lower income groups, both Saudis and migrant workers from South Asia and the Philippines.

Fears that WTO entry would end exclusive agency arrangements were unfounded, although Saudi Arabia's consumers might have benefited from the ending of monopolistic distribution agreements. What was agreed with the United States was that foreign firms could own 51% of retail and distribution businesses on WTO entry, rising to 75% three years after accession.

The major gain from WTO entry for Saudi Arabia was that being part of the international, rules-based, trading system would facilitate commerce, reduce transactions uncertainties and increase the confidence of investors. This includes not only foreign investors, but also Saudi Arabian investors who might otherwise have exported their capital. WTO entry has already resulted in the processes of commercial arbitration being streamlined, with the likelihood of more consistent judgements and a greater degree of legal and contractual certainty.

Macroeconomic Management

The major success of the Ministry of Finance and the Saudi Arabian Monetary agency for over 20 years has been in controlling inflation, which has been negligible for the last decade, varying between 1.3% and −1.0%. This has been achieved by maintaining the fixed rate of the Saudi Riyal against the United States dollar at 3.75. The Kingdom, like the other GCC countries whose currencies are also pegged to the United States dollar, has no independent monetary policy, as interest rates simply move in line with those set by the Federal Reserve. Discrepancies between the Saudi Inter-Bank Offer Rate (SIBOR) and the London Inter-Bank Offer Rate on dollars (LIBOR) seldom arise, the only recent exception being in 1998 when low international oil prices resulted in doubts about whether the Kingdom could maintain the riyal's peg to the dollar, and consequently SIBOR was raised temporarily to prevent speculative attacks on the riyal. In the event this proved sufficient to stabilize the riyal.

Although it might seem inappropriate for Saudi Arabia to be

subject to United States monetary policy, which is designed primarily for America's internal needs, in practice, as dollar inflation has been low, this has been helpful for the Kingdom. The only significant inflation was in 1995 when the dollar depreciated temporarily against other major currencies, and Saudi Arabia's inflation rose to 4.8%, which although unwelcome, was certainly not a major problem.

There is little discussion of monetary policy issues in the Kingdom, partly because inflation has not been an issue, but also because the use of interest rates is a sensitive topic in a country where *shariah* law is supposed to apply, which implies a prohibition on *riba* or interest. In practice, standard debt-financing instruments are used by the government, including development bonds for longer term funding that pay interest, and repurchase agreements (repos) for short-term funding. These instruments are held by the commercial banks and are used for treasury management by the authorities, but not as tools of monetary policy. Islamic banks such as the Al Rajhi Banking and Investment Corporation are exempt from holding these instruments, but they would be prepared to hold Islamic securities or *sukuk* if Saudi Arabia followed the example of other Muslim countries such as Bahrain and Malaysia and used these as an alternative funding source.

The recent oil revenue boom has meant that debt management has become less of an issue than it was in the late 1990s when government debt as a proportion of GDP peaked, as Figure 1 shows. Saudi Arabia has little external debt apart from supplier credits, but the government borrows from the domestic banking system, mainly through the issue of development bonds. The difficulty is that government borrowing from the banks inhibits their ability to finance the private sector, the expansion of which is important if the Kingdom's unemployment problem is to be reduced. In other words government debt is crowding out the private sector, arguably the more productive part of the economy.

Although by 2005 the level of debt was less than half what it was only six years earlier, it could easily climb again if oil revenue falls. The opportunity has not been taken to reform debt management, by, for example, as indicated above, issuing some of the debt in the form of sovereign *sukuk* that Islamic banks and *shariah*-compliant investment companies would willingly hold. If the debt burden was spread more widely, the risk of crowding out would be reduced. Furthermore, one way of reducing the debt would have been through the privatization of state-owned companies that would have raised revenue for the government. With more revenue in any case, due to international oil price rises, there is less pressure to privatize, and not surprisingly it is evident that the pace of privatization is extremely slow despite buoyant stock market conditions.

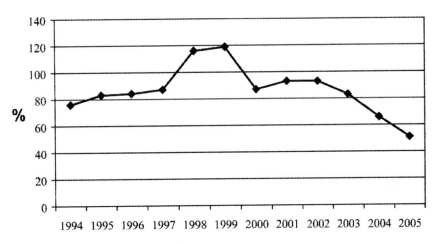

FIGURE 1
Government Debt as a % of GDP

In addition to the absence of a monetary policy, the Kingdom also lacks the tools to pursue an effective fiscal policy that could help with macroeconomic stabilization. The economy remains highly vulnerable to oil revenue shocks in the absence of other revenue streams from taxation. The major sources of non-oil revenue are customs duties and corporate taxes, but the former were reduced significantly when the former import tariffs, which were up to 20% in some cases, were reduced to 5% following the customs union agreement that provided for a common GCC external tariff. With minimal or very low corporate taxes in other GCC states, notably the UAE, the Ministry of Finance in Saudi Arabia was also pressurized into cutting these taxes to prevent a leakage of business to other GCC countries. Rates of corporate tax have been reduced from 35% to 20%.

The IMF has recommended that Saudi Arabia should introduce value added tax, which would contribute to the stabilization of government finances, as consumer spending fluctuates much less than oil revenues.[6] There is however a reluctance to introduce this type of expenditure tax as it would be unpopular with consumers and would have a one-off upward impact on retail prices. It would also prompt the general public to ask more questions about government spending, and demand greater accountability. Arguably this would be a desirable development. As Figure 2 shows, there was a budget deficit in the late 1990s, and if that had continued, the introduction of VAT would have been more likely. Since 2003, however, with much higher levels of government revenue from oil, there has been a substantial budgetary surplus. This has undoubtedly resulted in the postponement of fiscal reform and enabled the Ministry of Finance to avoid difficult and controversial choices.

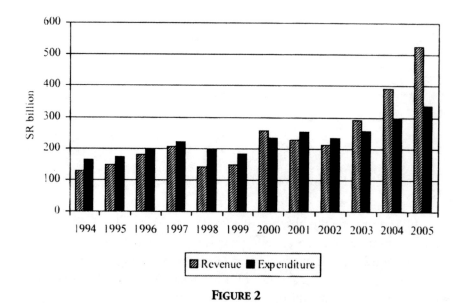

FIGURE 2
Government Budget

There have been proposals to introduce income tax in Saudi Arabia, most of which have been to apply this form of taxation to expatriate workers only rather than local citizens. Saudi Arabian businessmen have been opposed to this however, arguing that this would deter the best managers and workers from coming to Saudi Arabia, as they could seek employment elsewhere in the Gulf where there also are no taxes. Furthermore, as private sector employers already have to pay increasing amounts for work permits to enable them to recruit expatriate labour, there is resistance to yet more taxation. The *majlis al-shura*, on which the business community is well represented, has consistently rejected proposals for income tax, and the chambers of commerce and industry, which have strong lobbying power, are also opposed.

Most people in Saudi Arabia pay *zakat*, which is sometimes described as being an Islamic tax, as paying it is one of the duties of being a Muslim. In reality it is a form of alms giving as the proceeds of *zakat* are used for social purposes for the benefit of the poor and needy. *Zakat* is applied to wealth, usually defined as liquid assets such as funds in bank accounts or securities, rather than fixed assets such as real estate or business equipment. Muslims typically do not pay it on the value of their homes, as this could result in the family home being sold to meet a *zakat* obligation, which would be unjust.

Often in Saudi Arabia, the argument is used that there is no need for personal income taxes, because *zakat* is paid instead. If this argument is accepted, then there would be a strong case for including *zakat* in the public accounts, and for much more transparent reporting on its administration. At present the distinction between *zakat* and charitable giving is blurred, with some people even administrating it themselves, and making their own unilateral charitable donations, often in a somewhat arbitrary manner. There is much that Saudi Arabia could learn from the systems of collection and administration of *zakat* in other Muslim countries, notably in Malaysia, where Muslims receive a government certificate of payment that entitles them to an exemption from income tax for the amount they have paid. Any introduction of personal income tax in Saudi Arabia should arguably be accompanied by the reform and modernization of the *zakat* system, a move that could gain the support of the more progressive and financially aware religious scholars.

Economic Diversification

The declared development strategy in all eight development plans has been to diversify the economy, but this is easier said than done. An obvious question is what is actually meant by diversification, a minimalist interpretation being that it is about adding more value to crude oil by, for example, establishing refineries and augmenting petrochemical production capacity. These can reduce the share of crude oil exports, which has already happened with the Saudi Arabian Basic Industries Corporation (SABIC) becoming a major international producer of petrochemicals, and the largest company in the Middle East. Refining was more problematic due to the higher costs of transporting refined products to distant markets because of the increased risk of fire or explosions with refined rather than crude oil, but as the gap between prices of Saudi Arabia's heavy crude oil and refined products has increased in recent years, more investment is being planned in refineries. During the recent oil boom it has become apparent that it is the lighter oils that enjoy sharply rising premium prices, whereas crude oil prices have risen more modestly, partly reflecting the worldwide demand for cleaner fuels.

Much of the diversification in Saudi Arabia has been into manufacturing and services focused on the domestic market, and more recently with the customs union, the wider GCC market. The manufacturing involves a range of activities, from building supplies, including reinforcing rods for concrete structures, to food processing. Under the import substitution policy, industrial licences were granted based on ensuring that each supplier had an assured market. This policy reduced business risk because the stress was on limiting competition in the interest of producers rather than encouraging competition in the interests of consumers. Those who were awarded industrial licences were entitled to apply for subsidized credit from the Saudi Industrial Development Corporation, although they were expected to augment this with commercial bank financing.

Any competitive advantages private sector businesses in Saudi Arabia enjoy come largely from the relatively cheap migrant workers they employ rather than because of government subsidies. The policy of replacing these workers with more expensive and often less flexible Saudi workers potentially undermines this competitiveness. This partly explains why over 4000 Saudi businesses are now located in Dubai where there is less pressure to restrict work permits. The danger is that the replacement of expatriate labour could actually damage employment rather than increase employment opportunities for local citizens.

In recent years it is the growth of the domestic and wider GCC market that has facilitated the development of the private sector, with the Kingdom itself having by far the largest market for consumer goods in the Middle East. This has aided the expansion of distribution and retailing that accounts for a major proportion of private sector activity. As Figure 3 shows, the growth of the private sector has been higher than that of the public sector, although this is not to imply that there is a trade-off, as periods of higher public sector growth are usually accompanied by higher rates of private sector growth rather than vice versa, and both are dependent on oil sector developments, although with some lags. This highlights the fact that private sector growth should not simply be interpreted as evidence of greater economic diversification, as trends in the oil sector still have a significant influence on all sectors of the economy.

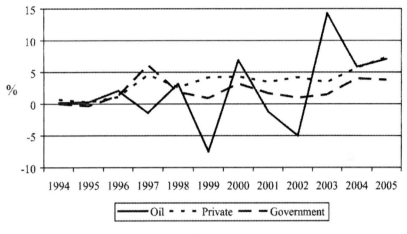

FIGURE 3
Sectoral Growth

The Role of the Private Sector

A very direct means of promoting the growth of the private sector would of course be through the privatization of state-owned companies. Progress with privatization has been painfully slow however, and there seems little likelihood that this will be accelerated in the near or even distant future. There is no ideological objection to privatization in Saudi Arabia, rather the objections are practical.

First the government sees it as being in its strategic interests to control the oil sector through its ownership of Aramco, and this is unlikely to change as decisions on production levels and investment in spare capacity are made by the Petroleum Ministry, and not by the company. Given Saudi Arabia's pivotal role in OPEC, and the major part played by the Petroleum Minister in its deliberations, this is unlikely to change. Secondly, the government's major holdings in SABIC, Saudi Telecom, the Saudi Electricity Company and the National Commercial Bank are through the State Pension and Social Security Fund, and these represent valuable and profitable assets. If these were sold off there is not an alternative ready supply of riyal-denominated assets for these government funds to hold. Thirdly there is a potential conflict between privatization, which implies a focus on profits and value added for shareholders, and the policy of replacing expatriate workers with local citizens. This adds to costs through training and higher salaries, and at present the state sector employs mainly Saudis, while the private sector employs a much higher proportion of expatriates.

The major privatization to date was the sale of one-third of the shares of Saudi Telecom that brought in over US$4 billion in revenue for the government. The formerly private electricity companies were merged through the establishment of a state holding company when a national grid was established, but this is seen as a strategic asset that the state is unlikely to sell, although a minority share remains in private hands.

Despite government control of electricity distribution, power generation in the future is to be undertaken by independent private companies. The largest venture to date of this type is the Shuaiba Water and Electricity Company plant south of Jeddah, which the German firm Siemens is constructing at a cost of SR 8.1 billion. From 2009 the plant will supply 900 MW of power to the national grid, together with 880,000 cubic metres of fresh water to Jeddah, Mecca, Taif and Al-Baha.[7]

In other sectors such as airlines the dominant state-owned company, Saudi Arabian Airlines, is escaping even partial privatization, but the Saudia monopoly of domestic and Gulf air routes is ending with licences being granted to private operators of both budget and business-class-only airlines, opening the sector to competition. Similarly in telecommunications, although no further shares in Saudi Telecom have been offered since 2002, when there was a partial sell-off, a second mobile licence was awarded to Ettihad Ettisalat, the UAE telecommunications company, introducing welcome competition into the market that soon resulted in better services and lower communications tariffs. Broadband services are to be opened up to competition, further augmenting the Kingdom's internet capacity.

Foreign operators have been brought in where it is thought that efficiency can be improved. In the case of Jeddah Islamic Port, the Kingdom's major port facility, a management contract was awarded to Dubai Ports World, the operator of the largest transit facility in the Gulf at Jebel Ali. As a result the throughput at Jeddah Islamic Port now compares with the best in the world. An even more ambitious venture involving a partnership with Dubai is the SR100 billion development north of Jeddah to be called King Abdullah Economic City.[8] The first phase of the project involves the construction of a 2.6 million m² seaport, the major developers being the Binladin Group of Saudi Arabia and Emaar Properties, the company responsible for some of the largest construction projects in Dubai.[9] When fully operational, the port will become the largest in the Red Sea and a hub for light industry and distribution. Eventually, it is hoped over 500,000 new jobs will be created in the new city, a development as ambitious for the new millennium as the industrial cities of Jubail and Yanbu were in the 1970s and 1980s.

Financial Restructuring

The major restructuring during 2004 and 2005 has been in the financial infrastructure of Saudi Arabia, with the creation of a new Capital Markets Authority to regulate the stock market, investment companies, managed funds and stockbrokers, while the Saudi Arabian Monetary Authority retained its responsibilities for the regulation of the banking system. The regulatory model adopted was similar to that of Malaysia, which is rightly perceived in Riyadh as one of the most successful economies in the Muslim world, and which in some respects the Kingdom seeks to emulate. There, a separate Securities Commission regulates stock market activity, while Bank Negara, the Central Bank, regulates the banking sector.

In Saudi Arabia, the banking system was structurally frozen for the two decades from 1979 with no newcomers permitted to enter the Kingdom after the local incorporation of foreign banks that meant a majority of the shareholding had to be Saudi. As the GCC evolved from being simply a free trade area, however, banks from other GCC countries were permitted to enter the Saudi market, the first being the Gulf International Bank of Bahrain followed by the National Bank of Kuwait in 2003. By 2005 other institutions were entering the market, including Muscat Bank from Oman, Deutsche Bank and BNP Paribas of France.[10] These banks aim to provide investment rather than retail banking services, as the former were relatively underdeveloped whereas there was already much competition in retail banking, with a modern and relatively sophisticated level of service provided.

At the retail level the major development over the last decade has been the spread of *shariah*-compliant banking products, provided not only by the Al Rajhi Banking and Investment Corporation and Al Jazeera, exclusively Islamic banks, but also by the conventional banks, notably the National Commercial Bank. In 2005 the former money-changing establishments were merged into one entity, Al-Bilad Bank, which was subsequently floated on the Saudi stock market. Al-Bilad is also an exclusively Islamic bank. It is evident that there is a strong demand by the public in Saudi Arabia for Islamic banking facilities, as illustrated by the fact that the Al Rajhi Banking and Investment Corporation has become the largest listed *shariah*-compliant bank in the world in terms of assets managed.

The responsibility of the Capital Markets Authority for regulating the stock market in Saudi Arabia is enormous, as the market has become by far the largest in the Islamic world in terms of capitalization, having overtaken the Kuala Lumpur market in 2003. By 2005 over one billion shares worth SR300 billion were being traded every month with the figure in excess of SR400 billion in June, August, October and November.[11] The market capitalization exceeded SR2 trillion by the end of 2005, but only 76 companies are listed, compared with over 1000 on the Cairo Stock Market. Over 45% of the market capitalization is accounted for by just three companies, SABIC, Saudi Telecoms and the Saudi Electricity Company, with many of the agricultural and manufacturing companies being relatively small. The listed banks account for around 25% of market capitalization. Given this narrow base and the amount of liquidity generated in the economy by the oil price boom, it is not surprising that share prices rose dramatically in 2004 and 2005 as Figure 4 shows, but the key question is how far such a rise is sustainable.

A major correction or slump in share values would cause considerable damage to the economy and bring ruin to many Saudi Arabian investors who have foolishly borrowed substantial amounts from their banks to buy shares. Some have assumed that the government would intervene to save them from bankruptcy if the market collapsed, but the amounts are too large even for the Saudi Arabian government to take corrective action. Past experiences in the Gulf are not encouraging, the *souk al manakh* in Kuwait crashed in 1982 and it took more than a decade for the country to recover from the shock, which in financial terms was as bad as the Iraqi invasion.[12]

Ironically, one problem may have been that listing requirements are too rigorous, and hence there are too few quoted stocks to mop up

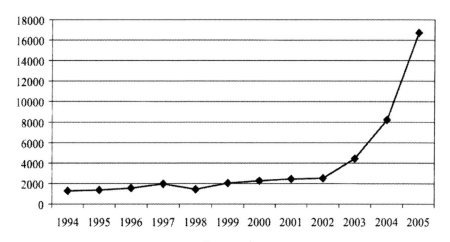

FIGURE 4
Saudi Arabia Share Price Index

the available liquidity. In October 2005 it was reported that 15 firms were seeking a listing from the Capital Markets Authority, but that although most had completed 80% of the requirements to obtain a listing, it was not clear when the remainder of the conditions could be met, and only one was likely to be approved for listing.[13] Stock prices might not have risen so far if there had been a market in government bonds or Islamic *sukuk* securities where investors could have 'parked' liquid funds and earned a return, but, as already indicated, government bonds are simply held by the banks and not traded. An Alternative Investment Market (AIM), where small and medium-sized companies could have sought equity capital without high compliance costs, would also be attractive for the more venturous investors and provide an additional outlet to the stock market. In the absence of such a market, some Gulf companies have sought a listing on the AIM in London.

Employment and Training Challenges
Estimates of unemployment in Saudi Arabia have to be treated with caution, as there is no unemployment benefit, and the Ministry of Labour figure of 8.8% male unemployment in 2005 refers only to job seekers who have registered. There are many who have given up seeking employment and are dependent on other family members, and as there

are few employment opportunities for women, most do not even attempt to seek jobs. The unemployed are mostly school and university leavers, many of whom are drop-outs without formal qualifications, and therefore not well suited for employment.[14] Young Saudis often have unrealistic expectations, hoping for a secure job in government rather than wishing to take the risks associated with the private sector; ideally they also want to be near their homes, family and friends.[15]

As Figure 5 shows, the population continues to increase, although the United Nations predicts a decline in birth rates, which has already started to occur, but this will take many years to feed through to a reduction in the rate of increase of those entering the workforce.[16] Contrary to what was anticipated in the Seventh Five Year Plan, the numbers of foreign workers has continued to increase over the 2000–2005 period from 5.59 to 6.29 million, and there is no reason to expect a reduction during the period of the Eighth Plan up to 2010 despite attempts to replace expatriates with local nationals.[17]

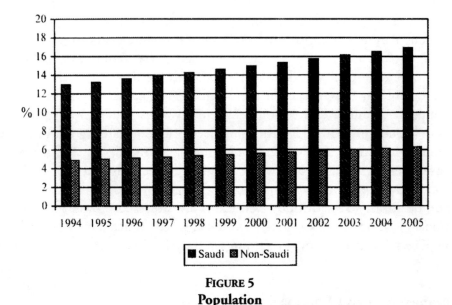

FIGURE 5
Population

The government currently recognizes that the employment problems in Saudi Arabia can only be solved in the long term, and therefore the emphasis has been on reducing expectations. The target for the Ministry of Labour is to achieve full employment by 2030 and raise the productivity of

the Saudi Arabian workforce. These are very long-term and rather impre-
cise targets. In the short run the emphasis is on containing unemployment
by trying to create an equivalent level of employment for the numbers
entering the workforce. By 2007 career offices are to be established at
educational institutions, job information systems are to be improved and
greater coordination introduced between high schools, universities and the
job market.[18] Advice will be given on the establishment and running of
family businesses and the employment of women will be encouraged.
There could however be a trade-off between this latter objective and
increasing male employment. Many doubt the Ministry of Labour's ability
to carry out the short-term measures effectively given the limited administrative capacity of most of the government bureaucracy to deliver on
specific programmes.

There is much evidence that many Saudis who find or are placed in
private sector jobs quit when they are faced with the reality of what the
work involves. Mecca Chamber of Commerce and Industry has reported
that two-thirds of Saudis in its area leave their jobs complaining about
long hours and low salaries.[19] Elsewhere there is evidence that some
young Saudi men have been letting their names be used to falsely fulfil
Saudi-ization quotas in return for a fee. As the Ministry of Labour has
only 20 inspectors for more than 300,000 businesses subject to the rules
concerning the percentage of Saudis in their employment, the possibility
of being discovered breaking the law is remote.[20]

The Eighth Development Plan envisages the establishment of
seven new universities and the expansion of the number of women in
the workforce by 30%.[21] There is little doubt that the universities will
be built, which should reduce the potential number of immediate job
seekers, but achieving the target for women in employment will be more
problematic; the issue being social attitudes, including those of educated
women towards employment. Even housekeeping is regarded as undig-
nified by many Saudi families, hence the large number of foreign maids
employed from the Philippines, Indonesia and India, despite the low
proportion of women in formal employment.

Towards a Post-Rentier Economy
Although there are significant differences between Saudi Arabia's economy
during the second oil price boom and that of the first boom during the

1970s, it is arguably premature to describe the Kingdom as a post-rentier economy. Much has been achieved in building industrial capacity at the new cities of Jubail and Yanbu, and a further expansion of the latter, Yanbu II, includes new industrial projects worth SR115 billion by 2019. The expansion will involve 34 basic and secondary industries and 224 light industries – SABIC and ExxonMobil being the partners for one of the major new petrochemical development.[22] The strategy for all these projects is still the top-down model of the 1970s, however, with the government taking the initiative and much of the spending being directed through state agencies, notably the Royal Commission for Jubail and Yanbu.

State agencies such as the Royal Commission do at least have a greater capacity to deliver than the government ministries themselves, and this also applies increasingly to the Saudi Arabian General Investment Authority, established in 2000 as a 'one stop shop' to encourage foreign investment. Foreign investment worth over SR119 billion was attracted in 2004, more than for the rest of the Middle East combined. Public–private partnerships are likely to raise foreign direct investment further in the coming years, including the ambitious land bridge project valued at SR19 billion that involves the construction of a rail link between Jeddah and Riyadh, connecting with the existing railway to Damman and a new extension to Jubail.

Foreign critics such as Matthew Simmons, who believe that Saudi Arabia is facing a Malthusian crunch as oil production peaks and population growth results in ever-rising unemployment and potential political instability, are simplistic in their analysis.[23] The economy has a capacity for continued growth that should not be underestimated, and the massive investments in infrastructure have improved efficiency, although admittedly investment in physical assets has proved more successful to date than investment in human capital that takes longer to yield results. Local Saudi Arabian observers are more measured, and probably correct, in their criticisms, with Ghassan Al-Sulaiman, Chairman of the Jeddah Chamber of Commerce and Industry and the US Arab Chamber of Commerce, arguing that policies towards foreign direct investment and security have been successful, but that only modest improvements have occurred with respect to economic diversification and the role of women in economic activity.[24]

Brad Borland, the seasoned Chief Economist at Samba, argues that

Saudi Arabia still exhibits many of the characteristics of a rentier economy, notably the stress on state-owned infrastructure that the government has little problem in financing from oil revenue, the minimal alternative tax base, and the lack of reliance on its own people or the local private sector for revenue and growth. Collecting economic grants from the export of natural resources has served economies such as Brunei, Qatar, Norway and Abu Dhabi well, but the jury is out on whether this rentier model will equally serve Saudi Arabia with its larger population, or if it will experience the problems of more populous oil exporters such as Algeria, Nigeria, Iran or Venezuela.[25] Clearly the post-millennium period has again been a good time to be a rentier economy, but the current favourable circumstances may not last. At present the major post-rentier aspect of Saudi Arabia's economy is the diversification into overseas productive assets that yield substantial incomes for many Saudi citizens of high net worth, which makes them more economically independent of government. Whether similar earnings can be generated from the domestic economy in the medium or long term remains open to question. In the short run the sustainability or non-sustainability of the capital gains in the local stock market may provide an indicative answer.

NOTES

1 Rodney Wilson (with Abdullah Al-Salamah, Monica Malik and Ahmed Al-Rajhi), *Economic Development in Saudi Arabia* (London: Routledge Curzon, 2004), pp. 41–50.

2 Sharaf Sabri, *The House of Saud in Commerce: A Study of Royal Entrepreneurship in Saudi Arabia* (New Delhi: I.S. Publications, 2001), pp. 15–34.

3 Clement M. Henry and Rodney Wilson, *The Politics of Islamic Finance* (Edinburgh University Press, 2004), p. 294.

4 P. K. Abdul Ghafour, 'WTO will open new markets for Saudi products', *Arab News*, Jeddah, 21 December 2005.

5 John Sfakianakis, *Saudi Arabia: Third Quarter Economic Update* (Riyadh: SAMBA Bank), 22 October 2005, pp. 2–5.

6 Rodrigo de Rato, 'IMF Managing Directors statement at the conclusion of a visit to Riyadh', *International Monetary Fund Press Release*, Washington, 24 October 2004.

7 Javid Hassan, 'SR 8.1 billion Shuaiba deal signed', *Arab News*, Jeddah, 29 December 2005.

8 MEED staff writer, 'Emaar Unveils King Abdullah Economic City', *Middle East Economic Digest*, 23 December 2005.

9 Javid Hassan and Ali Al-Zahrani, 'Abdullah launches mega city project', *Arab News*, Jeddah, 21 December 2005.

10 Saudi Arabian Monetary Agency, *Economic Developments First Quarter 2005* (Riyadh: 2005), p. 5.

11 Saudi Arabian Monetary Agency, *Monthly Bulletin of Statistics* (November 2005), Riyadh.

12 Rodney Wilson, *Banking and Finance in the Arab Middle East* (London: Macmillan, 1983), pp. 172–176.

13 Khalil Hanware, 'Saudi stocks continue to fall', *Arab News*, Jeddah, 18 October 2005.

14 Mohammed Bosbait and Rodney Wilson, 'Education, School to Work Transitions and Unemployment in Saudi Arabia', *Middle Eastern Studies*, Vol. 41, No. 4 (July 2005), pp. 533–545.

15 Mai Yamani, *Changed Identities: The Challenge of the New Generation in Saudi Arabia* (London: Royal Institute of International Affairs, 2000), pp. 81–87.

16 Anthony Cordesman, 'Saudi economics and Saudi stability: the facts behind the speculation', *Free Muslims Coalition Press Corner*, Washington, 8 August 2005.

17 Brad Borland, *The Saudi Economy at Mid-Year 2005* (Riyadh: SAMBA Bank, 2005), p. 1.

18 Maha Akeel, 'Mechanisms reviewed to implement employment strategy', *Arab News*, Jeddah, 27 December 2005.

19 Waheeb Soofi, 'Problems of Saudization', *Al-Watan*, Riyadh, 18 December 2005.

20 Unnamed reporter, 'Companies rent names to beat Saudization rules', *Al-Watan*, Riyadh, 20 December 2005.

21 P. K. Abdul Ghafour, 'Seven new universities to be set up under 8th Plan', *Arab News*, Jeddah, 24 November 2005.

22 Khalil Hanware, 'Turning the economy into a global powerhouse', *Arab News*, Jeddah, 30 December 2005.

23 Matthew R. Simmons, *Twilight in the Desert: The Coming Saudi Oil Shock and the World Economy* (New York: Wiley, 2005), pp. 1–29.

24 Usamah Al-Kurdi and Ghassan Al-Sulaiman, 'Opportunities for Economic and Political Reforms in the Kingdom of Saudi Arabia', *Middle Eastern Institute Policy Brief*, Washington, 12 August 2005.

25 Brad Borland, 'Arab World Economies: Prosperity amidst Political Uncertainty', *Saudi–US Relations Information Service*, Washington, 23 September 2005.

8

The Impact of Economic Reform on Dubai

Christopher M. Davidson

Throughout the Gulf region, Dubai is regarded as a pioneering model for economic reform and liberalization. As an emirate with dwindling hydrocarbon reserves and an increasingly skilled and employment-seeking national population, there has been an acute need for foreign direct investment, a diversification of the economy and the establishment of self-sustaining non-oil-related sectors. With these objectives in mind, a number of executive-level 'emiri' decrees and carefully worded directives have, over the past 15 years or so, facilitated the setting up of industrial and export processing free zones that have circumvented existing local sponsorship systems. These decrees and directives have helped to establish Dubai as one of the Middle East's premier tourist destinations; and have also attempted to reform the labour market and integrate Dubai nationals more fully into the private sector. In addition, they have created a flourishing real estate market by allowing freehold land ownership for both nationals and expatriates; and, very shortly, they will also allow for more relaxed residency visa requirements, more flexible mortgaging, and perhaps also the right of association for residential communities. At first glance, these reforms have been highly successful; in so far as Dubai has managed to reduce its dependency on oil exports and now boasts a multi-sector economy and non-oil GDP contributions of around 94%.[1] However, given the host of previous restrictions in Dubai, it is important to appreciate just how far-reaching these reforms are considered to be, and to understand that they have not been implemented without a significant political and social cost.

This chapter will therefore not only consider Dubai's diversification and the nature of its economic liberalization, but will also assess the implications of the reforms on Dubai's particular version of the ruling bargain between its government and national population, and, inextricably connected to this bargain, the direct impact on these citizens. It will also consider the level of enthusiasm or otherwise that citizens now display towards the foreigners and the foreign wealth that is now being so vigorously courted by the Dubai government. In addition to this analysis, given that Dubai is not a state as such, despite its enormous international recognition, but rather a member of the somewhat loose federation of United Arab Emirates, the study will also attempt to place Dubai's reforms within the context of its neighbours, most notably Abu Dhabi, the largest of the seven constituent emirates, and crucially an emirate that remains oil rich and is therefore able to follow a considerably more cautious path towards diversification.

Early Diversification – Agriculture and Light Manufacturing

As early as the mid-1970s, following a series of oil price booms and slumps, it was already evident to Dubai's planners that the emirate would need to diversify away from oil, so as to offset its chronic dependency on the major oil-purchasing economies. The first two sectors earmarked for development were agriculture and light manufacturing. Crucially, given that neither of these sectors required extensive or problematic reforms, sectoral growth was relatively fast and painless: existing oil wealth could be channelled into constructing the necessary infrastructure for such activities, and the necessary machinery and equipment could be imported and set up as and when required. While agriculture was never likely to provide a particularly high non-oil GDP contribution, the sector's improvement was nevertheless viewed as not only helping to reduce Dubai's reliance on foreign foodstuffs, and thereby achieving greater food security, but also as a means of expanding the domestic market and complementing the growth of other local non-oil-related industries, especially Dubai's many dairy and poultry industries which rely heavily on agricultural foodstock.[2] Moreover, it is important to note that by this stage the agricultural sector, which employs a higher percentage of Dubai nationals than any other sector (85% of all farm workers and 75% of all fishermen),[3] had assumed great socio-economic significance in an emirate which, as will be described later in this chapter, has become increasingly overwhelmed by expatriate workers.[4]

Indeed, in 1976, the directive documents of the UAE's federal Ministry of Planning emphasized the need to increase agriculture's contribution to the GDP, either by improving the productivity of the land itself or by increasing the total cultivatable area.[5] With regard to the former, there was substantial government investment in the form of considerable subsidies which were used to slow the migration of farmers to the cities, and to provide for superior equipment, irrigation and water wells. Moreover, in practice, the subsidies have often extended far beyond these initial objectives and, as one can witness in Khawaneej and other rural areas of Dubai, it is now possible for new farmers to walk into almost ready-made farms complete with housing, fencing, roads, and of course all the necessary farming machinery.[6] In addition, there was considerable investment in the development of new crop strains, with a number of agricultural trials stations set up so as to produce hardier crops better suited to the harsh desert conditions.[7] As far as increasing the productivity of the land went, there was a massive increase in agricultural output during the 1980s and 1990s. Certainly, vegetable production in Dubai more than tripled from less than 2000 tonnes in 1990 to over 6000 tonnes in 1999.[8] Similarly successful was the emirate's fruit production over this period, which rose from just over 1000 tonnes in 1990 to nearly 17,000 tonnes in 2000.[9] Most impressive, however, was the growth in Dubai's dairy production, which rose from just 300 tonnes in 1981 to nearly 32,000 tonnes in 2000, representing a hundred-fold increase in less than 20 years.[10] Equally promising, though undoubtedly far from cost-effective given the region's unforgiving climate, were the results of Dubai's various land cultivation strategies. Certainly, with figures made available by the Ministry of Agriculture, it can be demonstrated that there has been a substantial 82% increase of arable land since the mid-1980s. Further related to the growth of the agricultural sector has been the modest increase in fishing. Fishing has always been one of the region's main economic activities[11] and, although cautious of over-fishing, the industry has nevertheless also benefited from productivity gains and government subsidies in recent years. Indeed, over the past decade the catches for Dubai and the other northern emirates have risen from 12,500 tonnes to 21,300 thousand tonnes, thus representing a 70% increase in their annual fish production.[12]

With regard to manufacturing, Dubai's modest oil reserves dictated a strategy concentrating on lighter industries that would not be reliant on vast supplies of cheap energy and thereby would be less dependent on associated oil sectors. Thus, with the exception of Dubai's highly successful DUBAL aluminium operation,[13] the main focus was always on import substitution industries in which simple goods would be produced that would otherwise be expensive to import. It was planned that the technologies required for such activities would be imported as a temporary stop-gap measure until Dubai could substitute these with its own domestic technologies. Most notably, construction goods such as piping and cement could be manufactured and sold at competitive prices given the high cost of importing such bulky freight into Dubai.[14] Certainly there was an appreciable reduction in these imports, even during massive construction booms in the 1980s, with the cost of imports being held in check at around 20 billion dirhams (at fixed prices) until the early 1990s.[15] Although the importation of such goods has risen in more recent years, and of course continues to pose a serious structural problem for the economy, this does not necessarily indicate the failure of this early diversification strategy. Indeed, there continues to be a significant rise in the number of new import substitution projects, especially in the packaging and bottling industries, many of which initially licensed foreign technology but have now made success-ful substitutions. Other particularly notable successes have included Dubai's clothes manufacturing sector (especially the production of uniforms), and its ice cream industry.[16] As such, the perceived slowdown in Dubai's manufacturing in the late 1990s may have simply been due to the unsustainable growth of the early 'easy stage': import substitution industrialization was originally applied to relatively straightforward industries requiring only minor technology injections and minimal planning, but recent attempts to apply the strategy to more technologi-cally advanced industries may take more time and greater investment.

Early Diversification – Commerce and Tourism

In a further effort to diversify the economy and attract foreign currency, the 1980s and 1990s witnessed significant expansion of Dubai's commercial and tourist sectors. Capitalizing on Dubai's historical attrac-tiveness as one of the region's premier entrepôts, and by promoting Dubai's attractive climate and relatively unspoiled beaches, the planners were able to improve two additional non-oil-related sectors while again avoiding the need for any significant or controversial economic reforms. Indeed, following the construction of Dubai's Mina Rashid and Mina Jebel Ali, Dubai's ports have become some of the busiest in the world, shifting over 15 million metric tonnes of non-oil-related traded goods per year, and accounting for nearly US$31 billion in trade receipts per year (compared to just $2 billion in 1975).[17] Boosting trade further, the emirate hosts two major shopping festivals each year, 'The Dubai Shopping Festival' which runs from January to February and is targeted at international buyers, and the 'Dubai Summer Surprises Festival' which runs from July to August and is targeted at visiting GCC buyers. Most famously of course, Dubai's enormous commercial expansion has transformed it into a city of shopping malls, with some of the largest in the world and with many catering for the highest possible end of the international market. Remarkably, with the recently opened Mall of the Emirates and Reef Mall, and with the forthcoming Dubai Mall, the city's tally of such centres will soon be approaching the 30 mark.

With reference to the actual growth of Dubai's commercial sector, perhaps the clearest indicator of expansion has been the sheer increase in the value and volume of international non-oil-related trade. Indeed, quite remarkably the emirate's total non-oil foreign trade rose from a modest 8 billion dirhams in 1975 to nearly 112 billion dirhams after 2001 (measured at fixed 1995 prices), representing over 15 million tonnes of traded goods.[18] However, in addition to this fifteen-fold rise in the total value of non-oil foreign trade and a 140% rise in the total volume of foreign trade since 1980,[19] the emirate's substantial increase in re-exporting foreign goods imported into Dubai over the past 25 years must also be taken into consideration. Certainly, given the historically high levels of imports in the oil-rich Gulf states,[20] the value and quantity of re-exports together with their relative contribution to total trade may provide an even more accurate indicator of the recent commercial expansion. Thus, with a massive increase in the value of re-exported goods between 1975 and 2001 (and with the volume of re-exported goods more than doubling between 1980 and 2001 from 0.9 million to 2.5 million tonnes[21]) and, as the above trend line indicates, with re-exports accounting for a much higher proportion of total trade, it is evident that the emirate is indeed generating considerable non-oil-related commercial activity. Moreover, when compared to the value of foreign trade and re-exports for the other GCC States,[22] these figures clearly confirm Dubai's position as one of the main trading hubs of the Persian Gulf and the greater Middle East.

With regard to tourism, the emirate is now home to over 300

hotels and draws nearly 3 million visitors per annum (compared with just 40 hotels and 0.4 million visitors in 1985),[23] many of them flown in courtesy of Emirates, Dubai's semi-government owned and award-winning airline.[24] Moreover, given the major hotel developments that have taken place since 2000, including the Dubai Fairmont, the Dusit Dubai, Madinat Jumeirah's hotels and the Grand Hyatt, and given the only temporary decline in tourism following the September 2001 terrorist attacks in the United States, these positive trends seem set to continue.[25] Crucially, it is also important to break down this sector and to show how the most rapid growth has occurred in the luxury tourist market, thus underscoring Dubai's objective of transforming itself into an important winter sun resort for affluent Western holidaymakers. Indeed, of the hotels operating in Dubai, most are either 'deluxe' or 'first-class' rated, with many of the most prestigious Asian and international chains having chosen Dubai as the location for their flagship hotels.[26] Also, given that these deluxe hotels are far larger than most of the other hotels, they actually provide the bulk of tourist accommodation in the emirate. In fact, about 78 of these luxury hotels account for nearly 20,000 of the total 31,000 hotel beds in Dubai and, more importantly, have enjoyed much higher occupancy rates than the other hotels, averaging nearly 70%, compared with less than 36% for some of the lower-class hotels.[27] These occupancy rates have therefore translated into a high and growing number of luxury tourists staying in Dubai: about 2 million of the 3 million annual visitors, representing nearly 66% of the sector total and almost double the size of the emirate's resident population.[28]

Supporting this international tourism strategy has been the increasing number of cultural and sporting activities offered by Dubai. Certainly, the many museums, local art galleries, reconstructed forts and 'heritage villages' provide educational and charming distractions for the numerous tourists, most notably the pearling village, the Bedu village and the Sheikh Sa'id art gallery, all of which line the creekside in Shindagha and provide visitors with a pleasant open-air network of live entertainment, sights and sounds. The emirate is also becoming a major stop-off point for many of the world's most popular acts, and in recent years has hosted the likes of Elton John, Bryan Adams, Blue, Enrique and Julio Iglesias, Luciano Pavarotti, Mariah Carey, Dire Straits, Pink Floyd and Phil Collins. Moreover, the growing numbers of sporting events, many of which have achieved world-circuit status, have attracted

wide audiences and have greatly enhanced Dubai's international reputa-
tion for potential tourists sitting in front of their television sets in Europe.
Key examples include the European golf tour's Dubai Desert Classic, the
annual ATP and WTA tennis tournaments, and most notably the Dubai
World Cup – the world's most lucrative horse race. In the near future
these may be joined by the Dubai Grand Prix: Dubai has already constructed an impressive autodrome, and may soon launch its own Formula
One team. Hosting an actual race will be the natural progression.
Similarly, Dubai is in the process of constructing an international sports
city, complete with stadia that may allow it to make an Olympic bid in
the near future, or at the very least a bid for the Asian Games.

Complex Diversification – Freezones and Foreign Direct Investment

Another important component of Dubai's diversification strategy has
been the creation of free zones allowing foreign investment to flood
into the emirate and in which foreign companies can operate alongside
Dubai's indigenous light manufacturing and other non-oil-related
sectors. However, unlike the encouragement of Dubai's agricultural,
industrial, commercial and tourist sectors, the creation of these free
zones has been far more problematic, as it has required Dubai to under-
take significant reforms so as to encourage foreign direct investment.
Most notably, there had to be considerable liberalization of the
pre-existing 49% cap on foreign business ownership and the much
maligned *kafil* sponsorship system that required all foreign businesses to
take on an Emirati partner. Very often this sponsorship system led to
sleeping partners and a heavy and off-putting burden for potential
investors. At the forefront of such developments has been the Jebel Ali
Free Zone, south-west of Dubai. Although the original 1975 decision to
create Jebel Ali envisaged the zone as simply being Dubai's second port,[29]
in 1985 the Dubai Department of Industry began to operate it with the
objective of supplying foreign clients with all necessary administration,
engineering and utility services.[30] Thus, in the same year, a local Dubai
law was passed with the express aim of providing the Jebel Ali authority
with greater freedom and exemptions from existing business regulations.
Specifically, the law empowered Jebel Ali companies to be released from
all export fees and turnover taxes, and most crucially allowed all of the
zone's foreign companies to be exempt from local partner conditions

and to claim full repatriation of the invested capital.[31] Since then, the zone has expanded from around 300 companies in 1990 to over 2000 companies today (30% of which are European, and 14% of which are North American) and has attracted about US$4 billion in investments.[32]

In recent years a number of innovative development projects have attempted to follow this pattern, with many of the new free zones and parks also claiming to permit 100% foreign ownership. Indeed, Dubai Investments Park Development Co. (DIPD) can be regarded as the pioneer of this approach in the 1990s. In 1998 the firm was seeking approval to allow foreigners to hold a majority stake in ventures in its business park situated close to Jebel Ali. Although general manager Khalid Kalban accepted that the park was likely to remain distinct from Jebel Ali and its free zone status, he nevertheless stated his "hope for 100% foreign ownership in the business park".[33] Since then, DIPD intensified its marketing campaign to attract foreign investors and businesses by offering them first-rate infrastructure with complete freedom from any restrictions,[34] and, backed by a new Dubai decree in 2000 to promote such freedom in commercial developments, these promises were soon realized. Essentially the Dubai Technology, Electronic Commerce and Media Free Zone Law No. 1 was the first of its kind in the Gulf, again underscoring the emirate's strong commitment to the liberalization of its economy. Indeed, by expanding upon the earlier Jebel Ali enabling legislation, this new local ordinance responded to the needs of the business community by allowing for a number of significant amendments and relaxations of the existing restrictions:

Article 9. "Entry into leases of plots and buildings may extend to periods of up to 50 years, with any establishment in the free zone, to enable it to carry on its activity according to terms and conditions agreed upon."

Article 15. "Free zone establishments shall be exempt from all taxes, including income tax, with regard to their operations in the free zone. They shall also be excluded from any restrictions on repatriation and transfer of capital, profits and wages in any currency to any place outside the free zone for a period of 50 years . . ."

Article 16. "Assets or activities of the free zone establishments shall not be subject to nationalization or any measures restricting private ownership throughout the period of their activities in the free zone."

Article 17. "Free zone establishments may employ or hire whomsoever they choose in their operations in the free zone, provided that such employees are not subject to any countries politically or economically boycotted by the UAE."

Article 18. "The operations of free zone establishments or employees, within the free zone, shall not be subject to the laws and regulations of Dubai Municipality, the Department of Economic Development of the Government of Dubai, or the powers and authority falling within their jurisdiction."[35]

Thus, these articles formalized the practice of granting long-term leases to foreign firms while guaranteeing them exemption from any possible nationalization of industry and from any future implementation of taxation, such as corporation taxes.[36] Furthermore, they also granted all free zone companies exemption from municipal laws, thereby effectively placing them outside of greater UAE and GCC laws.

Benefiting from this custom-made legislation, a flurry of new ventures have sought to maximize these new advantages. One such example would be the Dubai Airport Free Zone which became operational in late 2000. Close to the city centre, the zone began to offer prospective high-tech companies a number of incentives, many of which relied heavily upon the recent relaxations. Indeed, in much the same way as Jebel Ali, but without needing a specific Emiri decree, the zone was able to promise tax exemptions, 100% foreign ownership and 100% repatriation of capital and profits.[37] Even stronger examples of such developments have of course been the Dubai Internet and Media Cities, which are now home to branches of Microsoft, Hewlett Packard, CNN and many other high-profile multinationals. Certainly, Dubai Internet City (DIC) would seem intent to capitalize on all of the benefits granted by the new law, as its marketing brochure reads:

> 100% foreign ownership, 0% problems! To attract IT and internet-focused companies, Dubai Internet City will offer an extremely attractive set of benefits. In addition to 100% foreign ownership, companies will also get land on renewable leases of up to 50 years. They can move into ready-to-operate-from offices or build their own offices. The aim is to facilitate immediate commencement of

business operations. Towards this end there will be a 'single-window' for all government clearances, including those pertaining to trade licences and work permits.[38]

Thus, given the many similarities between these objectives and the described articles, developments such as the DIC can be regarded as direct products of this new legislation. Moreover, it is also worth noting that as these new free zones grow in size and number, they may catalyse further amendments and reforms to existing regulations. Indeed, it is believed that the DIC's requirements for more comprehensive internet access may soon even lead to a relaxation in the telecommunications restrictions. For a long time the topic of internet access has been a delicate issue in the UAE, with freedom of use currently being sacrificed for state control. However, with a clear reference to the DIC, a spokesman for the federal government recently raised this very issue of censorship by stating that

> . . . the current regulations enforced in the UAE may need to be examined and even dropped altogether as a concession to the fact that electronic information knows no borders and it is virtually impossible to stop its flow in and out of the UAE . . . businesses located in the Dubai Internet City would soon be able to by-pass the Etisalat proxy server [the imposed intermediate server and information filter] for the purposes of sending and receiving electronic information.[39]

Foreign investment has also been channelled into Dubai's rapidly growing invisibles sector, as the emirate has rapidly expanded its international banking and insurance zones. As late as the 1960s, only two foreign banking houses operated in Dubai (Eastern Bank and the British Bank of the Middle East),[40] whereas today, fuelled by enormous demand and highly conducive conditions, Dubai is now home to dozens of Western and Asian banks including Paribas, Citibank, HSBC, Barclays, and Lloyds. Moreover, in 2000 Dubai was the first of the emirates to provide an integrated financial market, and more recently it has opened up the Dubai International Financial Centre (DIFC), housed in a 21st-century 'Arc-de-Triomphe' style monstrosity close to Sheikh Zayed Road. As Sheikh Muhammad bin Rashid al-Maktoum, Dubai's ruler, has claimed, the Centre will allow the emirate to join the international markets of

London, New York and Tokyo; and, as Anis Al-Jallaf, the chairman of the Centre's board has elaborated, ". . . it will be able to satisfy the regional needs of business and investors by building a hub in Dubai. We want to create a place for regional blue chips to find financial solutions and a place for international banks to seek regional investment opportunities."[41] Crucially, with regard to reforms, it has been reported that the Dubai International Finance Centre will attempt to defy current UAE laws in much the same way as the aforementioned free zones and industrial parks. Moreover, this challenge will be especially significant given that the Centre, lacking any official free zone status, will not be able to rely upon the Dubai 2000 legislation and, as is widely believed, has not yet received support from the Central Bank. Certainly, as Sultan Al-Suwaidi the governor of the Central Bank has stated, the Centre remains "entirely a Dubai initiative, with no connection to either the Central Bank or any other UAE institution".[42] However, despite its ambiguous status, the chairman of the DIFC, Al-Jallaf, has confidently stated that the centre's offices and banks ". . . will not be operating under the laws and regulations of the UAE", and that, "100% foreign ownership will definitely be permitted".[43] Unsurprisingly, Al-Jallaf's bold statement soon received support from Sheikh Muhammad who reiterated that the Centre would parallel international laws and conventions similar to those in the US and the UK, rather than local UAE laws.[44] It would therefore seem likely that the Centre, in a similar fashion to the DIPD, will at first be operating outside of UAE law, perhaps until fresh legislation is introduced in order to disable the existing restrictions.

Complex Diversification – Real Estate

Attracting foreign investment from individuals has of course been the secret of Dubai's much publicized real estate sector. Significantly, the reforms required for the take-off of this sector have been the most controversial of all. Since the late 1990s Dubai has been deliberately circumventing a long-standing federal law which bans property ownership for non-nationals, and, with the backing of Sheikh Muhammad, a number of the city's major developers have launched large-scale multi-phase residential projects aimed specifically at either Western or expatriate Arab clientele. Perhaps the first example of such an endeavour was the result of a strategic alliance formed between Sheikh Muhammad and Muhammad

Al-Abbar's Emaar Properties. Importantly, for much of the early and mid-1990s, Emaar Properties had confined its activities to the construction and letting of condominiums on the Sheikh's donated land, and both parties had been content to restrict the sale of completed apartments to UAE nationals, thereby upholding the foreign ownership ban. However, by 1997 an important change had taken place. Emaar announced the launch of 'Emirates Hills'; a 700 million dirham golfing-cum-residential project which would overlook the Emirates Golf Club close to Dubai's busiest commercial centre. Given the scale of the project, Sheikh Muhammad began to take a more active role by personally supervising its progress.[45] Thus, with a powerful supporter and benefactor, Al-Abbar finally began to contradict publicly the existing laws by underscoring his commitment to foreign ownership:

> We have had a strong response [for Emirates Hills] from citizens of Abu Dhabi, Dubai, Saudi Arabia, and Kuwait, and even from expatriates. We will also allow locally incorporated companies to purchase the villas.[46]

Thus, for the first time in the UAE's history, residential plots were not only being marketed to Emirati and GCC citizens, but also to ". . . those 'others' that can either buy fully built-up villas or plots".[47]

Moreover, Emaar's much-publicized follow-up project, the Westside Marina, further consolidated the reformist Al-Abbar/Sheikh Muhammad position. Indeed, in much the same way as Emirates Hills, the project's stated objective was not so much to meet the needs of the local population, but rather to increase the attractiveness of Dubai to foreign investors. Specifically, it was to comprise of:

> A marina complex with mixed usage low, medium and high-rise buildings along with comprehensive infrastructure features, complete with shopping centres, swimming pools and golf courses . . . which would accommodate the expected growth of Dubai for tourists, international expatriates, and UAE and GCC citizens. Properties within the community complex would also be available for UAE, GCC and other companies.[48]

Thus, by condoning the long-term leasing of property to all interested parties, regardless of nationality, the marketing aims of these two projects have, strictly speaking, been outside of UAE law. However, given that both Emirates Hills and the Marina have been resounding successes for Dubai's real estate sector, Emaar appears to have set a precedent with many other developers having followed their lead.

By far the most ambitious and noteworthy of these new property developments have been the creation of three vast 'Palm Island' complexes built on man-made atolls off the coasts of Jebel Ali, Jumeirah Beach and Dubai's Deira suburb. With their 120km of artificial sandy beaches, a monorail linking their palms' various fronds, high-rise hotels and 3000 luxury villas, the Palm Islands will join the Great Wall of China as being among the few man-made structures visible from space. The project has reportedly cost over 15 billion dirhams and has been funded primarily by the government of Dubai along with a number of local and international banks. Crucially, although not under the auspices of Emaar Properties, this project is also being personally supervised by Sheikh Muhammad. Furthermore, in much the same manner as the groundbreaking Al-Abbar developments, the properties on the Palm Islands are being made available to overseas buyers on 100-year leases.[49] Accordingly, while this does not actually constitute foreign ownership, the semi-permanency of the proposed leases and the overall objectives of the project are best viewed as careful work-arounds of the law.

Significantly, it would appear that even the UAE's federal ministries are now beginning to recognize the importance of these successful developments in Dubai, and as a communiqué from the Abu Dhabi-based Ministry of Information and Culture indicates, it would seem that the reformers' strategies are gradually being accepted, even if not yet officially approved:

> In general, expatriates are not allowed to buy properties in the UAE, however it is now possible to do so in some emirates, for example, Dubai. The ambitious Palm Island Project – the world's largest man-made island shaped like palm trees, being developed by the Dubai Government, offers villas to be sold on a freehold basis.[50]

In addition, the pioneering role of Dubai-based companies such as Emaar Properties, and their use of long-term leases as legal loopholes, are now also being acknowledged by the ministry:

> . . . Dubai Lands and Properties Department has announced that expatriates, including non-resident foreigners, can now buy property

in Dubai in the form of 99-year leases with properties managed by Emār Properties. Earlier, only GCC citizens were entitled to this privilege, now foreigners are entitled to the same rights as UAE citizens and Gulf nationals as far as buying, selling and renting lands and property in Dubai is concerned.[51]

Tellingly, almost all of the adverts for these projects (which are plastered all over the emirate) feature either Western or distinctly non-Emirati nuclear families frolicking on beaches or in gardens in front of their new homes. With a new emirate-level law in place (allowing foreigners to hold residency visas based on property ownership rather than employment); and a new federal law having been introduced in late 2005, with greatly relaxed mortgaging requirements; plus the hint of residential associations being allowed (previously such civil society associations would have been subjected to strict state control), the sector continues to enjoy enormous confidence, boosted by the attraction of large premiums for property speculators, and the prospects of tax-free rent income for longer-term investors. While the number of these projects has now reached the stage where no single person can keep track, it is nevertheless useful to draw attention to some of Dubai's latest schemes, if only to give an idea of the sheer scale of the strategy and the extent of Dubai's commitment. Pioneering Emaar continues to lead the way and in the last few years has been concentrating on its 'Old Town' and Burj Dubai projects: with over 189 storeys and a dynamic design capable of adjusting to international competition, Emaar insists that the Burj Dubai will be the world's tallest building upon its completion in 2007. Similarly spectacular have been the projects of Nakheel, the developer of the three Palm Island Projects and 'The World': a series of man-made islands for high-end foreign investors. Providing downtown, business-centric residences, Dubai Holdings has now launched the 'Business Bay' project: a gigantic artificial canal connecting the creek to a multitude of emerging skyscrapers complete with Venetian-style waterways just behind Sheikh Zayed Road and close to the aforementioned Dubai International Financial Centre. Crucially, almost all properties in these developments are snapped up immediately, and demand is currently outstripping supply. Moreover, although there are undoubtedly long-term risks associated with what many believe to be an over-extension of the sector, given that most of the real estate funds are paid up front by investors (often before the buildings have even emerged from the sand), Dubai is presently in a win-win situation.

As a side note, and although more a legacy of Dubai's laissez-faire past than a conscious part of Dubai's current development strategy, it is worth mentioning how this greater flexibility in permitting private ownership of real estate must be regarded as another key factor behind the growth of the commercial sector and the proliferation of shopping malls. Unlike Abu Dhabi and the other Gulf states, where until very recently most of the land was under government ownership, in Dubai it has been much easier for one individual or a group of investors to buy up many adjacent plots of land, thereby securing enough space for 'megaprojects'. In Abu Dhabi (home to just two major shopping malls) such megaprojects are only really a possibility for powerful businessmen who are either part of, or closely linked to, the ruling family, the best example being Sheikh Surur bin Muhammad al-Nahyan – the proprietor of the Abu Dhabi Mall and Trade Centre.

Labour Reforms and Emiratization

Another key area of reform in Dubai has been its labour nationalization programme. With all of these diverse touristic, commercial and real estate sectors, the bulk of the emirate's employment opportunities are now to be found in the private sector, which is currently dominated by expatriates. As most are aware, expatriate labour has long been an important socio-economic characteristic of the lower Gulf, with the pearling industry and its associated activities having always attracted large numbers of Indians, Iranians and other nationalities to the main coastal towns.[52] However, by the early 1970s, Dubai's massive labour requirements for its oil-financed development projects soon led to far greater numbers of foreign workers, both skilled and unskilled, entering the workforce and assuming semi-permanent residence. Indeed, this influx continued more or less unabated right up to the 1990s, leaving the indigenous 'locals' a minority in their own country and, as most would agree, rendering them totally reliant on the millions of foreigners who have built, and continue to build, Dubai and the rest of the UAE. In much the same way as the need for diversification of the oil-dependent economy became apparent, the planners recognized the need to reduce their population's persistent dependency on foreign labour and skills, not only to help achieve a more desirable level of labour self-sufficiency, but also to control better the many other socio-economic problems that could result from the continuing presence of a large number of expatriate workers (both Arab and non-Arab). As such, the need for greater 'emiratization' of the workforce has not only been viewed within the context of labour nationalization, but also has other implications. First it is increasingly regarded as a necessary safeguard against the negative implications for Dubai's money supply growth, resulting from salaries and other payments being transferred out of the country; second it is seen as a check on the unhealthy gender imbalances arising from a predominantly male immigrant workforce; and finally it acts as a curb on the perceived erosion of cultural and religious identities.

To give an idea of the scale of this foreign presence it is worth noting that in 1968, three years before the creation of the UAE, a sizeable, but perhaps containable 38% of the region's workforce were expatriates.[53] By the year 2000, however, with a population of somewhere between 3 and 4 million, surveys in the big cities indicated that less than 17% of households were UAE national, and that over 70% of the municipal populations comprised either Asian households or Asian labour collectives.[54] These were the last official surveys before the (as yet unpublished) census of 2006. More worryingly, it is now privately estimated that over 90% of workers may be expatriates, with the head of the Planning Department's statistics unit having recently admitted that UAE nationals now account for less than 7.5% of the private sector workforce.[55] As Rawhi Abeidoh describes, this has of course been an enormous change over a relatively short period of time, a change which has led to increasing socio-economic concerns for the UAE's future, even at the highest levels of Emirati politics.[56]

It is worth noting that even in the 1970s the government had recognized the potential problem of such 'shackling',[57] with the Planning Department recommending in 1977 that there needed to be state-sponsored encouragement for far greater nationalization, or 'emiratization' of the workforce.[58] Essentially, in economic terms, it was felt that a continuing reliance on foreign labour would lead to persistently high development costs, and that the growing expatriate population would also adversely affect the money supply.[59] Today it is estimated that US$3.3 billion is being repatriated overseas annually by foreign workers sending remittances back to their country of origin.[60] Furthermore, by the mid-1980s there was also a growing consensus that without such an emiratization drive, the employment structure would become even more distorted with fewer nationals capable or willing to undertake jobs normally associated with expatriate labour. Certainly, as Malcolm Peck observed:

> . . . as in the other wealthy oil states of the Arabian Peninsula, there is little evident connection in UAE society between wealth and work. As one analyst remarks, 'the message is clear: without effort or self-denial one can simply accept a world made by others'. As a result, there are incipient signs of the kind of social malaise already evident in Kuwait with its long history of very high per capita wealth and advanced welfarism. Some young men with large amounts of money and leisure at their disposal are tempted to spend them on such things as expensive cars and mistresses and to avoid meaningful employment.[61]

Greater emiratization has also been seen as an essential measure in lessening the growing gender imbalance in Dubai. Given that the vast majority of expatriate labourers are Pathan bachelors or married Keralite men unable to bring their spouses and families to the UAE (a minimum salary is required before a worker is eligible to invite family members to accompany them), this has inevitably led to a skewed demographic structure and a rather unpleasant atmosphere, with adult males vastly outnumbering adult females. As such, even though there were slight improvements in the 1990s, it is evident that of the population registered in the census of 2000, more than two-thirds were male, making Dubai's population one of the most imbalanced in the world. Moreover, the proportion of males is probably even higher than this official figure given that many short-term contract workers are not included in census data. Also, given that the vast majority of the expatriates are based inside or close to the major cities, it is important to note that the gender imbalance will be much greater in these areas. If more Dubai nationals, both men and women, can be brought into the workplace and eventually be used to fill positions previously requiring expatriates, then it is hoped that this disparity and its negative social implications can be somewhat reduced.

With regard to the socio-cultural impact of such a large population of foreign workers residing in the emirate, although not an official aim of the emiratization process, there is little doubt that the need for a preventative check on the perceived cultural and religious erosion resulting from the massive influx of expatriates is seen to be increasingly necessary. Indeed, it is important to emphasize how many Dubai nationals voice not only their misgivings over their minority status in the workforce and their reliance on foreign labour, but also their very deep concerns over their increasing cultural marginalization in a country dominated by non-Arabs and, in many areas, by non-Muslims.[62]

Finally, although of less direct interest to the Dubai government and the planners, it is perhaps also worth considering that the emiratization strategy and indeed 'Saudification' and the various other labour nationalization initiatives in the Gulf states are being increasingly viewed by both indigenous and Asian scholars as necessary measures for correcting what have developed into serious two-way population problems. Certainly, it has been argued that massive labour migrations on the scale such as that between the Gulf and the subcontinent have caused marked gender imbalances and other socio-economic problems for the supplier countries as well as the host. Indeed, as Peck noted in the early 1980s, severe strains were already beginning to emerge in these South Asian supplier countries with the cause often being dubbed 'the Dubai syndrome':

> . . . social strains are generated not only in the host societies by the presence of foreign workers, but in the latter's societies as well. Although many of the Asian labourers live in physically and psychologically difficult situations in the UAE and in its neighbour states, their wives left at home fall victim to frustration and attendant disorders dubbed 'Dubai syndrome' (as coined by a Pakistani psychiatrist). The prolonged absences of heads of families cause a breakdown of social controls in some Asian settings, and the remittances that are sent back often create resentments and divisions in the workers' home communities.[63]

Moreover, 20 years later, these psychosocial problems are still very much in evidence, with recent UAE-based studies concluding that the majority of the millions of Asian expatriate workers not only suffer from some sort of psychological depression themselves, but also, due to their long periods of absence, are beginning to cause significant socio-economic problems in their home country.[64] If therefore, as part of a broader labour nationalization policy, there can be time limits or other restrictions placed on foreign workers, especially those unable to bring their families to Dubai, it is theorized that these pathologies can be somewhat reduced before conditions further deteriorate.

With regard to the emiratization strategies and reforms themselves, the encouragement of nationals' participation in the workforce actually has a long history in the region and, as such, the present-day emiratization initiative can be viewed as an extension of existing ideas and practices, albeit on a much more comprehensive scale. Indeed, with the beginning of *Al-khawiya* (the oil exploration by foreign firms in the early 1930s) the rulers had already begun to insist that as part of their concession agreements, the firms should be obliged to recruit and train up some of the local population, rather than simply importing all of their labour.[65] Moreover, by the late 1930s, the ruler of Dubai had taken this agreement one stage further by insisting that Petroleum Development Trucial Coast Ltd (PDTC) employ only Dubai subjects.[66] Following the decline of the pearling industry, and faced with the prospect of unemployment, it was reasoned that Dubai locals needed far more stable jobs, and with the training provided by the foreign oil companies this early emiratization was seen as a suitable long-term solution.[67]

By the late 1970s and 1980s the emiratization strategy became far more extensive, with the official economic and social development plans outlining a comprehensive programme aiming to rehabilitate as many nationals as possible by educating them, training them and giving them added incentives to participate and become an active part of the workforce.[68] Indeed, as has been described elsewhere, the development of the education system was always a key priority,[69] and, with specific regard to emiratization, a special emphasis was placed on courses and subjects relating to business practices and the professional skills demanded by other areas of Dubai's diverse development. This commitment to investment in education was to be matched in the workplace by a number of government-sponsored schemes to encourage greater work experience and full-time employment. Prominent examples in recent years have included the Al-Futtaim Trading Group's summer courses offered to young nationals, with the group claiming it intends to "pioneer the training of national personnel";[70] the work of the UAE Women's Federation which aims to bring more young Emirati women into the workplace;[71] and the various Emirati-specific training programmes offered by the major banks. Indeed, speaking about Mashriq Bank's role in the emiratization process, Abdul Al-Ghurair, Chief Executive Officer of Mashriq Bank in Dubai, explained why the bank was the first to launch such a programme:

> In our continuous quest for excellence, Mashriq Bank has never neglected to play the role of the responsible corporate, forever striving to create practical and innovative solutions in response to the direct needs of the UAE market. The contributions of Mashriq Bank in the process of emiratization has been quite significant as we go ahead with our plans to increase the presence of UAE nationals in our bank.

Moreover, Mohammed Al-Sayari, chairman of the bank's human resources department, explained how such a programme would actually contribute to the emiratization process:

> Our aim is to train sixty UAE nationals every year by running four courses throughout the year. The first fifteen passed out in March and completed the programme successfully. Some are now working in Mashriq and some have started careers in other banks. The course concentrates on improving practical skills through on-the-job training rather than theory work. The course runs for five full working days to give the young nationals a feeling of the workplace. They learn how to write a professional CV, how to behave in an interview and where to go if they have a problem. The training is definitely more practical than theoretical.[72]

In addition to these educational programmes, there have also been more direct and in some cases more controversial strategies, many of which have focused on the granting of specific privileges to nationals with the aim of assisting their introduction into the workplace and reducing competition from expatriates. Certainly, as Abdullah Sultan Abdullah, the secretary general of the Federation of the UAE Chambers of Commerce and Industry has explained, although Dubai's chamber does place great emphasis on training and qualifying nationals, this can only go so far, and in certain cases the government has had to intervene in order to provide additional incentives and encouragement.[73] Most recently this strategy has been reinforced by a new labour law aimed at regulating the employment of nationals in the private sector. As part of the new law, nationals will benefit from special pension funds and better guarantees of their rights as employees in the private sector.[74] Alongside these initiatives there have, of course, been more restrictive schemes, including the aforementioned *kafil* sponsorship system in which all non-Emirati entrepreneurs require a local partner, thereby ensuring that nationals, even as parasites, have at least some involvement in the management and profits of the domestic economy. In addition, there have also been specific emiratization quotas introduced, requiring certain companies to increase their percentage of Emirati employees over a set period. Once again, the banking sector provides a strong example, where up until the late 1990s nationals accounted for just 12% of the workforce. To redress this situation, the government chose to impose quotas, requiring all banks to increase their percentage of locals to 40% over the next ten years.[75] As such, Mashriq Bank and many of the other banking houses have publicly stated their intention to have an 'emiratization growth rate' of over 4% per year in an effort to meet these targets.[76] Moreover, it is worthwhile noting that in certain circumstances there have also been more extreme measures including, for example, highly contentious directives such as the Ministry of Agriculture and Fisheries' decree that nationals must captain all fishing boats. Explained by the Minister as being a necessary step in order to "help check over-fishing and eliminate illegal practices resorted to by expatriate fishermen at sea", in practice it is simply a part of the government's overall drive for emiratization in the agricultural sector.[77]

Thirdly, and also deserving mention, are those emiratization reforms concerned not so much with the encouragement of UAE nationals, but rather the discouragement of expatriates, or more specifically, the discouragement of employers intent on hiring foreigners. Indeed, an important example is the draft law that was released by the Ministry of Labour which will require companies to pay a fee for every foreigner they hire, thus making UAE nationals a more attractive alternative.[78] In addition, other more severe laws have aimed at stemming the flow of immigrant labour and actually reducing the size of the current expatriate population. Examples include the restrictions placed on new visas requested by unskilled workers from India and Pakistan,[79] and the introduction of lengthy immigration amnesties which have allowed all foreign workers without valid visas to leave the UAE with only minimal penalties. Indeed, it has been estimated that during the 1996 amnesty as many as 200,000 workers unexpectedly took advantage of the favourable terms and left before its deadline, thereby creating massive labour shortages.[80]

Given the enormity and complexity of the challenge, the results of these various emiratization strategies have, however, been far less impressive than most would have expected (although it is important to note that many serious observers had always remained sceptical[81]). Certainly, the original objectives of the early 1980s, which proposed that national management and labour in all sectors should reach at least 25% of the total within five years,[82] have clearly not been met. Thus, unlike the comparatively straightforward early diversification objectives, the nationalization of the workforce has not been solved with financial packages and massive investment. Indeed, the experiences of the 1990s point to the opposite, given that the improved incentives, higher salaries and pension schemes encouraged by the emiratization initiative may have actually priced national graduates out of the market. Certainly, many employers baulked at paying the US$26,000 average salary for a local graduate in addition to the obligatory 12.5% pension contribution,[83] and much preferred to hire well-qualified and experienced South Asians at a fraction of the cost.[84] Nevertheless, although few of the official targets may have been reached, there has undoubtedly been a rise in the number of nationals participating in very diverse areas of the workforce and, with the rapidly increasing number of young Emiratis entering higher education, it is likely that emiratization, especially in managerial positions, will mushroom in the near future. Thus, although lacking the immediacy of the incentives, quotas and sponsorship systems, the various emiratization education programmes and Dubai's considerable investment in higher education may lead to important long-term results, especially in the nationalization of professional occupations which is, after all, a far more realistic objective than nationalizing 25% of the total workforce. Indeed, there are already important glimmers of hope, as the proportion of nationals gaining such positions, in both the private and public sectors, has appreciably increased. Again referring to the banking sector, the emiratization process has really taken hold since 2000, with nationals now accounting for around 20% of the workforce, thus representing a rise of nearly 8% over just a few years. Moreover, some banks have been particularly successful and, in the case of EIBFS, the general manager confidently expected their proportion of UAE nationals to rise to 23% in the near future as a direct result of fresh Emirati graduates.[85]

Implications for Security, Identity, and the Ruling Bargain

The upshot of all of these diversification, foreign investment and labour nationalization strategies, and their associated reforms, is that Dubai is now undoubtedly less reliant on its dwindling oil reserves and expatriate population, and is clearly the most integrated into the international system of all of the Gulf states. It can claim the highest share of all foreign investment in the UAE, much higher than neighbouring Abu Dhabi, it now boasts one of the Middle East's most successful tourist industries, and it continues to position itself as a major international trading hub. On paper therefore, Dubai is succeeding. With regard to stability and security, however, Dubai's eagerness to integrate itself into the international system is likely to have serious consequences in the very near future, and unless properly managed and contained, these may well outweigh the raw economic benefits of its development reforms. As other studies have demonstrated, many of the world's surviving traditional monarchies (most of which are Gulf states) rely upon an extremely delicate balance of legitimacy resources which together make up something of a 'ruling bargain' with the national population.[86] Dubai is definitely no exception, as its very survival has rested upon a combination of personal, patrimonial, cultural and religious resources, combined with massive distributions of oil-rent-derived wealth to its citizens, and of course the discreet backing of its oil-purchasing superpower friends.[87] Dubai's diversification does not of course upset the wealth distribution component given that it is still the nationals who own the plots of land that the residential properties, hotels and foreign business parks are built upon.[88] Indeed, although there are a few hidden taxes creeping up on Dubai's nationals (including higher parking fees, uncompetitive monopoly-controlled telecoms prices, and a 10% tax on utility payments), and although they may no longer be receiving such blatant oil-financed handouts from the government (as is still the case in Abu Dhabi where nationals receive much larger 'marriage funds', and can expect very generous allowances and free residences[89]), it is important to understand that the vast majority of Dubai nationals are still elevated above the wealth creation process and can still enjoy a rent-based income, albeit a different form of rent.

What Dubai's diversification does upset are the patrimonial, cultural and religious resources of the bargain. With accelerating foreign ownership, many of the nationals, both young and old, feel that Dubai's

[175]

development is not really for their benefit any more. As foreigners are beginning to make vast profits out of real estate and other activities that were formerly the preserve of the indigenous population, the monarchy and its cronies are beginning to appear as very obvious clients or intermediaries in a metropole-satellite chain of dependent relations. Moreover the aforementioned Jebel Ali Free Zone and many of the more recent free zones do not really target Arab investors and are therefore becoming seen as fragile products of globalization rather than regionalization. In other words, although the money still flows, Dubai nationals realize that their previous membership of a distinct patrimonial elite is now under threat and in some cases they even feel unwelcome in certain parts of their city. Not only are formerly exclusive privileges being eroded, but so too is their way of life, as the government continues to bend rules to accommodate the increasing number of non-Arab and non-Muslim foreigners. Most obviously, following an emirate-level decree, the volume of loudspeakers on mosques has been reduced in many residential areas (including those with mixed national and foreign communities such as Umm Suqeim and Jumierah), and previous restrictions on food and drink normally observed during the month of Ramadan are now rarely monitored, in an effort to boost non-Muslim tourism. Indeed, in many of Dubai's hotels it is perfectly possible to consume alcohol during this month and all other Islamic holidays. Remarkably, during the official mourning period following the ruler of Abu Dhabi's death in November 2004, Dubai chose not to adhere to the UAE-wide prohibition of live music and alcohol lest its tourist industry be affected. Similarly shocking to the local population has been the explosion in prostitution. Now firmly established as an international centre for sex tourism, the authorities allow thousands of street hookers, escorts, hotel hostesses and all manner of sex workers from China, Russia and the former Soviet republics to flood into the emirate and reside there, unchecked, on perpetual tourist visas. Also worthy of note is the tolerance of homosexuality (which is officially illegal in the UAE and often leads to imprisonment and corporal punishment in Abu Dhabi, Sharjah and the other emirates), including public displays of homosexuality and the widely acknowledged existence of Dubai-based gay bars and nightclubs. Perhaps most controversial of all has been Dubai's increasing communication with Israel. With its rising profile in the international banking system, Dubai chose to host the 2003 annual meetings of the World Bank and the IMF[90] and given that Israel is also a member of these organizations, a delegation had to be invited. When one considers that for more than 30 years all of the GCC states have upheld a total boycott of all Israeli relations and trade,[91] and that one of the UAE's primary foreign policy objectives (and ideological legitimacy resources) is its support for Palestine against its illegal occupation,[92] one can begin to imagine how dangerous Dubai's package of reforms has become.

NOTES

1 Personal interviews, Dubai, January 2006.
2 Abu Dhabi Planning Department Economic Division, Directive Documents for the Preparation of the Economic and Social Development Plan, 1977–1979 (Abu Dhabi: June 1976), pp. 21–22.
3 GCC Development Plans, United Arab Emirates (Abu Dhabi: 1982), p. 46.
4 Economist Intelligence Unit, United Arab Emirates (London: 2000), p. 28.
5 Abu Dhabi Planning Department Economic Division, pp. 21–22.
6 Personal interviews, Dubai, April 2001; personal interviews, Al-'Ayn, April 2001.
7 Kevin Fenelon, *The United Arab Emirates: An Economic and Social Survey* (London: Longman, 1973), pp. 46–50.
8 Dubai Department of Economic Development, Development Statistics (Dubai: 2001), p. 75.
9 Ibid., p. 78.
10 Ibid., p. 80.
11 Christopher M. Davidson, *The United Arab Emirates: A Study in Survival* (Boulder: Lynne Rienner, 2005), pp. 5–6.
12 Dubai Department of Economic Development, p. 83.
13 Economist Intelligence Unit, p. 33.
14 A prime example being Portland Cement (with nine factories across the UAE and a tenth under construction in Ra's al-Khaimah), see Oxford Business Group, *Emerging Emirates* (London, 2000), pp. 90–91.
15 Dubai Department of Economic Development, p. 110, imports valued at fixed 1995 prices.
16 A good example would be 'London Dairy'. As an ice cream manufacturer and packager, the firm originally licenced British technology, but in recent years has substituted domestic technology.
17 Dubai Department of Economic Development, p. 109.
18 Ibid., p. 109, values for non-oil foreign trade given at fixed 1995 prices.
19 169% increase in volume calculated from 1980 to 2001, as 1975 remains unavailable. Ibid., p. 109.
20 Ibid., p. 109; imports currently account for around 75% of the total value of non-oil trade.

21 Ibid., p. 109.
22 Personal interviews, Dubai, May 2006.
23 Dubai Department of Economic Development, p. 167; p. 172.
24 Davidson, *The United Arab Emirates*, p. 167.
25 Ibid., p. 134.
26 Dubai Department of Economic Development, p. 167.
27 Ibid., p. 171.
28 Personal interviews, Dubai, May 2006.
29 Personal interviews with Frauke Heard-Bey, Abu Dhabi, January 2004.
30 Dubai Department of Economic Development, p. 241.
31 Federation of UAE Chambers of Commerce, *The Components of Investment and the Methods of Promoting Investment Opportunities in the UAE* (Abu Dhabi: 1994), pp. 36–37.
32 Dubai Department of Economic Development, p. 255.
33 *Khaleej Times*, 13 May 1998, 'Dubai investments to lift returns assets'.
34 *Khaleej Times*, 25 October 1998, 'Dubai investment park excites Dubai investors'.
35 Dubai Government, "Dubai Technology, Electronic Commerce and Media Free Zone Law No.1", issued by Sheikh Maktum Al-Maktum in 2000.
36 Economic Intelligence Unit, p. 23.
37 Al-Sharhan International Consultancy, *UAE Country Report* (Dubai: 2001), pp. 25–30.
38 Extracted from the Dubai Internet City's official brochure.
39 Al-Tamimi Consultancy, *The Development of the Dubai Internet City* (Dubai: 2001).
40 Fenelon, *The United Arab Emirates*, pp. 80–83.
41 *Middle East Economic Digest*, 8 March 2002, 'Bridging the Gap'.
42 Ibid., quoting Jamal Sanad Al-Suwaidi of the Emirates Centre for Strategic Studies and Research (ECSSR).
43 Ibid.
44 Personal interviews, Dubai, May 2006.
45 *Gulf News*, 25 November 1997, 'Emaar to set up Dh700 million complex'.
46 *Gulf News*, 26 February 1998, 'Emaar ups project outlay'.
47 *Gulf News*, 25 November 1997, 'Emaar to set up Dh700 million complex'.
48 *Gulf News*, 19 August 1998, 'Emaar flies high with mega project'.
49 *The Times*, 5 January 2002, 'Biggest man-made isles rise from the Gulf'.
50 Personal interviews, Abu Dhabi, March 2002.
51 Ibid.
52 Davidson, *The United Arab Emirates*, pp. 13–14.
53 *Dawn Magazine*, 28 October 2000, 'Arabs: a shrinking minority in the UAE', calculations based upon quoted figures.
54 Dubai Municipality Statistics Centre, Results of income and expenditure survey – Dubai city, 1997–1998 (Dubai: 1999), p. 133, with regards to Dubai the survey indicated that 17% of households were local, 8.9% were non-local Arabs, 3.2% were European, 41.9% were Asian, and the remaining 29% of the population were collective labourers (based in labour camps).
55 *Dawn Magazine*.
56 Ibid.
57 For a further discussion of the demographic problem see (in Arabic) Muhammad

Bilal, *Changes in Population and Power among Immigrants and Citizens of the UAE, 1976–1980* (Sharjah: Sharjah Sociologist Society, 1990).

58 Abu Dhabi Planning Department Economic Division, pp. 14–16.

59 GCC Development Plans, United Arab Emirates, p. 17.

60 Al-Sharhan International Consultancy, p. 54.

61 Malcolm Peck, *The United Arab Emirates: A Venture in Unity* (Boulder: Westview Press, 1986), p. 68.

62 Personal interviews, Dubai, May 2006.

63 Peck, *The United Arab Emirates*, p. 72.

64 *Gulf News*, 11 January 2003, 'Majority of expats suffer from some sort of depression', reporting the findings of Dr Ali Harjan, a leading Sharjah-based psychologist.

65 Frauke Heard-Bey, *From Trucial States to United Arab Emirates* (London: Longman, 1982), p. 252.

66 Donald Hawley, *The Trucial States* (London: George Allen & Unwin, 1970), p. 212, for details on article 14 of 1937 agreement with PDTC.

67 Ibid., p. 212.

68 Abu Dhabi Planning Department Economic Division, p. 14.

69 Davidson, *The United Arab Emirates*, pp. 139–144.

70 *Khaleej Times*, 26 July 2000, 'University Students take Al-Futtaim Trading Courses', quoting Jassim Al-Banay, Al-Futtaim's 'Emiratization Manager'.

71 *WAM*, 17 May 2001, 'New avenues for UAE women'.

72 *Gulf News*, 3 September 2000, 'Mashriq Bank joins hand with NHR to promote Emiratization'.

73 Chamber of Commerce and Industry, *Business in Dubai*, Volume 1, Issue 6, June 2001, p. 26.

74 Gulf News, 14 December 2002, 'New contract rule to benefit nationals', as explained by Dr Khazraji, undersecretary of the Ministry of Labour and Social Affairs.

75 Al Sharhan International Consultancy, pp. 12–13.

76 *Gulf News*, 3 September 2000, 'Mashriq Bank joins hand with NHR to promote Emiratization'.

77 *Khaleej Times*, 26 July 2000, 'Only Nationals to be Captains of Fishing Vessels', quoting A. Abdulrazzaq, the Director of Fisheries in the Ministry of Agriculture and Fisheries and head of the Fishing Regulations Committee, speaking to *Khaleej Times* about the Ministry's plans.

78 Al Sharhan International Consultancy, pp. 12–13.

79 Ibid., pp. 12–13.

80 Economist Intelligence Unit, p. 5, also, with regard to the 2002 amnesty see Business Monitor International, *The United Arab Emirates*, second quarter report (London: 2002), p. 8.

81 Personal correspondence, June 2003.

82 Personal interviews, Dubai, May 2006.

83 Economist Intelligence Unit, p. 14.

84 Personal interviews, Dubai, April 2002.

85 Dubai Chamber of Commerce and Industry, *Business in Dubai*, Volume 2, Issue 15, March 2002, p. 2, quoting from Humaid Al-Qutami, general manager of EIBFS.

86 See Jill Crystal, *Oil and Politics in the Gulf: Rulers and Merchants in Kuwait and Qatar* (New York: Cambridge University Press, 1995); Davidson, *The United Arab Emirates*; and Michael Herb, *All in the Family: Absolutism, Revolution, and Democracy in the Middle Eastern Monarchies* (New York: State University of New York Press, 1999).

87 For a full discussion see Davidson, *The United Arab Emirates*, pp. 65–118.

88 For a discussion of 'new rentiers' see ibid., p. 225.

89 Ibid., pp. 73–77.

90 Ibid., p. 252.

91 Ibid., pp. 81–82.

92 Ibid., p. 81.

9

ICT and the Gulf Arab States: A Force for Democracy?[1]

Emma Murphy

To the surprise of many, the last few years have witnessed significant political reforms in the Arabian Peninsula. The regimes of Qatar, Bahrain, Kuwait, Oman and even Saudi Arabia have been introducing constitutional reforms and new electoral practices which appear to have substantively altered the dynamics of political space in countries previously thought to be perhaps uniquely impervious to pressures for democratic change.

In their seminal 1980s work on the nature of rentier states, Beblawi and Luciani had asserted that the distributive functions of states which accrued such vast sums of externally derived rent protected them from domestic demands for popular representation.[2] Citizenship was characterized by access to distributed rent and a consequent political passivity. Rent was used constantly to reinforce those traditional modes of social organization which bolstered the legitimacy and capacity of ruling dynasties. As such, and contrary to the claims of modernization theorists like Walt Rostow, they could achieve a variant of economic development (albeit based on consumption rather than production), without progressing to a liberal democratic political structure.

This perspective was shaken by the fiscal crisis of the late 1980s which resulted from falling oil prices. As revenues declined, Gulf Arab regimes were forced to focus their energies on economic diversification and liberalization. If economies reduced their dependence on rent-derived income, if they encouraged a truly independent and dynamic private sector to flourish, and (most importantly) if governments began to tax their populations, the political equation would surely be reconstructed. It was supposed that economic reform would broaden demands for an input into policy making and require a more rational bureaucracy of a Weberian ilk in place of autocratic, personalized and monarchical systems of government.

However, the Gulf Arab regimes proved extraordinarily resilient: economic reform was inconsistently implemented and painfully slow. Surrendering the power of patronage proved unattractive to regimes and, with China progressively adding to revived global demand for oil, economic liberalization largely stalled before it could generate a corresponding political impact. Like the rest of the Arab world, the Gulf Arab states were written off as somehow having evaded the so-called 'third wave' of democratization, and a discourse of exceptionalism evolved invoking historical, structural, cultural, even religious explanation.[3] But while academics have been writing epitaphs for the short-lived hopes for regional democratization, these five Gulf states have quietly revived the process of political liberalization. Starting in 1992 with the introduction of Basic Laws in Saudi Arabia, but dynamized by the accession to power of a reforming Emir in Qatar in 1995, the region has seen the introduction of new processes (municipal and national parliamentary elections and referenda), new institutions (municipal and consultative councils, national legislative assemblies, constitutional monarchies), new or reformed constitutions embodying civil and political rights, the introduction of women's suffrage, a greater freedom for the media, and a new discourse of democracy and reform led by national elites. The reforms are by no means consistent across the region, and even where they seem to have made most progress, they are accompanied by repressive measures which test their credibility. One cannot claim, therefore, that democracy has actually taken root. The reforms may mark major progress in political development, as some have suggested,[4] but others are more sanguine. Jill Crystal, for example, has argued that the Gulf rulers remain engaged essentially in an exercise of regime survival based on opening political space sufficiently to either co-opt opposition or better target repression.[5] Daniel Brumberg has suggested that this equates to a liberalizing of, rather than transition away from, autocracy.[6] Whether the reforms place the regimes on a trajectory towards democracy is thus still a moot point, as is the nature of the engine behind their new dynamism. Certainly many of the reforms predate the current American efforts at regional democracy promotion. While external political pressure may have fuelled the fires of reform, it did not provide the early spark!

This chapter does not seek to examine the full range of explanations for the current wave of political reforms in the Gulf Arab states. Rather it seeks to test whether some contribution towards that momentum might have been made by a particular feature of the economies of the states in question: their relatively recent, but rapidly increasing, penetration by state-of-the-art information and communication technologies (ICTs). In doing so, I am returning in essence to the debate as to whether economic development necessitates political change in the direction of democracy, if not democratization itself. The last 20 years have witnessed a revolution in ICT technology which is transforming the global economy, and the place of national economies within it. National development strategies around the world increasingly assume ICTs to be the new engine for growth, but – as has been argued extensively elsewhere, ICTs are not politically neutral. They impact upon political, social and cultural environments, empowering some actors, possibly at the expense of others. This impact may contain its own contradictions, and it may engender both political opening and *fermature* simultaneously. I will argue that in the case of the Gulf Arab states, the overall trajectory of consequent political change has been in the direction of political liberalization. However, claims that the global ICT revolution would lead to a rapid and uncontrollable diminution of the power of the state over its citizens have proved, in the Gulf Arab countries at least, to be wildly off the mark. The particular configuration of the agents which have brought ICTs to the region, determined their role in national development strategies, shaped the selection and diffusion of specific technologies, and utilized choice in consumption of the product, has restricted their political and social impact. While we are able to identify political spaces which have been created, expanded or liberalized as a consequence of the dissemination of ICTs, it is equally possible to establish how these spaces have been delimited by the role of agents in the process.

ICTs and Development

There is nothing new in the notion that ICTs play a fundamental role in both the economic *and* political development of countries. The newly independent states of the post-Second World War era identified ICTs as a means for propagating new political cultures based on national and civic (as opposed to localized, traditional and tribal) identities. The development of, and more importantly control over, ICTs became a pillar of development planning, usually being managed through state-owned monopolies overseeing telecommunications and the mass media. The media played a particular role, inculcating new citizens with notions of civic responsibility, impressing upon them the urgent need for modernization and industrialization regardless of the disruption to traditional forms of social and economic organization. Modernization itself, along with accompanying urbanization, transferred a greater part of the socialization process to the mass media and away from informal agents like the extended family. Thomas McPhail has argued that information is the basis of culture[7] and, with regimes presiding over both access to, and the content of, the information available to citizens, political cultures were arguably more restrictive when the information that would generate or facilitate contestation was limited.

The mass media was also used as a weapon in the post-colonial struggle against perceived cultural imperialism. Transnational media companies, primarily located in the West, promoted consumer cultures which asserted the primacy of the Western product as well as the Western 'way of life'. They were viewed as agents of a double agenda, economic exploitation and cultural annihilation. The Western-dominated international media portrayed the developing world as culturally backwards, politically sterile and prone to natural disasters. This imbalance could only be redressed by excluding external media actors and using a state-managed or owned media to project images of local development and progress, as well as vibrant cultural diversity. Advocates of the New World Information Order proclaimed that Western advocacy of freedom of the press was simply a ruse for continued 'media-based colonialism' while government control was as vital for protection of national cultures as it was for promotion of national political identities.

By the 1980s it was becoming clear that ICTs were developing faster than the ability of governments to control them. As the units of technology became smaller, cheaper and more transportable, so the transmission of information became infinitely faster and harder to restrict. Mobile phones, fax machines, portable satellite dishes, all became the tools of political opposition movements. They spawned a whole new set of transnational identities, causes and aspirations which translated into new political demands on governments. The impulse of non-liberal regimes was to restrict rather than proliferate access to such innovation.

At the same time, however, new forms of production were as much about information as material goods. The *information society* represented the new highest stage of development, higher even than Rostow's age of mass consumer consumption. For American economists like Paul Romer, information had replaced land, labour and capital as the primary source of value![8] Crucially, writers like Edward Ayensu were arguing as early as the 1980s that ICTs could assist developing economies in 'leapfrogging' over the industrial stages of development, allowing them to catch up with more developed economies and to compete on a more level playing field.[9] ICTs did not always require massive new capital investments; knowledge-based patterns of production can be small-scale; they can utilize small, cheap units of technology and can be oriented towards individualized product spread (as opposed to old-style Fordist and post-Fordist production patterns). Low-cost technologies in particular can radically alter the economic prospects and quality of life of poorer populations. Mobile phones are more cost effective than landlines for rural areas; digital technology may be more appropriate for dusty or humid climates than electromechanical equipment.[10] The downside was identified as domination by primarily (but not exclusively) Western industrialized countries in the development, and sale of, the new technologies. Writers like David Lyon[11] and Gerald Sussman[12] pointed to the role of the multinational corporations, largely based in the Silicon Valleys of America, Europe and the Far East – the 'Brahims of the Global Village'. Their ownership of the patents, licences and delivery technologies (such as satellites) has allowed them to dominate the technology markets and perpetuate the gap between more and less advanced economies.[13] But whether one produces or consumes the technology, a consensus emerged that development required engagement with the new ICTs. Rejection or isolation from them resulted in relegation in terms of global economic positioning. Regimes were thus compelled to incorporate the integration of new ICTs into their development strategies.

The precise link between ICTs and development remains opaque. The 12th United Nations Human Development Report made it clear that there is no simple blueprint for how and what a developing country should embrace, how it can anticipate the associated costs or what risk management strategies work best. Moreover, there remain concerns over the priority given by new research to the needs and interests of developed countries and by the uneven spread of ICT penetration which sees "the majority of the world's population yet to benefit from the new technology".[14] Nonetheless, making the benefits of the new technologies universally available was included as one of the stated targets in the United Nations' Millennium Development Goals.

A Necessary Democratizing Impact?

It is not only in the realm of economic development that the full impact of contemporary ICTs is as yet unknown. A number of suggestions have been posited as to how they may contribute to social, cultural and most particularly political change.[15] These cannot be treated as isolated arenas but may be seen rather as *superstructure* to the developmental *base*. In the following discussion, I shall use the term 'democratizing' broadly to include all political changes which enhance the power of citizens relative to the state, which improve equality among citizens – both before the law and in terms of their contribution to decision making – and which challenge the relative autonomy of the state from other social actors. This is admittedly not a wholly satisfactory use of the term, but suffices in the absence of anything which more closely approximates the intended meaning.

ICTs undoubtedly present an unprecedented challenge to the state. For a start, as governments use the internet to 'talk' to their citizens, providing information and services more efficiently, so too they are required to be more consistent, reliable and transparent in what they are actually saying. More information about what governments are doing (transparency) implies greater accountability, while governments find it increasingly difficult to control access to broader, and potentially challenging, realms of information when individuals have access to the technology itself. Both the internet and satellite television, for example, allow ideas and information to flood into a country, relatively unhindered by the sovereign body!

Writers like Manuel Castells[16] have argued that over time this will progressively lead to a more horizontally networked society in place of current top-down forms of organization. The power of the state is eroded while the individual citizen's capacity to engage directly with an un-bordered society is infinitely increased. Political mobilization is no longer confined to public space and thus cannot be physically constrained by the agents of the state. Indeed, space itself develops new dimensions beyond the public and private, what may be termed a *virtual* space, in which state and citizens engage and contest. Of course, for this to be true, universal access to the web is vital – anything less reinforces hierarchies of knowledge which translate into hierarchies of power![17] Furthermore, the *nature* of the virtual activity is crucial. For example, the *Democracy in Cyberspace Initiative*[18] has found that the majority of US and EU government-funded on-line activities have been directed towards G2C (government to consumer) uses of technology, which deliver passive information from state to citizen and which do little to challenge the relationship itself. Indeed, they may simply be reinforcing the state's role and power as primary provider of information!

A second arena for impact lies in the nature of this virtual political activity itself. Web-based ICTs enable individuals to relocate their participation out of the conventional public space and into this new space in which they may operate as private individuals but can engage with political society. They are empowered by their ability to connect with like-minded individuals elsewhere, to tap into transnational resources and to engage in political dialogue beyond the control of the state. Direct censorship of the internet is difficult, although not impossible, and individuals become more free to express opinions or identities which were previously politically or socially taboo. They become better informed, more able to articulate demands and interests, and gain a 'voice' where previously they were mute. Crucially, these ICTs do not just facilitate free flow of knowledge or information – they facilitate interactive behaviour. The act of engaging with the technology has significance beyond the function itself. It is a deliberate commitment by the individual to the global community, an act of self-identification with a world beyond local or national, physical or social borders. Yet simultaneously the relocation of specifically political activity to the *virtual* space may weaken local direct action and civil society groups. It focuses attention on single issues and arguably reduces mobilization in the public space.

The act of engaging with web-based ICTs has its own potential pitfalls. The process of communicating is altered by virtue of the fact that it utilizes a mechanical medium instead of taking place at the level of person-to-person exchanges. As such it is a potentially isolating and dehumanizing phenomenon. The EU's *FAST* programme identified this as a problem of *alienation*, suggesting that:

Alienation denotes a feeling of separation from society. It is a sense of being left behind by developments which, in effect, take on overtones of domination of the individual by the system.[19]

Moreover, although censorship becomes more complex, it equally becomes less tangible for the individual. Citizens may find the invisibility of modern ICT censorship more frightening simply because it is harder to see how, and where, it is being done (and by whom)!

The cross-border aspect of the range of ICTs has its own impact in so far as governments are forced to relinquish their monopoly hold over information and media networks. Integration into global networks requires compliance with international, rather than national, regulation. It requires engagement with an international network of technology developers and suppliers, and frequently with foreign investors who serve as conduits for the technology. Meanwhile compliance with the membership conditions of organizations like the WTO means introducing competition into national markets. In sum, ICT penetration necessarily brings economic liberalization, empowering national and transnational non-state actors through their control over information provision and ICT access. As agents of a national developmental mission, they become political actors by default. States meanwhile become subject to international scrutiny, even as their monopoly over the information delivered to their citizens slips away.

While populations may welcome this degraded state role, they may be less inclined to accept all the information that now comes their way! Information carries biases and Western cultural domination of ICTs is clearly evident and not always welcome. For a start, the language of cyber space is predominantly an Americanized version of English which has been compressed to exclude the complexities of political discourse and localized expression. In 2000, 69% of websites were composed in English, while 43% of web users were non-English speaking. After English, the most widely used languages were Japanese (5.85%), German (5.77%) and Chinese (3.87%). Twenty-four of the top thirty languages used were European and, interestingly for the purposes of this chapter, there were more websites in Icelandic than in Arabic![20] Search engines favour English language websites, mostly because they are designed, constructed and managed from the West.[21] One only has to use an academic reference database to realize how priority is given to American and

European academic publications over those that originate in the developing world. Western scholarship is given greater credibility by virtue of its inclusion, while non-Western scholarship is excluded on linguistic rather than qualitative grounds.[22]

The ownership and management (or 'gate-keeping') of ICTs by the developed world is also reflected in the content of the data, images and discussions which reach developing world consumers. These frequently conform to a liberal and permissive cultural mindset which rejects exclusionary practices. Consequently, contemporary ICTs have come to be seen by some as the new medium for Western cultural imperialism and domination, a means of eroding alternative cultural contexts through an unstoppable onslaught of alien words and pictures. Moreover, the commercial mega-giants of the telecoms world (IBM, Time Warner, Nokia, France Telecom, Bertelsmann and the like) now advise governments and INGOs on ICT policy, reserving the domain for themselves and crowding out smaller 'counter-hegemonic' groups which might be able to utilize ICTs for the purpose of challenging the national or international political status quo. The commercialization of ICTs further limits their potentially democratizing impact by making access dependent on ability to pay! This is as true of satellite television as it is of the internet.

When access to new ICTs is not universal, there are a range of potentially fragmenting social impacts. Access to the new ICTs in developing countries often remains limited to urban elites, consolidating status differentials and marginalizing still further the voices of the poor. When the telecommunications infrastructure which supports technologies remains confined to cities and large towns, access cannot be equitable or universal. This is true as much of regions of the world as it is of individual countries. Jason Abbott's study of the internet in Malaysia and China has argued for example that the internet-savvy population in Asia, as in America, is clearly defined by wealth, gender and race.[23]

Meanwhile development strategies which introduce ICT skills to a population via schools and universities empower the young in a way denied to many of the older generation. Economic initiative is relocated into their hands: they become more tuned in to the global economy, and less willing to accept state-imposed restrictions on their abilities to profit from that engagement than their parents. Like older ICTs, new technologies also impact on social and cultural structures. Youths can short-circuit traditional systems of socialization – they can download films, music, advertising, even shopping, evading parental or other social control. Consequent generational rifts in the cultural framework of what may be termed more traditional or authentic societies see ICTs challenging patrimonial social organization, and systems where status is related to age/generation rather than activity. Correspondingly, traditional elites and those with a stake in conventional socialization practices, frequently oppose the introduction of new ICTs on the basis that they represent a corrupting and culturally offensive influence. These groups may form a coalition with regime elites in terms of developing a restrictive rather than liberal response to technological advances.

There is one area which, more than any other, tests the democratizing credentials of new ICTs: military, security and intelligence forces have proved adept at integrating the new technologies into their own operations. Contemporary ICTs provide massively expanded capacities for data collection, storage and transfer which may as easily be used for oppressive purposes as for combating crime or terrorism. Indeed, the two functions fluidly coalesce when communications between agencies, nationally and internationally, are faster and more integrated. The ICT-embedded security agency will "give rise to fear on the part of others who conceive of its authoritarian power to control legal dissident behaviour".[24] Concern is compounded by the fact that the instrument itself is not necessarily reliable or authoritative: computer records can be interfered with, networks can be hacked into or corrupted. The more reliant society becomes on anonymous and distant ICTs for its policing, the less the police forces themselves are seen as a recognizable and indigenous part of society. Of course, ICTs also work to the advantage of political opposition groups. They allow virtually instant mass communication, with possibilities for anonymity, speedy access and unlimited distribution. The electronic maze of the financial world allows funds to be ghosted across borders, virtually traceless and beyond the clutches of those who would deprive opposition (or terrorist) groups of their economic assets. The race is on for both political authorities and those who challenge them to acquire ever faster and better ICTs and to penetrate or subvert those used by the other side.[25]

One aspect of the age of 'big brother' technologies is the institutionalization of concepts of, and rights to, privacy. The development of mass data storage, and the ease with which that data can be transferred, has led to a range of new actors having an ever wider knowledge about what we do, how we live, and who we are. This can potentially be abused by political and commercial agents – banks, credit providers, tax offices, employers, investigative bureaus . . . The individual no longer has the ability to control who knows what about him or herself. In many states this has led to new legislation to protect the individual, with the rights of the individual relative to the state and other institutions being progressively redefined. In this world, privacy assumes new significance for societies which may have previously considered the boundary between public and private to be porous and flexible. Equally, the introduction and implementation of property law and copyright protection, as it relates to knowledge and intellectual resources, acquires a new urgency in states where the rule of law has historically been either weakly upheld or entirely absent.

What are we to make then of libertarian suggestions that contemporary ICTs will usher in an era of unfiltered, universally accessible information which will equalize and empower individuals? I have argued here that they may indeed have impacts which serve to spread political power beyond the realms of government, or which challenge the power of non-democratic states over their citizenry. This is through their expansion of existing *public* space (through the multiplication of modes of broadcast communication) and through the creation of new *virtual* space (through web-based applications). In both instances, the technology allows the space to be un-bordered, limited neither by physical geography nor by identities which have evolved within that geography on the basis of culture, tradition or national construction. State–citizen relations are consequently being acted out on both an infinitely enlarged playing field and on a new adjacent pitch. The capacity of the state to extend its authority and power across this new arena is sorely tested!

Yet I have also suggested that any democratizing impact of the new ICTs must be limited by a combination of the following: the capacity of the state to utilize those same ICTs in its own defence; the current non-universality of access to, let alone ability to make use of, ICTs; the commercialization of ICTs on the one hand, and the economic capacity of national economic actors (both public and private) seeking to embed them in their own development strategies on the other; and ultimately, social and cultural resistance to the perceived content of newly available information. This leads to two further arguments.

Firstly, it points to the role played by agency. Jon W. Anderson, in his own study of internet technology in the Middle East,[26] has correctly pointed out that impact is determined by agency. Specifically the technology producers (which includes financiers, sponsors, regulators and administrators), play as great – if not greater – a role than end-users. He argues that technologies have a life which involves choices being made *before* they are consumed. Thus he demands analyses which examine the structures and processes whereby ICTs are introduced and utilized since these shape the subsequent product which is offered and the responses of consumers. While consumption itself may be passive, production is not; thus we must take account of who decides on what technology to embed, on how it is implemented, regulated, managed and delivered. Our analysis must, therefore, pay attention to the role played by the state, the public sector telecommunications companies, local private sectors, the transnational telecommunications corporations, international organizations like the United Nations, local mediators of cultural norms (such as Islamic and educational institutions), civil society organizations, regulatory bodies (both national and international) and populations themselves.

This takes us one step further, to Henri Lefebvre's argument that social space is not to be thought of simply as a medium or milieu. It is not only where activity happens or where relationships are enacted, and cannot be defined solely by its function.

> . . . its role is less and less neutral, more and more active, both as instrument and goal, as means and as end.[27]

Lefebvre's focus on the production of space finds resonance in Anderson's insistence that it is the production of ICTs rather than their consumption which is the key to understanding impact.

Specifically the Arab World

Before moving on to examine the particular experiences of the Gulf Arab states, and the role played by agency in determining the expansion or constriction of political space as a consequence of ICT dissemination, a word must be said concerning some specificities of the region in which they are located.

The 2003 Arab Human Development Report, compiled by Arab specialists for the UNDP and the Arab Fund for Economic and Social Development, identified a string of political and cultural 'blocks' that obstruct the building of a knowledge-based society in the Arab world, and which consequently impede the momentum of ICT penetration of the region. According to the report, Arabs are socialized away from knowledge generation through authoritarian and over-protective child rearing, a deteriorating quality of formal education which continues to encourage learning by rote and submission to established discourse, historically low levels of investment in research and development, intellectual capital flight to the West, the absence of a democratic value system, censorship and the persistence of corruption. Additionally, the political exploitation of religion has made original thinking a sin as well as a crime! In sum, the report's authors claim that the region has made a 'retreat' from knowledge and is consequently ill-prepared for the challenges posed by the unrestrained flow of information which will result from ICTs.

This is a painful indictment of both the regimes and the political cultures of the region and should be qualified by a recognition that the Arab world includes a diverse set of political systems and a mosaic of ethnic, linguistic, national and religious groupings which each exhibit their own cultural uniqueness. This is true as much between the Gulf Arab states as it is between them and the broader Middle East: there are variants in the domestic political cultures, structures and public policies of the Gulf Arab states which require attention if one is not to generalize to excess. Islam per se does not represent a barrier to full engagement with ICTs. The experiences of countries like Malaysia indicate that Muslim countries can be fully receptive to the developmental potential of ICTs and need not find them sufficient a threat to Islamic principles or identity as to establish barriers to their introduction or widespread use.[28] Equally, Islamist movements and individuals within the Arab world have been quick to adopt the new ICTs as a means for communicating with populations and with each other while evading the controlling impulses of the state. That is not to say that ICTs do not provide particular new challenges to Islam and Islamic identities: Peter Mandaville has outlined the possibilities for a virtual umma, as well as the tensions which arise from new channels of communication which bypass traditional sources of authority or even present alternatives.[29]

One might suggest that, in expanding or creating social spaces, ICTs present yet another forum within which the forces of tradition and modernity battle for the soul(s) of Islam, but it would be incorrect to generalize an outcome that reduces Islam to a monolithic and inflexible normative edifice which impedes the creation of a knowledge-based society.

The Arab cultural context may be of greater significance. Mamoun Fandy has suggested that their historical experiences have led Arabs to place far greater trust in information which is transmitted informally, through oral or unofficial mediums, than in that which is transmitted in formal, written or public contexts.[30] Just because new sources of information are available, it does not follow that Arab populations will necessarily afford them credibility or engage with them. He further argues that virtual communications will not create a single 'imagined' Arab community. There are linguistic and epistemological complexities which surround the relationship between communication and trust and which afford ICTs more credibility for some segments of the Arab population then for others.

This may in part account for the sluggish pace with which the Arab world in general has internalized the ICT revolution. In 2003, the management consultancy firm, Booz Allen Hamilton, conducted a survey which showed that ICT spend in the Middle East was lower than in any other region of the world, accounting for a mere 0.5% of GDP in 2001 compared with around 11% in the USA and Canada and 7% in Europe.[31] Industry analysts have argued that the MENA region lags up to ten years behind Europe and North America in its acquisition of and access to ICTs.[32] The wealthy Gulf Arab states are less daunted but are still apparently 'information shy' and are two to three years behind their Western counterparts. Table 1 illustrates this through a comparative regional survey of internet usage while Table 2 uses selected access indicators to demonstrate the advanced status of the Gulf Arab countries compared to the rest of the Arab World.

ICT Diffusion in the Gulf Arab Countries

Anyone travelling to Dubai Internet City, or watching one of the numerous available satellite television channels in the Gulf today might be surprised to learn that the Gulf Arab states were slow to buy in to the

TABLE 1
Internet Usage by Region

Region	Usage (Millions)	Usage (% of Regional Population)	Usage (% of World Population)
North America	223.8	68.8	28.2
Oceania	15.9	49.1	2.0
Europe	222.2	30.4	28.0
Latin America/ Caribbean	51.2	9.4	6.4
Asia/Pacific	252.6	7.0	31.8
Middle East	16.8	6.5	2.1
Africa	12.2	1.4	1.5
World Total	**794.8**	**12.4**	**100.0**

Source: Adapted from Table 6.6 Access Indicators by Region, *UN Global E-government Readiness Report 2004,* p. 98.

new technologies. With their considerable financial resources, delivered by the technically demanding hydrocarbons industry, they were well placed to buy in to the new ICTs and their modernized urban settings suggest that they have done just that. On closer inspection, however, and despite a recent acceleration in ICT diffusion, they cannot yet claim to have fully translated the potential of ICTs into reality. All the Gulf Arab states have incorporated ICTs into their strategic visions for their economic future to some degree, Bahrain going so far as to state its ambition to become a regional ICT hub, although Saudi Arabia has remained notably cautious. Ironically then, Saudi Arabia today represents the largest ICT market in the region, worth a still modest US$533 million in 2004. This is set to double by 2010[33] but will not make Saudi Arabia, or the Gulf Arab states as a group, a major market player. For them, ICT activity remains only a small proportion of both public and private expenditure, facilitating just 5% of business-to-business transactions in 2002.[34]

The delayed status of ICT diffusion in the Gulf Arab states is central to this story. It can be traced to the twin problems of political and infrastructural constraints which manifested themselves through agency. The recent acceleration of diffusion can be similarly accounted

TABLE 2
ICT Diffusion in the Arab World and Comparator
Countries – Selected Access Indicators, 2003

Country	PCs per 1000 persons	Internet Users per 1000 persons	TV sets per 1000 persons
Algeria	7.7	16.0	114.0
Bahrain	**160.4**	**247.5**	**446.0**
Egypt	16.6	28.2	217.0
Iraq	8.0	0.0	83.0
Jordan	37.5	57.7	111.0
Kuwait	**120.6**	**105.8**	**482.0**
Lebanon	80.5	117.1	336.0
Libya	23.4	22.5	137.0
Morocco	23.6	23.6	159.0
Oman	**37.4**	**70.9**	**563.0**
Qatar	**178.2**	**113.4**	**866.0**
Tunisia	30.7	51.7	198.0
Saudi Arabia	**136.7**	**64.6**	**264.0**
Sudan	6.1	2.6	386.0
Syria	19.4	12.9	67.0
UAE	**119.9**	**313.2**	**252.0**
Yemen	7.4	5.1	283.0
United States	658.9	551.4	835.0
United Kingdom	405.7	423.1	950.0
Japan	382.2	448.9	731.0

Source: *United Nations E-Government Readiness Report 2004.*

for. The pace and manner of ICT production and diffusion in the region is determined by the decisions and actions of a number of key agents, and the relationships which exist between them. These processes have shaped the impact of that diffusion, generating or restraining their democratizing effects.

Political Constraints: The State Versus Society?

Inevitably, the state is perhaps the single most important agent in ICT production and diffusion. The developmental mission suggests that the state may decide which technologies are permissible and to be encouraged. The state may even determine how they should be facilili-tated. This role may be direct (through budgetary expenditure and development planning) or indirect (through regulation and legislation). The state can also restrict or prohibit technologies which it perceives to be politically, culturally or socially threatening. Historically, the auto-cratic quasi-monarchies of the Gulf have taken a restrictive position, allotting to themselves or their state-owned monopoly-status telecoms and media corporations the task of controlling information and communication. The new ICTs have presented an unprecedented challenge to this arrangement.

Perhaps the clearest example has been from satellite television channels. Until 1991, television coverage in the Gulf Arab states was largely provided by state-owned national networks which offered a diet of heavily censored local news, limited foreign coverage (usually revolv-ing around overseas visits of heads of state), Arab soap operas, religious programming and limited, culturally conservative entertainment. An Arab satellite system (Arabsat) did exist by the mid-1980s, but was not used as a direct broadcast media. Satellite television-viewing was limited to a few, wealthy individuals with dishes which could receive signals from a rather dodgy Soviet satellite. This changed with the 1990 Iraqi invasion of Kuwait, when regional allies of the US-led coalition realized that their own populations were vulnerable to propaganda beamed at them by Iraqi television. To counter this, Saudi Arabia began installing hardware close to the borders which allowed the American news channel CNN (considered to be more professional and attractive to viewers) to be downloaded and rebroadcast (after some editing) via terrestrial means. At the same time the Egyptian company, ESN, took a position in a European satellite which allowed it to broadcast across the region. Its programme content included news coverage purchased from other international stations and it was soon proving a hit across the Gulf region. As it became clear that Gulf Arab viewers preferred the modern, uncensored news of international satellite stations, a group of influential Saudis close to the King established their own station, MBC, based in London. Its programming was transmitted via satellite to Bahrain, and rebroadcast terrestrially from there. Its audiences grew rapidly but were soon poached by the Qatar-based Al Jazeera in 1996[35], which proved to be more critical, professional and lively than its Saudi-backed com-petitor. Al Jazeera's challenge to the state-owned media companies of the region soon became news in itself, stimulating a wave of new Arab satellite stations which raised the general quality of programming and journalism generally.

Much has since been made of the impact of Al Jazeera and its peers. Edmund Ghareeb has suggested that they are helping form a new Arab public opinion, from the bottom-up instead of from the top-down. They are not confined to local audiences but reach out to broader Arab and international constituencies, changing the way Arabs think about themselves and their governments,[36] a point echoed by Najib Ghadbian:

> Not only is government media rendered less relevant by the new satellite channels, but also the introduction of freer and more independent sources of information may be an additional tool for civil society in its struggle with states over such issues as freedom of expression, human rights and democracy.[37]

Such channels challenge traditional social norms as much as they do the state, breaking taboos by discussing controversial topics such as homo-sexuality, religious conversion, and domestic violence. In so doing, they force such issues into the mainstream coverage. For example, the Saudi Arabian government has recently established a fourth national television news station which aims to rival international news channels broadcast by satellite. Although al-Ikhbariya still presents a very Saudi take on the world, its presenters include women, in traditional headscarves and wearing make-up and Western clothes, something which would not previously have been contemplated in the Kingdom. The channel has proved popular, attracting a third of all satellite viewers in Saudi Arabia (or nearly 30% of the population). It employs female journalists and has covered sensitive issues such as the exclusion of women from voting in the municipal elections and the attack on presenter Rania al-Baz by her husband. Clearly, satellite television has opened up realms of what may be discussed, with the state being complicit in this liberalization.

However, although Gulf Arab regimes have now fully opened their airwaves to privately owned and international satellite channels, and encouraged national state-owned media companies to make a qualitative leap in their own programming which involves a degree of greater edito-rial freedom, they have also found occasion to resort to repressive means to contain criticism of themselves. All Qatar's partners in the Gulf Cooperation Council have had occasion to ban Al Jazeera from reporting in their countries, with the result that the channel is unable to draw sufficient advertising from local companies (which remain reliant on good relations with political elites for their own welfare) to become financially independent from its al-Thani sponsor. The degree to which the channel's coverage of Qatar is self-censored to avoid losing the financial support is consequently a highly problematic issue.

Financial backing is a crucial part of understanding who provides what via satellite to the region. Al Jazeera's main regional rivals are Abu Dhabi TV (a state-owned company), the private Saudi-owned Orbit and MBC's al-Arabiya, and the part Saudi-owned LBC. Gulf Arab-owned satellite channels now dominate the wider Middle East,[38] and while they have followed Al Jazeera's lead in improving the quality of programming, particularly of news coverage, and in pushing editorial boundaries on social and political affairs, they have equally stayed within a culturally familiar domain, not least by virtue of the fact that they broadcast in the Arabic language and cover events and issues familiar to the Arab world. Their criticism of regional governments is restrained, with emphasis being given to bureaucratic failures rather than the controversial activities of prominent individuals within the ruling families. They aim to project a positive image of the Arab world, to counter 'misperceptions' propagated in the West, and to preserve local cultural integrity. As such, they serve gradual and selective rather than revolutionary change of the status quo. The fact that they have proved popular with local Gulf audiences suggests that this is not out of sync with social preferences and that populations are happy to see satellite TV opening up the political space but equally content to see it localized and its content moderated. Whether the audiences will find their own perspectives subverted by the coverage given by these channels to matters beyond the Arab world remains unknown. Will the extensive and informed Al Jazeera coverage of the American elections or of British parliamentary debates inspire them to demand more representative political processes at home? Will images of Palestinian and Iraqi women putting voting slips into boxes make Saudi women more vocal in demanding the franchise? As yet, we only have anecdotal evidence to suggest they might. What we can say is that in the case of satellite television technology, the state, private financiers, the commercial sector and audiences have collaborated to create a domain in which the public space is more open than previously and in which contestation between state and society – and indeed between elements within society itself – has emerged. They have equally conspired to 'localize' that space, to exclude from it influences which are so culturally subversive or politically revolutionary as to threaten the legitimacy of regimes or the stability of societies. Of course, international satellite channels offer a more diverse diet which may have its own effect, but the linguistic barrier to mass consumption continues to play a part in limiting their impact.

Extending internet coverage across the Gulf Arab countries has been equally problematic in political terms for national regimes. There is no 'ownership' of the internet through which its content can be controlled, and the infrastructure that enables access is more extensive and expensive than the relative simplicity of purchasing a dish. On the other hand, putting information *on* the web is a relatively easy task and one which can be done by literally anyone with on-line access and the necessary skills.

The Gulf Arab states were again relatively early users in the MENA region but tardy in global terms. Although the internet was available in selected universities previously, public access became available when Kuwait went on-line in 1994, followed by Bahrain and the UAE in 1995, Qatar and Oman in 1996 and Saudi Arabia in 1999. Table 3 shows that usage is still limited and unevenly distributed among the countries. It should be pointed out that low usage may be attributed in part to the still limited amount of material available in Arabic: Arabic speakers represent 4.6% of the world's population yet only 1.4% of internet users, with Arabic sites representing only a tiny proportion of the 7% of sites in languages other than the top nine used.[39]

It may also be that the content available on the web is not entirely relevant to potential users. Early Arabic-language sites were frequently developed by expatriate or diaspora Arabs, who had acquired the necessary web-skills abroad and who sought to introduce their own political or social agendas to the region. Jon Anderson has suggested that they coloured their websites with a cultural nostalgia, presenting an idealized version of their homelands.[40] Alternatively political dissidents used the web to give profile to human rights abuses, or to mobilize opposition at home and abroad. Neither approach necessarily reflects the interests or concerns of the majority of internet users in the Gulf Arab states.[41] Anderson suggests that a second generation of facilitator-visionaries developed within the Arab world itself, comprising information service providers like newspapers and news services, businesses interested in

TABLE 3
Internet Usage in the Gulf Arab states

Country	No. of Internet Users	Internet Users (% of Population)	Internet Users Index*
Bahrain	180,000	24.73	0.4
Kuwait	245,000	10.13	0.2
Oman	165,000	5.98	0.1
Qatar	75,000	9.32	0.2
Saudi Arabia	1,920,000	8.03	0.1
UAE	1,100,000	29.73	0.5
North America		57.00	
Europe		24.00	
Latin America		5.00	

Source: *Madar Research Journal,* May 2003, quoted in *Middle East Economic Digest,* 27 June 2003.

*from *United Nations Global E-Government Readiness Report 2004,* New York: United Nations, 2004, Table 4.

experimenting and translating the new technology, and visionary public sector officials eager to import its potential.

In the Gulf Arab countries, a number of agents have played a role in the diffusion of internet technology. A report by the International Telecommunications Union in 1998 highlighted a number of features of the initial period of internet development. Governments were reluctant to license independent internet service providers, relying on the monopoly state-owned telecoms companies to offer the service. In some cases these became the national top-level domain managers (Bahrain, the UAE and Qatar) while elsewhere the domain was managed by the Ministry of Communications (Kuwait) or the Ministry of Telecommunications and Information Technology (Saudi Arabia). In Oman, a dispute between the Ministry of Posts, Telegraphs and Telephones and the Ministry of Information allowed the Foreign Minister to slip in and register the *.om* national TLD (top-level domain) in his own name!

Development of the service in Bahrain was driven by commercial interests, although security considerations led to what was thought to be pervasive monitoring of internet traffic by the government. In Qatar the initiative came from the telecoms monopoly (Q-*Tel*). The Emir was vocal in his support for the growing infrastructure but discussion at government levels was confined to questions as to how to filter out material that was contrary to local culture or laws. In Kuwait the government was the major force behind the introduction of the technology, with the internet being made freely available to all university students. Filtering was directed at pornography and 'politically subversive' material. In Oman the business community lobbied the Ministry of Commerce and Industry until the state-owned monopoly (GTO) was entrusted with internet development. Again this has enabled the internet provider to restrict access to servers and sites which are deemed to be politically or morally offensive. There was not much public debate about this, with a consequent widespread belief that government surveillance of internet use was pervasive. In the UAE, public debate was much greater. When the web first became accessible, it was the public who complained about the nature of the material available on it. Universities subsequently joined with the police, the Ministry of Information and the service provider to discuss the possible hazards and recommended procedures for minimizing the risks associated with internet use.[42] As a consequence and with the support of the community of users, proxy servers were installed to filter and monitor internet traffic. The government made no effort to hide this fact and there has been very limited criticism for its doing so.

The Saudi official response to the internet was still more cautious. When it was made publicly available in 1999, the government sought to restrict its potentially threatening features by allowing access only through one of 26 approved internet service providers (ISPs) which received information after it had first been filtered by the Internet Services Unit at King Abdul Aziz University. The ISPs have complained that this slows the service down and discourages subscribers. It also makes the service prohibitively expensive and cuts profit margins to a minimum. ISPs argue that demand is now flattening off because of these constraints and that we can expect to see the sector consolidate into fewer, bigger firms in the near future. Yet, again consumers have not been entirely displeased with the system. When the government asked for suggestions as to which sites to block, they received 500 recommendations to every 100 requests for sites to be unblocked.

The clearest indication that the regimes of the region find full engagement with ICTs politically problematic is their own failure when it comes to introducing meaningful *e-government*. The United Nations Global *E*-Government Readiness Report 2004 (shown in Table 4) ranked the Middle East region below South and Central America and the Caribbean in terms of *e-government readiness* (a composite measurement of the demonstrated capacity and willingness of governments to use *e-government* for ICT-led development). When it came to *e-participation*, which measures the usefulness of government on-line services in enabling public participation in the deliberative process, not a single Arab government was recognized as encouraging citizens to engage in on-line participation. Four of the Gulf Arab states actually fared worse than Afghanistan and Iraq!

TABLE 4
Regional Levels of *E-readiness* and *E-participation*

	E-readiness Index (2004)	E-participation Index (2004)
North America	0.8751	0.9180
Europe	0.5866	0.2856
South and Eastern Asia	0.4603	0.2280
South and Central America	0.4558	0.2172
Caribbean	0.4106	0.0369
Western Asia	0.4093	0.0654
Bahrain	0.5323	0.0400
UAE	0.4736	0.0400
Qatar	0.4005	0.0100
Saudi Arabia	0.3858	0.0400
Kuwait	0.3649	0.0100
Oman	0.2884	0.0000
South and Central Asia	0.3213	0.0661
Oceana	0.3006	0.1284
Africa	0.2528	0.0309

Source: *United Nations E-government Readiness Report 2004,* New York.

The weakness of *e-government* in the region may be attributed as much to the lack of appropriately trained manpower within government bureaucracies as to deliberate neglect or indifference. The rankings were brought down by inconsistent provision rather than absence of provision. But one can also argue that the marked disparity between *e-readiness* and *e-participation* indicates a willingness to use ICTs to talk *to* citizens, but not to allow them a means to respond. It should be noted, however, that demand for *e-government* services has come primarily from the business community which seeks rapid and reliable access to government information services,[43] not from civil society groups seeking greater transparency or participation (although this may yet come). The nature of the demands will inevitably shape what on-line services are made available and thus any political impact here is likely to be a by-product of the further development of the business sector rather than of direct political reform. On a positive note, *e-government* initiatives in the region are driving a new vogue for building specifically Arabic-language storage and retrieval systems rather than Arab companies simply importing and translating English-language resources. With the Gulf Arab firms like Kuwait's Sakhr leading the way, and the Arab Gulf states accounting for a round 25% of sales for such systems, this represents an important milestone in the Arabization of digital technologies.

This discussion of the political constraints on ICT dispersion in the Gulf Arab states has identified a number of agencies involved in producing and shaping that diffusion, with consequent implications for the political impact. The major agency is clearly regimes themselves, and the bureaucracies that serve them. Ruling dynasties are aware of the potential for opposition movements to use ICTs for subversive activities, and of the possible impact on public opinion of exposure to unrestricted political information. However, with the exception of Saudi Arabia, they have progressively reduced their intervention. This has been the result of a number of factors. The recent privatization of national telecoms providers and the introduction of competition to the sector has reduced direct government control over internet provision for a start. Internet use has been driven by commercial interests, who have lobbied for the reduction of filtering mechanisms which increase the cost and slow down the delivery time of provision. Finally, far from pressing for a more liberal approach to internet provision, Gulf Arab society has proved an ally of the regime in its active demands that the state should play a role in controlling the influences to which the public may be exposed. Social actors are concerned with potential morally or culturally corrupting influences rather than political subversion on the web, but they have nonetheless been co-opted into a developmental vision which delegates a censoring role to the state! As with satellite television, the consumer has clearly played an active rather than a passive role, exercising choice and in doing so restricting potential impact.

Of course, there are social actors who do seek to use the web or satellite television to mobilize for political change. For them, the new technologies have undoubtedly offered new opportunities and new space for activity. Regimes have not resisted the creation of this space, since it serves their economic and developmental interests. However, they have sought to control what takes place within that space as much as they can without jeopardizing their alliance with commercial interests. In the case of satellite television, those commercial interests have acknowledged the alliance by stepping in to use their ownership of the technology to limit its politically or culturally subversive potential. The relationship between state and commercial interests is one of uneasy mutual accommodation. Consumers of the technologies have demonstrated their approval of the new space which it offers them, but have equally been content to delegate the task of moderator to the state or its allies in the interests of protecting cultural and moral integrity. In doing so, they have resigned themselves to the fact that the state will use the technology, or censor it, where it can to prevent it from being hijacked by political competitors. Overall, the relationship between the relevant actors here is clearly different from that existing in the more developed countries of the world where ICT-diffusion has been led by the multinational corporations in liberalized economies and liberal democratic political environments. It is not surprising then that there is variance in both producer and consumer expectations as to how free the new or expanded spaces will be.

Infrastructural Constraints: Running Before You Can Walk!

Of course, all agencies in this equation are constrained by the limitations of the infrastructure available to them. The table below clearly illustrates that, for all their wealth, the Gulf Arab countries – like most of the MENA region, remain handicapped by underdeveloped telecoms infrastructure.

The reason for this lies in the historical reliance on state-owned monopolies to develop what were seen as social development components. Planning and investment followed commercial logic and monopoly status allowed company management to be of variable quality. As a result, fixed

TABLE 5
Telecommunications Infrastructure Index 2004

Country	Telecoms Index	Fixed Lines Index	Mobile Subs Index
Bahrain	0.332	0.3	0.6
UAE	0.386	0.3	0.7
Qatar	0.297	0.3	0.4
Kuwait	0.230	0.3	0.5
Saudi Arabia	0.139	0.1	0.2
Oman	0.135	0.1	0.2
USA	0.770	0.6	0.5
Denmark	0.790	0.7	0.8
UK	0.693	0.6	0.8
Egypt	0.066	0.1	0.1
Jordan	0.097	0.1	0.1

Source: *UN E-Government Readiness Report 2004.*

line coverage is surprisingly low relative to per capita income. Quality of service is poor and costs are high. In the Gulf Arab countries, it was those same telecoms monopolies which were initially tasked by government with leading the way in ICT development and dispersion.

It is true that the last few years have seen them making some efforts to expand fixed-line coverage[44] but over the last two years spending on GSM services has overtaken this as telecoms companies respond to immediate customer demand. WTO membership requires the Gulf Arab states to liberalize their telecoms markets by 2005. They have started by privatizing their monopoly providers and introducing competition into the GSM rather than fixed-line market. With comparatively low existing penetration rates and affluent populations eager to purchase the latest mobile phones with all the additional value-added services, there is room for growth and therefore for interest from other providers. By April 2005, only the Qatar and UAE markets were still dominated by state-owned monopolies, although both had set up regulatory bodies as a first step towards the introduction of competition. The result has been an astonishing boom for the regional telecoms companies. Profits for the former-monopolies have soared: Bahrain's Batelco by 36.2% in 2004, Qatar's Q-Tel by 25.3% and even Saudi Arabia's Saudi Telecom by 9.2%. But this growth is fuelled by the GSM market, leaving investment and growth in the fixed-line sector a poor second. Only Bahrain is anywhere near introducing competition into the fixed-line market. The consequence is that only those technologies which utilize GSM systems are making real inroads to the region, while those dependent on fixed-line and cable technology are lagging behind. The consequences can be significant: Dubai Internet City, for example, is hailed as a model for ICT-led development planning, yet it is serviced by Etisalat. Service delivery is slow and inconsistent, reducing the impact of all the state-of-the-art technology imported by companies locating themselves within the facility.

Even the introduction of competition to GSM markets is not as clear-cut as it first appears. In 2004 the six Gulf Cooperation Council communications ministers agreed that they would all select regional telecoms operators in preference to international companies when putting licences out to offer, confirming a trend which had already become apparent. Kuwaiti-owned MTC competes with Batelco in Bahrain, Qatari-owned Q-Tel with the Omani Telecommunications Corporation (Omantel) in Oman, Etisalat with Saudi Telecom in Saudi Arabia and so forth. International companies have been largely confined to the role of equipment suppliers or sub-contractors. As yet, this role may suit them given the risks attached to a still poorly regulated Gulf market.[45] For the Gulf telecoms companies it is a necessary move as their own markets come closer to saturation. But the exclusion of international companies also means that the region remains untouched by the business practices and associated cultural innovations that they might have brought.

If customer demand has shaped investment by preferentializing GSM over fixed-line platforms, it has also featured in overcoming government efforts to control associated technologies. The classic example of this was the Saudi government's effort to declare camera phones illegal in 2002 on the grounds that they were being misused to circulate photographs of uncovered women. Despite the ban on such phones, and the fines which were levied for illegal use, trade flourished on the basis of smuggled-in hardware. An estimated 40% of all phones sold in Saudi Arabia were camera phones, with retailers blatantly advertising them on billboards and in shopping malls. In December 2004 the government caved in and repealed the ban, under pressure from four of its own ministries (Commerce and Industry, Interior, Communications and

Information, Technology and Finance), operators, manufacturers and retailers, but against the demands of the religious authorities.[46]

In terms of infrastructural platforms for ICT dispersion, there are clearly a number of key agencies in the Gulf Arab countries. The state remains important, although its role will diminish as privatization, competition and ultimately independent regulation take root. Regional telecoms companies play a fundamental role in determining where investment is located and what services are available to whom. International companies have as yet to make their mark beyond their retailing and supply functions, although here they can influence consumer demand, which in turn is also an increasingly important agency. Other actors which mediate between the new technologies and cultural norms may play a less significant but nonetheless visible role.

E-commerce, the Private Sector and the Culture of ICT

One agent which has featured less in this story than might have been expected, is the private commercial sector. ICT spend by the private sector is growing rapidly, most notably in Saudi Arabia, which is now the largest regional market.[47] There is even a nascent local IT sector, although it currently provides only few niche services and is outpaced by Egyptian and Jordanian competition. But in general, *e-commerce* has been slow to take off. Analysts have identified a low level of trust in electronic systems for communicating sensitive financial information.[48] This is not least a result of the booming industry in internet fraud in the region which has seen Gulf banks in particular proving to be vulnerable and ill-prepared. Regional companies are reluctant to entrust their financial security to external third parties, what are termed managed security services (MSS) providers, but lack the skills to do the job themselves. This is particularly a problem for small and medium-sized enterprises with fewer connections to the international economy that might encourage them to outsource their security or fewer resources to buy in the skills. Small-to-medium enterprises (SMEs) have also been slow to utilize electronic data services. So far that market has been dominated by government departments and large corporations. Even relatively large conglomerates in Saudi Arabia remain unaware of data products which are 'common currency' for Western firms.[49]

Both the awareness and trust problems may be ameliorated over time, particularly as local applications services providers (ASPs) offer more 'Arabized' packages which can be leased (rather than bought) and which adapt international business practice to local conditions and language. Such ASPs offer a forum for 'negotiating' the culture and practices of international business with local knowledge and ways of doing things. In doing so they both moderate and catalyse the impact of ICTs on the region.

One problem they cannot resolve, however, is the absence of strategic IT planning and the resistance among middle managers to the introduction of new forms of business activity by younger colleagues. Analysts have pointed to a disconnection between the people running firms and the people who understand ICTs. The result is an approach to ICTs that sees them as support platforms, not as strategic assets. This is compounded by the fact that much of the skilled labour is imported: local companies are geared to a 'plug-and-play' approach, recruiting ready-trained employees rather than investing in in-house training and development. The result has been that much of the ICT-competent manpower in the Gulf is imported from Jordan, India or elsewhere. Not only is this labour increasingly hard to retain given international salary opportunities: it is also less trusted and less likely to penetrate the senior management tiers than Gulf Arab employees.

These generational and staffing issues have been faced and overcome elsewhere. Neighbouring Jordan, for example, has adopted a strategic plan which sees US$500 million being ploughed into reforming the national education system over the next three years. The idea is to create a national labour-force with the skills to utilize the new technologies which can be integrated with a supportive infrastructure and an ICT-friendly regulatory environment. The Gulf Arab regimes have yet to take such a proactive position – the drive for ICT diffusion is being led by commerce rather than government, the latter choosing to intervene to control rather than produce the technologies. If and when they take a more creative position, educational actors will become important agents in their own right.

Technologies, Agents and Impacts
The discussion above allows us to reach a number of preliminary conclusions.

Firstly, it can be seen that some political opening has been generated by the diffusion in the Gulf states of contemporary ICTs. While this cannot be conceived of as democratization in a narrow sense, one can argue securely that ICTs have expanded existing political spaces, and offered new ones. Citizens can use them to access a wider range of information, to interact with new political communities and to express political demands. Regimes have had to accommodate these to some extent, either by allowing greater freedom of the media and supporting improved professionalism, or by facilitating the expansion of the infrastructure which offers the platform for such ICTs. They do so because of their awareness of the developmental potential of the ICTs and as a result of demands coming from allied commercial classes. On the other hand, regimes and those same allied business classes have sought to 'capture' ICTs through ownership and control over provision. They use what control over the technology they can muster to limit the direct political impact of ICT diffusion, filtering web sites or banning satellite channels when the criticism hits a nerve. Crucially for the Gulf Arab states, this political function overlaps with a cultural function, with an obligation handed to regimes by their own populations and interest groups within them, to protect the country from morally corrupting or excessive Westernizing influences. But the nature of the technologies means that there is little regimes or their allies can do to prevent the more gradualist impact which arises from exposure to, and awareness of, political alternatives. The existence of the space itself provides a political challenge, independent of the activity which fills the space!

The national telecoms companies are interesting in so far as they were originally entrusted by regimes with the developmental task of rolling out ICT provision. Increasingly, however, they are themselves challenged by the international requirements for the introduction of competition into local markets and by the demands of private commercial actors wanting faster, cheaper and more reliable services. As they themselves become increasingly privately owned entities, and as they move into more competitive arenas, it will be interesting to see whether the alliance with regimes is weakened and whether they too become advocates of a less politically restrictive approach to ICT diffusion. This is unlikely to be the case until privatization is complete, local demand is saturated, regulation is fully independent and international companies are allowed to complete equally in Gulf Arab markets.

The private sector in the Gulf states has played a role in pushing for better quality, lower cost delivery, freer competition and greater integration with the global economy. All of these suggest progressively excluding the government from an interventionist role. However, the interdependent relationship between regime and business elites in the Gulf Arab states has so far seen them accommodating one another. Together they are stakeholders in both the process of ICT diffusion and the political stability of the national arenas and as such they see mutual interest in balancing the two requirements for sustainable growth. The commercial sector has also played a role in localizing ICTs, diminishing the impact of globalized Western culture, particularly through translation into the Arabic language (although this might equally diminish the status of minority languages or local dialects). This in itself is a filtering role, and one which may ultimately serve to counter the politically liberalizing impact of the new ICTs.

Gulf Arab populations have played their own role, both as consumers and as filtering agents. They have used choice, exercised through dialogue with governments and subscriptions to ICT providers, to decide what technologies they want and what political openings they expect to enjoy. Equally, they have at times rejected any universality of the contents of the expanded or new political spaces, particularly when they have perceived it to be culturally threatening. This statement generalizes of course, and there have undoubtedly been social agents which have sought precisely to use that space to issue both political and cultural challenges. Society is not a single unitary agent but rather an agglomeration of agents which constantly negotiate their responses to the new ICTs amongst themselves as much as with government or the business classes.

Other relevant actors identified in this narrative include international regulatory bodies, the multinationals which initially produce, supply and retail the technologies, the skilled migrant labourers who provide the crucial link between local producer and consumer, the public sector bodies which plan, coordinate or regulate ICT provision, the international media companies which compete with local providers: the list is too long to do justice to all.

It has not been the task of this chapter to map precise political reforms in the Gulf Arab states onto the regional production and diffusion of ICTs. Nor has this been a comprehensive survey of either political or technological developments in these countries. It has shown, however, that the regional penetration of new ICTs has been a driver in opening up existing public space, and creating new *virtual* space, in which political activity has had the opportunity to adopt broader dimensions. It has also shown that this is unlikely to lead to revolutionary political transformation; there will be no flood of unfettered liberalism sweeping across the region simply by virtue of borderless technologies. The configuration of agents, of both producers and consumers of those ICTs, has so far served to restrain the political impact of the new spaces. However, the relationships between agents are not set in stone, they are themselves constantly metamorphosing and ICTs play a part in that process. We may therefore understand the technologies and the agencies which produce and diffuse them as being dialectically bonded with each other, set on a liberal trajectory by virtue of the expansion of political space but fraught with implicit tensions and resistances that seem likely to be playing out for years yet to come.

NOTES

1 A revised and updated version of this article can be found at: Emma Murphy, 2006, 'Agency and Space: The Political Impact of Information Technologies in the Gulf Arab States', *Third World Quarterly*, Vol. 27, No. 6 (2006), pp. 1059–1083.

2 Hazem Beblawi and Giacomo Luciani (eds.), *The Rentier State* (London: Croom Helm, 1987).

3 Structural analyses has been provided by Mehran Kamrava, 'Non-democratic States and Political Liberalisation in the Middle East: A Structural Analysis', *Third World Quarterly*, Vol. 19, No. 1, pp. 63–85, 1998. Explanations based on oil wealth precluding a necessity to liberalize are provided by Kiren Chaudhry in *The Price of Wealth* (Ithaca: Cornell University Press, 1997); and Dirk Vandewalle in *Libya Since Independence: Oil and State-Building* (Ithaca: Cornell University Press, 1998). Samuel Huntington argued that Islam was not compatible with democracy in 'Will More Countries become Democratic', *Political Science Quarterly*, Vol. 99, No. 2 (Summer 1984), pp. 193–218. Adam Garfinkle, meanwhile, claimed that Arab societies lacked in varying degrees three vital prerequisites for democracy; a belief that political authority lay with mankind rather than God, a concept of majority rule and the notion of universal equality. See A. Garfinkle, 'The New Missionaries', *Prospect* (April 2003), pp. 22–24. Alfred Stepan has likewise argued for a specifically Arab cultural resistance to democracy. See Alfred Stepan with Graeme Robertson, 'An Arab More than a Muslim Electoral Gap', in *Journal of Democracy*, Vol. 14 (July 2003), pp. 30–59. Eva Bellin has argued that the strength of the coercive

apparatus in the Arab world has inhibited democracy but also that the process of state-led development has created an ambivalence towards democracy among key elements of capital and labour. See Eva Bellin, 'The Robustness of Authoritarianism in the Middle East: A Comparative Perspective', paper presented at *Bringing the Middle East Back In*, Yale University, December 2001. Also *Stalled Democracy: Capital, labour and the Paradox of State-sponsored Development* (Ithaca: Cornell University Press, 2002). Volker Perthes has meanwhile concluded that Arab elites have successfully managed to circulate, regenerate and co-opt to the point that they can successfully neutralize demands for democracy from the wider masses; Volker Perthes (ed.), *Arab Elites: Negotiating the Politics of Change* (Boulder: Lynne Rienner, 2004). Ellen Lust-Okar keeps the emphasis on elites, arguing that in the Arab world they have proved particularly adept at exploiting and manipulating cleavages between opposition groups, notably along the secular–Islamist faultline. Ellen Lust-Okkar, 'Divided They Rule: The Management and Manipulation of Political Opposition', *Comparative Politics*, 2002. Frédéric Volpi has suggested that the Muslim world has specifically spawned what he terms 'pseudo-democracies' as a stalemate is reached between three political currents: liberalism, republicanism and Islamism. See F. Volpi, 'Pseudo-democracy in the Muslim World', in *Third World Quarterly*, Vol. 25, No. 6 (2004) pp. 1061–1078.

4 See, for example, A. Ehteshami, 'Is the Middle East Democratising?', *British Journal of Middle Eastern Studies*, Vol. 26, No. 2 (November 1999), pp. 199–219. Jean-François Seznec has suggested that the reforms in Saudi Arabia amount to 'proto-democratic stirrings' which place it on a trajectory towards polyarchy. See Jean-François Seznec, 'Stirrings in Saudi Arabia', *Journal of Democracy*, Vol. 13, No. 4 (October 2002), pp. 34–40. Michael Herb has argued that Gulf democracy may not be full parliamentary democracy, but it retains the virtue of monarchical domination which prevents Islamist subversion of democratic processes and thus retains stability. See M. Herb, 'Emirs and Parliaments in the Gulf', *Journal of Democracy*, Vol. 13, No. 4 (October 2002), pp. 41–47.

5 Jill Crystal, 'Political Reform and the Prospects for Democratic Transition in the Gulf', *Working Paper for Fundación Para Las Relaciones Internacionales y el Diálogo Exterior* (July 2005). The International Crisis Group has likewise argued that the Saudi regime is reluctant to do more than talk the talk. See 'Can Saudi Arabia Reform Itself?', *ICG Middle East Report No. 28*, Cairo/Brussels, 14 July 2004.

6 Daniel Brumberg, 'The Trap of Liberalised Autocracy', *Journal of Democracy*, Vol. 13, No. 4 (October 2002), pp. 56–68.

7 Thomas McPhail, *Electronic Colonialism: The Future of International Broadcasting and Communication* (London: Sage, 1981), p. 244.

8 Paul Romer, 'Endogenous Technological Change', *Journal of Political Economy*, Vol. 98, No. 5 (1990), pp. 71–102.

9 Edward Ayensu, 'International Management', quoted in Brian Murphy, *The World Wired Up* (London, Comedia, 1983), p. 119.

10 Jeffrey James, 'The Global Information Infrastructure Revisited' in *Third World Quarterly*, Vol. 22, No. 5 (2001), pp. 813–822.

11 David Lyon, *The Information Society: Issues and Illusions* (Cambridge: Polity Press, 1988).

12 Gerald Sussman, *Communication, Technology and Politics in the Information Age* (London: Sage, 1997).

13 There have been suggestions of a New International Division of Information Technology, comprising a wired core and a less wired, or wireless periphery! See Jason Abbott, 'Democracy@internet.asia? The Challenges to the Emancipatory Potential of the Net: Lessons from China and Malaysia', in *Third World Quarterly*, Vol. 22, No. 1 (2001), p. 111. Linda Main has discussed the opposing scenarios of either a Global Information Infrastructure which massively accelerates economic and social development the world over or a concentration of activity in one privileged group creating a two-tier technology society; Linda Main, 'The Global Information Infrastructure: Empowerment or Imperialism?', in *Third World Quarterly*, Vol. 22, No. 1 (2001), pp. 83–97.

14 'United Nations adopts resolution in the World Summit on the Information Society', Press release of the International Telecommunication Union, 21/1/02. Speech by Kofi Annan, Secretary General of the United Nations.

15 See, for example, D. H. Perrit Jr, 'The Internet as a Threat to Sovereignty? Thoughts on the Internet's Role in the National and Global Governance', *Indiana Journal of Global Legal Studies*, Vol. 5, No. 2 (1998), and B. Warf and J. Gromes, 'Counterhegemonic Discourses and the Internet', *The Geographical Review*, Vol. 87, No. 2 (1997).

16 Manuel Castells, *The Internet Galaxy: Reflections on the Internet, Business and Society* (Oxford: OUP, 2001).

17 For example, this is fundamental to European institutional ideas as to how the information society will impact upon European and partner states. Hence we see initiatives such as the 1999 European Commission's '*e*Europe: An Information Society for All' initiative, the tenth action area of which was entitled Government Online, and which aimed to 'ensure that citizens have easy action to government information, services and decision-making procedures online'. See http://europa. eu.int/ISPO/basics/I_europe.html. The EU also endorsed the Yale University-based *Information Society Project* which explicitly seeks to promote democratization, participation and decision making through the development and spread of ICT. Meanwhile the World Information Society Summits (Geneva December 2003 and Tunis November 2005) have placed dissemination of ICTs to all villages, hospitals and schools around the world, including all populations having access to radio and television by 2015, as their principal target. Clearly, for them, universal access is considered a prerequisite for a democratizing impact!

18 This initiative is part of the Yale University Information Society project. Its preliminary results can be found at http://www.law.yale.edu/isp/strongdem/overview.html.

19 William Martin, *The Information Society* (London: Aslib, 1988), p. 59.

20 See Jason P. Abbott, 'Democracy@internet.asia?', p. 107.

21 See discussion in Anthony Wilhelm, *Democracy in the Digital Age* (London: Routledge, 2000).

22 Even the French have been complaining about Google's plans to create a digital library which will give priority to English language material. French scholars have termed their resistance to this 'the first cultural war in cyberspace', claiming Google will be in a position to 'hijack the thought of the world'.

23 Abbott, 'Democracy@internet.asia?', p. 106.

24 Gerald Sussman, *Communication, Technology and Politics in the Information Age* (London: Sage, 1997), p. 194.

25 A report by *The Economist* suggested that American and European companies have been falling over themselves 'in their eagerness to sell the latest surveillance gear and software' to countries like China and Saudi Arabia, which Western governments are simultaneously eager to portray as authoritarian and repressive. The tension between commercial interests which restrict the democratizing impact of ICT and political interests which might seek to promote it is once again evident. 'Digital Dilemmas: A Survey of the Internet Society', *The Economist*, 25 January 2003.

26 Jon W. Anderson, 'Producers and Middle East Internet Technology: Getting beyond "Impacts"', in *Middle East Journal*, Vol. 54, No. 3, Summer 2000, pp. 419–431.

27 Henri Lefebvre, *The Production of Space* (Oxford: Blackwell, 1991 edition), p. 411.

28 See, for example, Toby E. Huff, 'Globalisation and the Internet: Comparing the Middle Eastern and Malaysian Experiences' in *Middle East Journal*, Vol. 3, Summer 2001, pp. 439–458.

29 Peter G. Mandaville, 'Reimagining the *ummah*? Information Technology and the Changing Boundaries of Political Islam', in Ali Mohammadi (ed), *Islam Encountering Globalization* (London: Routledge Curzon, 2002), pp. 61–90.

30 Mamoun Fandy, 'Information Technology, Trust and Social Change in the Arab World', *Middle East Journal*, Vol. 54, No. 3 (Summer 2000), pp. 378–394.

31 *Middle East Economic Digest*, 27 June 2003, p. 33.

32 *Middle East Economic Digest*, 27 June 2003, p. 33.

33 *Middle East Economic Digest*, 27 May 2005, p. 37.

34 *Middle East Economic Digest*, 19 April 2002, p. 6.

35 Al Jazeera had an audience of approximately 50 million in 2005. S. Abdallah Schleifer, 'Satellite TV and Democracy' in *bitterlemons-international.org Middle East Roundtable*, Ed. 19, Vol. 3, 26 May 2005.

36 Edmund Ghareeb, 'New Media and the Information Revolution in the Arab World – an Assessment', *Middle East Journal*, pp. 395–417.

37 Najib Ghadbian, 'Contesting the State Media Monopoly: Syria on al-Jazira Television', *MERIA Journal*, Vol. 5, No. 2 (June 2001), p. 1.

38 Although most Arab countries have now moved to satellite broadcasting per se.

39 *United Nations Global E-Government Readiness Report* (New York: United Nations, 2004), p. 111.

40 Jon Anderson, 'Producers and Middle East Internet Technology: Getting Beyond "Impacts"', *in Middle East Journal*, Vol. 54, No. 3 (Summer 2000), p. 424.

41 Jason Abbott has argued, for example, that his own survey of progressive websites on Yahoo.com and Yahoo!Asia indicates that Asian internet users have different priorities in their website selection than users in mature, democratic societies with well-developed civil societies. Abbott, 'Democracy@internet.asia?', p. 101.

42 International Telecommunications Union, *The Global Diffusion of the Internet*, March 1998.

43 *Middle East Economic Digest*, 23 November 2001.

44 Between 1999 and 2003 fixed-line penetration in Saudi Arabia rose by just 1.7% while it actually declined in the UAE. *Middle East Digest*, 27 May 2005.

45 *Middle East Economic Digest*, 24 September 2004.

46 *Middle East Economic Digest*, 18 February 2005.

47 The GCC ICT market is currently worth an estimated US$5000 million a year, depending on who you talk to, with 60% of the spend taking place in Saudi Arabia.

48 *Middle East International*, 6 February 2004.

49 For example, according to Abdallah al-Musa, the head of Saudi data research for Saudi Telecom, some 91% of Saudi medium-sized businesses had no knowledge of virtual private network (VPN) systems. Third MEED Middle East Telecoms Conference, Bahrain, 9 February 2005.

10

The Future of Reform in the Societies of the GCC Countries

Mohammad Al Rumaihi

More has been written on reform in the Arab world than on any other geographic region around the world. Indeed, in the past few years alone, there have been several conventions held calling for reforms to be made.

Reform is a subject that is close to the Arab and Muslim heart. I recently stumbled on a school play entitled *Reform*. It was performed in the early 20th century in one of Kuwait's first ever schools. The oldest and most significant Islamic cultural association in Kuwait is still the Association of Social Reform. It has been run by the Kuwaiti branch of the Muslim Brotherhood since the early 1980s.

Arabs as well as foreigners have written substantially about the need for urgent and significant political, economic and social reform. All have written about its urgency and significance. However, the Arab countries differ in their perception of reform. The GCC countries (Saudi Arabia, Kuwait, UAE, Bahrain, Qatar and Oman), for example, are not all at the same point on the road to reform. In addition, the opinion of what is needed for the reform agenda bears little resemblance to what the existing predicaments and aspirations actually are.

The influential elites in the GCC countries have their own views on comprehensive reform. They also have their own assessment of the reform steps that have been implemented thus far. The Development Forum, a civil society group that was established more than a quarter of a century ago by a number of intellectuals in the GCC countries, has held annual meetings. The purpose of the meetings was to examine the shape and extent of the needed reforms in the Gulf states, as well as to review the political future of these countries. The debate continues to rage, and much has been written and published by those interested in the subject, whether with regard to the Gulf states as a whole or in each country separately. And while the elites may share approximate views and recognize the existing shortcomings, they do not necessarily share a similar vision over the needed steps and programme.

The issue of reform may be related to several points that can be summarized as follows:

1. Fundamental or partial change.
2. Defining reform and the steps to achieve it.
3. The hurdle presented by whether reforms should be inspired from within or from without, or both?
4. The attitude of Islamic political jurisprudence toward modern reform.
5. Economic or political reform.

And although such issues are being debated in other Arab countries, where the priorities and needs may differ, the core issues remain the same. While, for example, the GCC countries do not suffer from a scarcity in public income, especially after the hike in the prices of oil, nor suffer from a high population, as other Arab countries, they share with other Arabs the ailment of corruption. Moreover, there are several factors that make the GCC countries vulnerable. Their economies depend largely on the diminishing commodity of oil, and they suffer from a negative imbalance in population, as well as from a primitive educational system. In addition, their public administration is plagued with considerable backwardness.

Some Arab observers argue that history offers us two models for progress, especially toward democracy.[1] The first is along the Western model (Europe and North America), while the second emulates the Asian model, which encompasses Singapore, Taiwan and Malaysia. The former is the cautious and slower path, while the latter is the fast lane. Democracy and reform advocates urge adopting the fast lane, which they regard as possible in the Gulf states because of the presence of primary resources (mainly oil) and funds. What is lacking, they argue, is the will and determination to formulate a common Gulf agenda. Such an agenda remains absent despite the fact that the Gulf Cooperation Council has been in existence for more than a quarter of a century.

Fundamental or Partial and Programmed Change?
Views differ in the Gulf area over the issue, but there are two main ideas. The first argues that fundamental, or revolutionary, change has

taken place in a number of neighbouring Arab countries but was not followed with real reform; instead it reached a dead end. At the same time, the Arab peoples that were burdened with it are today the least free and most deprived. They give the examples of Egypt, Syria, Iraq, Yemen, Libya, Sudan and neighbouring Iran. They maintain that all these countries experienced revolts that ended up changing regimes without changing the rules, and in some cases the situation actually worsened. The peoples lost much of their inherent abilities for change because of the rule of the military or the clergy. Thus, we have to adopt the idea of changing the mindset of the rulers rather than simply replacing them with another ruling tribe. This is without doubt a lengthy process, but one which, at the end of the day, is the most suitable.

The structural reforms that are underway (including constitutional and human rights reforms), may improve as the middle class increases due to economic restructuring. Such reforms may also lead to wider reforms. Consequently, this school of thought argues in favour of seeking common national ground between the governments of the region and their peoples, as well as between individuals and groups seeking change. It also argues that common ground should be sought between the nationalists and the religious groups at all levels. The way to achieve such an aim is through objective and responsible dialogue at all levels and among all those concerned.[2]

On the other hand, there is an opposing view that argues that the ruling families in the Gulf states cannot carry out the needed reforms. Those who subscribe to such a view believe that one of the main political flaws in the Gulf countries is the absolute power that the ruling families enjoy. Such power allows them to manipulate the political as well as economic decisions of their countries.[3] The ruling families regard the citizens as subjects, and some of them even believe that it is within their rights to control their livelihood. They regard talk of sharing power as heresy and even when others do accept to share power they endorse constitutions that allow them to have their way.

Defining Reform and the Steps to Achieve It
While the debate rages over whether fundamental or gradual reform should be implemented, elites in the Gulf countries stand almost united

in demanding some sort of reform. Most of them view reform within the parameters of five basic demands:

- National security: the absence of fear from foreign threat and military struggle.
- Social security: liberation from fear of violence. This also involves the enforcement of the law, which is enacted by an elected institution, fairly upon all citizens within the framework of an impartial, independent and effective judicial system.
- Individual freedoms: guaranteeing the freedom of movement, expression and right to congregate and to live in a country with dignity without discrimination with regard to race, creed or social background. Such a demand also includes the right to own media outlets and the freedom to become politically active. Moreover, it involves the right of a citizen to choose freely who in their society they want to represent them in the decision-making process.
- Personal security: liberation from destitution, and including the ability to secure an income, housing and medication, as well as the provision of equal opportunity in education and employment in the public sector.
- Environmental security: the provision of a healthy environment that allows the public to work and enjoy a balanced life.[4]

Those five demands are hardly local or regional; they are universal. They can be found in the literature of reformists throughout the Gulf area.[5] Some have been implemented by some countries in the Gulf, while others remain totally non-existent. The priority of the demands varies among the Gulf states. Some regard political reform as having higher priority than other issues. Others argue that change should start with judicial and legal reforms, or that economic reform should be the first priority.

No one denies that there are reforms that are underway. Some are visible, such as the modern constitutions in Kuwait, Bahrain, Qatar, the UAE and Oman. There are also economic and administrative reforms in Saudi Arabia and Oman, such as the establishment of a *shura* (consultative) council and holding local elections in Saudi Arabia. Yet even the moderates among the elites in the Gulf states continue to express criticism, and there is a general disagreement on the type and pace of reforms in the Gulf area.

Abdulatif Al Hamad is an economist and the Director of the Arab Development Fund and former Finance Minister in Kuwait. He maintains that responding to political reform in the Gulf states has been slow and limited.[6] He notes that there are four areas in which the Gulf countries need to implement urgent reforms:

1. Improving the performance of the public administration and its institutions. Al Hamad believes that the development of public administration in the Gulf countries was handicapped by increased restrictions on access to information, lack of responsibility and excessive centralization in decision making. Such a state of affairs, he argues, represents a considerable threat to the performance of the private as well as the public sector.
2. Disheartenment with democratic and civil rights reforms. It is not possible to achieve meaningful economic progress if the people are denied the right to think and act independently.
3. Reforming financial regulations. A developed financial system is the main component of open markets that allow increased competition. The weakness or inflexibility of the monetary system makes the Gulf states vulnerable to unpredictable financial crises. This makes reforming the financial sector an urgent necessity for the GCC countries.
4. Reforming the educational system by way of broadening its outreach and increasing its quality. Competition depends on knowledge and the use of technological means, as well as the employment of advanced administrative methods.[7]

Yet even such reasonable priorities for reform, which are called for by moderates, public servants and intellectuals in the Gulf area, have failed to generate any response that could transform them into real programmes. Political, economic, social and cultural barriers continue to impede the desired reforms.

Another writer, Vinan Zanubian, notes that the Gulf states were unable to carry out real reforms in the past three decades, especially when they had a surplus in oil revenues. The reason, he maintains, is that they faced considerable regional hurdles. These included the perpetual Palestinian problem, the menace of pan-Arabism, the recurring Arab military coups as well as the 'heat' generated by the Iranian revolution and the Iran–Iraq war that followed soon afterward. There was also the Iraqi invasion of Kuwait and its turbulent aftermath which produced the current instability in the area.

The Gulf states were thus busy preserving the status quo without introducing any real political or economic reforms.[8] The writer goes on to say that due to these events the Gulf states delayed taking difficult decisions with regard to reform, and with each delay the cost of implementing reforms increased.

Yet such a view is refuted at the highest levels. The Emir of Qatar, Sheikh Hamad Bin Khalifa Al Thani, insists that

> it is no longer acceptable that the Arab–Israeli struggle, or waiting for peace with the Jewish State, be used as a pretext to delay reforms. This has taken too long, and it may take even longer. This is especially true since the Arab rage is prompted not only by the Palestinian issue, but it has other deep offshoots that are related to the political and economic performance in the area.[9]

Others maintain that some of the reforms that have been carried out in the Gulf states are cosmetic, having assumed the characteristics of speaker's corner or a talking shop that failed to develop into a true democracy.

The Hurdle Presented By Whether Reforms Should be Inspired from Within or from Without, or Both?

As with the other Arab elites, a debate is raging among the elites of the Gulf states. At issue is whether to accept reforms that are driven by outside pressure, or insist that such reforms should be homegrown, and how to achieve such an aim.

A general intellectual trend has evolved in the Arab world, influenced by nationalist or religious ideology, which is strongly opposed to any reform imposed from the outside. An extreme school of this trend goes as far as saying that it is better not to have reform at all than to have one that is imposed from outside. Adherents to this school of thought may find some historical justifications for their uncompromising attitude. Such justification is rooted in the perception that the West, which is pushing enthusiastically for reforms, failed to provide any genuine reforms during the colonial era as well as afterwards when it allied itself with Arab rulers. Furthermore the attitude of the West toward the Palestinian issue has also totally undermined the reform movement.

Some of these thoughts find credence among the masses in the Gulf area. Some argue that change cannot be accomplished by subordinates, only the believers can inspire change. And while rejecting foreign influence on implementing change enjoys considerable popularity, there is another view that is shared by the elite in the Gulf states and in other Arab countries.

Such a view maintains that reform cannot be totally independent of either foreign *or* domestic influences. Adherents to this school of thought argue that had it not been for some recent Western pressure, the slow wheel of reforms would not have moved in the Arab world. Perhaps the experience of Iraq is the most significant event of change in contemporary Arab history. Its outcome will determine the fate of many reform efforts in the Arab world. The failure of reform in its modern concept, which involves the establishment of a pluralistic and democratic state that respects human rights, would deliver a crucial setback to the idea of a foreign-inspired reform. It would be a long time before the Arab political culture would again accept such an idea.

Political Jurisprudence in Islam

This is a matter that is related to culture. In its political and economic meaning, reform cannot be achieved within the framework of a culture that is resistant to change or wishes to maintain the existing state of affairs. How change should be measured is a controversial subject within Arab culture. Some see the Iranian model as the one most worth emulating, while others regard the Western or Asian models as more fitting to Arab culture. There are no shared values in aspiring for change. Moreover, objective criticism is not yet developed enough through education and the media. Complaint about a lack of intellect in the political institutions has come from the highest level. Prince Saud Al Faisal, the Foreign Minister of Saudi Arabia, complained in a lecture about the absence of studies that address the question of political jurisprudence in Islam. He argued that the failure to entrench political jurisprudence made political understanding a fertile ground for conflict.[10]

The most addressed subject in contemporary Arab political culture is classified under the general topic: Islam and democracy.[11] There are three schools of thought on this subject.

One school argues in favour of accommodation between democratic principles and the ideals of Islam. Another has reservations about such a proposal. Its adherents maintain that the concept of the 'will of the people' is absent from the Islamic *shariah*, which makes it impossible for the legislator to override the will of God. A third school calls for the selection of alternatives that are based on what is evident in Islamic texts, as well as in the interpretations of the enlightened legacy of learned men, the *ulama*. There is an extensive heritage of interpretations that all students of the *shariah*, as well as of modern democracy, may utilize. However, such effort is undermined either by political considerations, which are the most apparent, or by failure to grasp the intellectual bases of such interpretations.

Jamal Al Bana once maintained that "had the *ulama* started where the second Caliph Omar bin Al Khattab had ended, they would have saved the Muslim nation a thousand years of fruitless debates, and we would not have found ourselves in the position we are in. But the *ulama* believed that what is permitted for Omar is not allowed for others."[12]

In addition to the complex notion of Islamic jurisprudence, there is also the social aspect. The argument in favour of the Western democracy of Westminster, or Jeffersonian democracy, which is in force in some Asian countries, may not be suitable for countries where the social culture could prevent its application. The social structure of such countries depends on the tribe, extended family and sectarianism. Those who have thin or no links to such a structure, such as women, are marginalized. Moreover, citizenship is meticulously weighed since it is considered a means to a much better way of life. All such factors are deeply rooted in the formation of social and business relations.

In such an environment the social fabric becomes contradictory to modern democratic values. This is because such values demand transparency and legal equality, as well as favouring public interest over personal concerns. Some maintain that 'clean hands crimes' are most widespread in such societies, and include bias toward a social class or tribe, while tribal or sectarian 'gallantry' could influence the outcome of the democratic process. Many observers express reservations over the application of democratic ideals in such societies. They cite such maxims as "there is no democracy without a democratic culture", or "there is no democracy without democrats".

Such an analysis applies to most, if not all, of the Arab countries, but it applies in particular to the Gulf states where the principle of "first among equals" has no real meaning. This is true in the context of a culture which maintains that wisdom lies only with the Sheikhs. However, such a way of thinking is not sustainable. Some maintain that without starting on the democratic ladder it will be impossible to achieve progress.

Political or Economic Reform?

Would a political reform that is imposed from above last or provide permanent results for the stability of the people? Or should priority be given to economic reform? This is a question that the elite in the Gulf states continue to debate. Some agree with the United Nations Development Report on development in the Arab world. The report calls for political reforms to be embraced to become the engine that drives all other reforms. While this may be true for some Arab countries, it is different in the Gulf region where oil revenue provides the state with control over all the forces of society. If one adds to that the nature of the structure of the Gulf societies, it is apparent that political reform will remain dependent on top-down measures, as is the case in Qatar and Bahrain even though they have recently adopted modern constitutions. Such countries have dressed their new constitutions with sizeable tribal clothing, which blocked the implementation of a constitutional mechanism that would have allowed such constitutional rights as the transfer of power, accountability and a vote of no confidence in the pillars of the regime. Such privileges were obstructed because of social attitudes.

The same argument applies with regard to the priority of economic reform. The state is the owner of the wealth and it controls the access of individuals and families to the club of the wealthy as well as to the middle class. Moreover, most citizens are employees of the state. This prevents the rise of an independent middle class that may demand a role in the political process, increased transparency, the encouragement of competition and equality before the law.

In light of such political, economic and social structure there is no alternative but to adopt a reform that accommodates two main necessities. The first is for a reformist who can lead society with vision and according to a true reforming agenda. The second is for some sort of external intervention to reinforce this agenda. Without such dual prescription, the Gulf state will remain hesitant, dealing in tactical ways with changes without making effective change on the ground, thus making the political scene more tense and vulnerable.

NOTES

1 Tariq Hiji, 'Hawamish ala Daftar al Islah', *Al-Ahram* of Egypt, 21 February 2004, p. 12.

2 Ali Al Kawari, paper entitled 'Mutatalibat Tahkik Agenda Al Islah Jazri min al Dakhel fi itar Majlis Al Tawon', 25th Development Forum meeting, February 2004.

3 See an expanded study on the subject by Abdurrahman Al Nueimi, Chairman of the National Democratic Action. The paper was presented to the 25th meeting of the Development Roundtable, February 2005.

4 See paper presented by Mohammad Al Rumaihi to the Conference on Democracy and Reform held in Doha, Qatar, 3-4 June 2004 (in Arabic).

5 The writer coins the phrase 'hard-line-reformists', since their programmes do not embrace democracy or human rights in their modern meaning.

6 See paper by Abdulatif Hamad, 'Political and Economic Reforms in the GCC Countries and Their Future Horizons', presented to a roundtable held by the Kuwaiti parliament under the title 'The Region and the Future', 15–17 May 2004.

7 Ibid.

8 Vinan Zanubian, a specialist in oil analysis. Paper entitled 'It is Time for Historical Decisions in the Gulf Area', presented to the Center of Strategic and Futuristic Studies, Kuwait University, November 2002.

9 Speech by the Emir of the State of Qatar, Sheikh Hamad Bin Khalifa Al Thani, during the opening of the Conference on Democracy and Reform in the Arab World, Doha, 3–4 June 2004.

10 Parts of the comments of Saud Al Feisal were published in *Al Hayat*, a paper he had presented to the Janadiria festival in Riyadh, 2004.

11 Jamal Al Bana, paper on Islamic reservations concerning democracy.

12 Ibid.

PART 3

REFORM IN A GEOPOLITICAL AND INTERNATIONAL CONTEXT

11

US Foreign Policy and the Changed Definition of Gulf Security

Steven M. Wright

In the wake of the trauma of the 11 September 2001 terrorist attacks, the United States has entered the new grand strategic era of the War on Terror, where unlike the post-Cold War era of the Clinton years, an identifiable threat exists under the spectre of Islamic terrorism. The response of the Bush administration to this threat draws not only from a conception that it is the lack of freedom and democracy in Islamic societies that has produced such radicalism, but also historically from the founding values of the republic. Such values have slowly evolved from, at first, being seen as a leading example for others to emulate, which had no substantive impact on the foreign policy agenda, towards a crusading moralism that has reached its zenith under the George W. Bush administration.

This historical trend towards an assertive crusade for the promotion of perceived universal values for mankind – stemming from an inherent conception of American exceptionalism – has often conflicted with a *realpolitik* understanding of the national interest. However, in this new era, the root causes of Islamic terrorism have become viewed as being the absence of freedom and democracy in the Middle East. Such an interpretation holds a unique synergy with the crusading moralism force which desires to promote these values for the benefit of all mankind that has existed in US foreign policy arguably since independence was achieved. Both are seeking a comparable objective but for different reasons and in this post-9/11 environment they have merged. This has changed the parameters of the debate on what American foreign policy should be. This chapter will aim to demonstrate the importance of these competitive, but at times complementary, streams of thought on contemporary US foreign policy in the War on Terror. It will aim to place them in a historical context whilst also showing how the Bush Doctrine has shaped US foreign policy in the era of the War on Terror, and will use the Middle East as a case in point. Finally, the chapter will seek to show how these important historical developments are setting the scene for new debates and lessons in US foreign policy.

US Foreign Policy Thinking: The Historical Context

To be sure, the United States has, since the early days of the republic, been heralded as a nation that is motivated by the dictates of enlightened rationalism, its very destiny tied to serving as a beacon of freedom, hope and advancement. In the isolationist years of the nineteenth century, two central themes came to dominate US diplomacy: the values on which the republic were founded were viewed to be universal moral maxims, and also, their global adoption was seen to become yet more certain once the United States had refined them at home and properly conceived a "shining city on the hill" for others to emulate – symbolic of the views articulated by Thomas Jefferson. Such moral maxims did, however, have to operate under observance of the accepted Westphalian doctrines of sovereignty and non-intervention and so did not successfully emerge as integral parts of US foreign policy. With Secretary of State John Quincy Adams famously stating in 1821 that the United States' role was "the well-wisher to the freedom and independence of all" but not a nation that "goes in search of monsters to destroy", the promotion of such moral virtues was largely to be a missionary affair with foreign policy confining itself to *realpolitik* statecraft. However, a fundamental break from this occurred under the fateful presidency of Woodrow Wilson, the legacy of which has had a defining resonance in contemporary US foreign policy.

After a century of feeling inhibited by the Westphalian order, the First World War presented an opportunity for Wilson to remake the international order based on the underlying political moral maxims that captured the essence of enlightened American rationalism. Indeed, Wilson explicitly justified America's involvement as premised on the objective of reordering the international system in its own image. This was a clear departure from the long-standing US foreign policy practice of conducting its diplomacy based on practical rather than ethical considerations. The pursuit of a national interest was thus rejected as selfishness and substituted with the broader doctrine of seeking the advancement of values which could benefit all of mankind; such an objective was thus in clear conflict with long-standing Westphalian notions on a nation's sovereignty over its internal polity.

The Wilsonian view left a defining impression on all subsequent US foreign policy through three interrelated themes. Firstly, it held the progressive view that the natural state of the international system was harmonious cooperation – the Hobbsian world view was largely rejected. Secondly, the use of force to achieve change was similarly abandoned in favour of international law and arbitration. Moreover, such normative values were extended to the sub-state level which upheld that people had an innate right to determine their own future; the principles of self-determination and democracy were therefore seen as the pillars on which a nation should be based.

Finally, and most importantly, Wilson upheld the view that nations that are built on such criteria would not only be stable internally – therefore ending the risk of carnage through civil war – but also that such nations would never opt for external war. Achieving a global adoption of such values was therefore upheld as not only a moral imperative but also a practical means of reducing the risk of war which could embroil the United States. Nevertheless, the driver was firmly seen as for the benefit of all mankind. Wilsonian doctrine therefore challenged the purely amoral *realpolitik* conception of statecraft by taking the founding values of the republic and applying them within a cogent foreign policy package.

The legacy of the Wilsonian world view on US foreign policy cannot be underestimated; it has served to challenge the very essence of an enlightened pragmatic or *realpolitik* conception of foreign policy. Although this thought has been an integral part of US diplomatic thinking since Wilson, the failure of the League of Nations showed that in the absence of a clear external threat to US national security, the political stomach for such a crusading morally grounded diplomacy was limited. It was only with the onset of the Second World War that such Wilsonian values came to be merged with a clear conception of threat to US security. Indeed, America's appetite for entry into the Second World War was largely wanting until Pearl Harbour. This teaches us that in such circumstances where US national security is challenged, a common cause emerges between those who seek to pragmatically safeguard the US and those that shape its objectives on a moral plateau. This affords wider support, but also errs towards John Quincy Adams's caution against the US seeking a crusading foreign policy.

The onset of the Cold War allowed the continuance of this alliance between Wilsonian values and what Walter Russell Mead describes as 'Jacksonians' who are primarily concerned with defending the US from an external enemy. The Soviet Union was an ideal enemy that posed not only a military threat but also an ideological one which allowed this synergy of streams of thought to mutually reinforce each other. Nevertheless, the danger posed to US foreign policy from the Wilsonian school is that within contexts where national security is challenged, a crusading messianic globalism is a genuine risk. Vietnam is a prime example where, within the Cold War strategic context, Wilsonian values, most notably under Johnson, ultimately triumphed over a *realpolitik* assessment of the geopolitical situation and thus propelled the United States into a misguided conflict that was hugely wasteful of life, financial resources and to the standing of the US in the international system. The unfolding failure of the Wilsonian mission in South East Asia ultimately heralded a short-lived return to a sophisticated *realpolitik* diplomacy under Nixon and Kissinger which not only saw them manage the US withdrawal from the conflict, but also achieve other notable successes through a revolutionary triangular diplomacy. Whilst this episode was a golden era for US diplomacy, the ensuing Watergate scandal and ending of the Vietnam conflict once again brought about a revival in Wilsonian forces on foreign policy with *realpolitik* strategy merely dismissed as amoral and too power-centric. Given this, the key lesson of the tragedy of US involvement in Vietnam had not been learned: that a rejection of the pursuit of a national interest in favour of an unselfish and universalistic Wilsonian mission, driven by American exceptionalism, may ultimately lead to costly adventurism – i.e., increased suffering, death and a rejection of US values as being alien rather than universalistic.

Under Ford and Carter, the Wilsonian vigour that had brought about Vietnam began to resurface – this occurred most significantly within Congress and amongst disillusioned left-wing intellectuals. For Congress, a watershed occurred in 1974 when, for the first time, legislation was passed that directly concerned the domestic policy of another state. Here, Congress's concern was the immigration of Jews from the

Soviet Union. Within the framework of the universal human rights agenda which coincided with this, the concept of a Westphalian system was clearly on the decline as the formerly sacred cow of a nation's internal affairs was increasingly seen as fair game. Moreover, this struck a cord with several of the key principles on which the republic was founded and thus provided a second coming for Wilsonians.

Compounding this, a new intellectual movement, neoconservatism, emerged from the controversy of the Vietnam antiwar context and struck a chord with the human rights activism that gained momentum initially under President Ford. As an intellectual movement, neoconservatism provided a synthesis between the universalistic Wilsonian morals and the Jacksonian need to safeguard US national security. In essence, neoconservatism advocated the pursuit of long-term national interest through Wilsonian values, as only by their global adoption could the United States achieve the security it so yearned for. In the Cold War, it bridged both the divide between those who wanted to combat the Soviet military threats and those who wanted to free its people enslaved by a hostile ideology. Neoconservatism advocated the objective of achieving freedom and human rights, as the adoption of such values would not only free an enslaved people, but would also nullify the risks posed to US national security. Democratic states were, at the end of the day, more used to resolving their disputes through international law and arbitration than through war so the global adoption of such values thus provided for US national security. In essence, neoconservatism had given Wilsonianism a new character of both a crusading messianic globalism whilst also serving the selfish national interests of US security.

Under Reagan, this neoconservatism took on a defining role as Reagan adopted the Wilsonian rhetoric of a crusading moralism against an "Evil empire" intent on challenging the very existence of the United States. Traditional *realpolitik* statecraft was thus deemed as an unworkable concept unless guided by this crusading moralism. Amoral *realpolitik* statecraft was relegated from defining the national interest towards helping achieve the crusading Wilsonian belief. A fusion of these historical schools of thought had thus occurred which captures the essence of neoconservatism. But with the ending of the Cold War, the loss of a clear external threat to the United States resulted in the demise of neoconservatism as a guiding ideology that fused a clear moralism with a security-based conception of Cold War grand strategy.

Victory over the Soviet threat saw the post-Cold War strategic environment characterized by a 'New World Order' absent of a clear threat to US national security. For neoconservatism, this translated into the loss of an essential pillar which made it largely redundant in the post-Cold War strategic context. With this onset of American hegemony and the lack of a clear external competitor, a clear-sighted political strategy did not emerge. The Clinton era maintained the Wilsonian theme by engaging in several humanitarian causes, but given the lack of a political strategy, its diplomacy was ad hoc and not geared towards a clear conception of the national interest along *realpolitik* lines. The foreign policy of the United States thus retained its Wilsonianism but lost the crusading zest that characterized previous eras. With the absence of a clear political strategy, foreign policy during the Clinton era largely gave way to a promotion of global economic integration as the cornerstone of day-to-day US diplomacy. This largely accounts for the unparalleled economic success that the 1990s bore for America. Nevertheless, the promotion of economic globalism is not a satisfactory substitute for a coherent political strategy as it lends itself to an ad hoc and, crucially, a reactive foreign policy that is absent of any recognition of the national interest and the statecraft involved in preventing geopolitical threats from emerging.

The trauma caused by the 11 September 2001 terrorist attacks fundamentally changed this post-Cold War conception of the 'New World Order'. The devastation and shock caused by a small number of Islamic fundamentalists to the US homeland was reminiscent of the Japanese attack on Pearl Harbour. The threat posed by Islamic extremism was viewed as akin to communism during the Cold War and thus the new grand strategic era of the War on Terror had begun.

The Context of the War on Terror

With the Bush administration comprising a number of key decision-makers who had clear neoconservative idiosyncrasies, the establishment of a comparable foreign policy was understandable; however, extremist political Islam constituted a threat unlike communism and thus produced a more nuanced Reaganite political strategy. Unlike the Cold War where the Soviet Union posed a clear ideological and military threat, with radical political Islam it was recognized to be an unintended offshoot of the social and political structure within autocratic Middle

Eastern nations. Specifically, the lack of fundamental freedoms were seen as resulting in Islam serving as the sole political mobilizing agent which, although Muslim politics has many faces, results in extremism directed internationally against the United States and the West in general. So unlike the communist threat, which was clearly state-centric, radical political Islam was simply viewed as an unintended by-product of the state structure having failed to adopt the universalistic pillars that captured the essence of the American republic: freedom of speech, equity and self-determination. Moreover, the failure of Middle Eastern countries in adopting such values was recognized as being initially a product of colonialism and later a result of the United States seeking maintenance of the status quo in order to ensure a secure flow of hydrocarbon resources from the region.

With the threat being an unintended by-product of the state structure, the manner in which neoconservatism approached this quagmire differed in important ways to the Cold War Reaganite strategy. Specifically, it meant that whilst at a state level the United States could have friendly relations with a given Middle East regime, the problem at hand was their political structure and practices rather than the rulers themselves – the strategic objective for the neoconservatives was therefore to elicit political change through them adopting some of the universalistic standards on which the American republic was based. Whilst a risk of this was that a hostile power could gain control over the existing friendly regime, it would, nonetheless, serve US strategic interests providing it upheld the key values that were deemed as an antidote to political extremism.

In a historical context, this translated to the George W. Bush administration adopting a nuanced Reaganite approach, or indeed neo-Reaganite strategy, as the purpose of military force was relegated in importance: only in circumstances where a state was an overt supporter of terrorism would a military, or Jacksonian, state-centric approach apply, otherwise the strategic focus was on achieving Wilsonian ends at a sub-state level. That is not to say that Bush's approach discounted *realpolitik* statecraft; as with Reagan, Bush saw such calculations as a tactical means of fulfilling the crusading Wilsonian strategic objective. So, therefore, the character of the threat had resulted in the adoption of a more nuanced approach when compared with Reagan's Cold War strategy: in essence an approach with a much greater Wilsonian character. Crucially, with the prognosis of the Islamic terrorist threat being a result of Muslim nations having largely failed to adopt universalistic values on which the American republic was seen to be based, the scope for variance in US foreign policy, whilst geared towards this strategic endgame, was limited to how the US should effect change within Muslim nations. Nonetheless, the US conception of threat and its strategy towards countering it became firmly premised on an abandonment of the Westphalian concept of sovereignty.

With the approach of the Bush administration in the War on Terror being firmly grounded in a global messianic Wilsonianism, historical observations can be made on the risks pertaining thereof. As the tragedy of Vietnam has shown, a preponderance of Wilsonian values, as a determinist force in foreign policy, risks adventurism and miscalculation in the application of military power. The dilemma facing US foreign policy is whether a sophisticated *realpolitik* strategy, which can convincingly deal effectively with the threats posed by Islamic extremism, can be developed which will determine the national interest over a currently preponderant and vigorous Wilsonianism.

The Bush Doctrine and the Middle East

The response of George W. Bush's administration to the attacks can be likened to a fundamentally new foreign policy doctrine. The Bush Doctrine was originally outlined in the National Security Strategy of September 2002, and has the following identifiable pillars:[1]

1. Preventing hostile states from acquiring unconventional weapons.
2. Promoting democracy and freedom on a global basis.
3. Maintaining the pre-eminence of the United States in the international system.

Although it has three pillars, this chapter will only concern itself with the first two as these are of direct relevance to the Middle East. Nevertheless, the nature of the Bush Doctrine can be described as ambitious, optimistic and long-sighted. Clear comparisons can be drawn with Wilson's vision in the aftermath of the First World War but, for the Bush administration, it is seen not only in moral terms, but, as outlined above, also through a clear definition of what the national security threats to the

United States are. The nature of its pillars reflect this as they include both immediate security concerns from states intent on producing unconventional weapons, to the more long-term goal of combating the root causes of extremist political Islam and politically motivated extremism with global reach in general. Given this, a more detailed analysis of its nature is warranted, which will begin with an analysis of the more immediate concerns of the doctrine, whilst the subsequent sections will look at its more long-term aspects.

The Preventative Use of Force

The first pillar of the Bush Doctrine emerged as a direct response to the realization that if terrorists armed with box cutters could use aeroplanes as a weapon to cause mass casualties, what would the scenario be if an unconventional weapon was used?

The response to this possible scenario saw the Bush Doctrine draw a linkage between terrorism and hostile states with the intent to produce unconventional weapons. It also rejected, in no uncertain terms, Kenneth Waltz's argument that proliferation can be equated with international stability.[2] This aspect of the Bush Doctrine was controversial as it called on such threats to be dealt with preventatively. This linkage went beyond the separate issues of states harbouring and supporting terrorist groups, which the Afghanistan campaign underscored.

Vice President Cheney argued that the casualties posed by terrorist groups actually using unconventional weapons would, if used to their greatest potential, have dwarfed those of 11 September 2001. Given the difficulties in manufacturing and deploying such weapons, Cheney is correct that the most logical means for terrorists acquiring such weapons would ultimately stem from 'rogue state' producers.[3] Indeed, this point was underlined by Bush:

> The gravest danger our Nation faces lies at the crossroads of radicalism and technology. Our enemies have openly declared that they are seeking weapons of mass destruction, and evidence indicates that they are doing so with determination. The United States will not allow these efforts to succeed. . . . [H]istory will judge harshly those who saw this coming danger but failed to act. In the new world we have entered, the only path to peace and security is the path of action.[4]

The significance of this pillar in the overall strategy is that it vastly broadened the target list from "terrorist organizations of global reach" to include "any terrorist or state sponsor of terrorism which attempts to gain or use weapons of mass destruction (WMD) or their precursors".[5] The scope was thus widened to include countries *defined by the United States* as hostile, which were viewed as procuring, or *attempting to procure*, unconventional weapons. This was in spite of whether they were legally entitled to produce such weapons under international law. The reason why this potential form of terrorism was placed onto the national security agenda is not only attributable to the logical projection in the nature of terrorist attacks, but also to the anthrax attacks which took place in the immediate aftermath of the 9/11 terrorist attacks. Although it is unclear what impact the anthrax attacks had on the national security agenda, it seems justifiable to infer that they were a factor which installed a level of fear within the domestic electorate of a mass casualty terrorist attack using such weapons.

The specifics of this strategy mean that in cases where hostile states are viewed as having *intention* or *actually* producing unconventional weapons, the United States would prevent their acquisition by resorting to anticipatory self-defence if a diplomatic/peaceful resolution in accordance with US zero sum demands proved elusive. In other words, the United States would ultimately resort to the use of force if a state did not comply with US non-negotiable demands. This is based on the belief that such weapons could be used directly or asymmetrically against the United States, and that the scale of the threat justifies the subjugation of state sovereignty. Bush actually unveiled this change in military strategy at the West Point Military Academy in June 2002 when he stated that "our security will require all Americans to be forward-looking and resolute, to be ready for pre-emptive action when necessary to defend our liberty and to defend our lives".[6]

In terms of the historical use of pre-emptive action, the National Security Strategy maintained that:

> The United States has long maintained the option of pre-emptive actions to counter a sufficient threat to our national security. The greater the threat, the greater is the risk of inaction – and the more compelling the case for taking anticipatory action to defend ourselves, even if uncertainty remains as to the time and place of the enemy's attack. To forestall or prevent such hostile acts by our adversaries, the United States will, if necessary, act preemptively.[7]

Bush's proposal, however, went beyond the traditional definition of *pre-emptive* war and encompassed the doctrine of *preventative* war.[8] It is important to recognize that *pre-emptive* warfare is a response in the face of an *imminent* attack whilst a *preventative* war is carried out long before a potential threat materializes.

The use of pre-emptive force was not a new concept by any means in the history of US foreign policy. Indeed, the Kennedy administration had acted pre-emptively in its establishment of a naval quarantine around Cuba during the missile crisis. However, Robert Kennedy reminds us that the naval quarantine of Cuba was premised on the call to action from the Organization of American States, and the administration purposely refrained from referring to it as pre-emptive self-defence.[9] Nevertheless, a policy of pre-emptive action had never been a *formally declared policy* of the United States, *despite* its actual usage. The adoption of the *preventative* war doctrine was, however, very much a new concept in US foreign policy.

The case of the invasion of Iraq in March 2003 underlined the application of this doctrine: Iraq was highlighted as having such weapons in its possession, and also intent on further production whilst being unwilling to comply with the demands of the international community in a peaceful manner, thus providing a casus belli. The key issue to understand about this pillar is, however, that the preventative use of force is not seen as applicable in every circumstance. The Bush Doctrine only saw this as applicable in cases where hostile states remain committed to acquiring unconventional weapons once diplomacy to reverse this situation had been tried and failed. But the significance of this pillar is that it reduces US diplomacy to a zero-sum game where compromise is not possible on this issue. Therefore, under its rubric, the preventative use of force would occur once diplomacy, leading to a *full* compliance with US demands, had been seen to have been tried and failed, which indicates that the notion of diplomacy in such circumstances is reduced to an anachronism.

Nonetheless, the Bush administration's adoption of the concept of the preventative use of force, premised on *unilateralism if necessary*, sets a precedent for states defining their security interests and applying unilateral measures to achieve them. But the willingness of the Bush administration to resort to unilateralism has some vintage in US foreign policy, particularly in Republican circles. Nevertheless, it is a course of action that holds the risk of setting a precedent in the international system. Henry Kissinger succinctly comments that:

> As the most powerful nation in the world, the United States has a special unilateral capacity to implement its convictions. But it also has a special obligation to justify its actions by principles that transcend the assertions of preponderant power. It cannot be in either the American national interest or the world's interest to develop principles that grant every nation an unfettered right of preemption against its own definitions of threats to its security.[10]

Although the administration did caution other nations from using pre-emption as a pretext for aggressive military action, the ambiguity of what exactly warranted such state practice, if it is taken as a precedent for international action, underscores that the Westphalian order is truly in systemic crisis.

A key implication of this pillar of the Bush Doctrine in the Middle Eastern geopolitical environment following the Iraq invasion specifically concerns Iran and its nuclear programme. A sober reading of the Bush Doctrine shows that Iran faces the risk of the application of the preventative use of force if it fails to comply with US zero-sum demands on its nuclear programme. That is not to say that such military action would be inevitable, but rather it is a risk if a diplomatic resolution fails to reach certain benchmarks deemed acceptable to the Bush administration by the time a military decision needs to be made, which is in turn contingent on the progress the Iranians make.

Democratic Promotion

The second key pillar is the adoption of the neoconservative position on the promotion of democracy and freedom. As discussed above, the desire to defend and spread such values draws from a historical vintage in US foreign policy which was most clearly articulated by Wilson and Jefferson. In contrast to previous administrations which saw its promotion as desirable, the Bush Doctrine classified the promotion of self-determination and other universalistic values which draw from a perception of American exceptionalism as national security *requirements*.

The key reason why the Bush Doctrine equates democratic promotion with national security is on account of the interpretation that the absence of democracy and freedom actually spawns extremism under the guise of terrorism. Therefore, in the post-9/11 context, the root cause of the terrorist attacks was viewed as the lack of legitimate representative institutions within the Middle East and elsewhere, which resulted in religious fanaticism being the only outlet for dissent.[11] The Bush administration thus embraced the intellectual position on radical political Islam that it is the very lack of democracy and freedom in given countries that results in the rise of political extremism and terrorist action.[12]

In addition to democratization actually combating the root causes of Islamic terrorism with global reach, the Bush administration also saw it as desirable on the grounds that representative democracies are more likely to engage in peaceful relations and thus democratization would provide stability and security for the international system. Indeed, this is a thoroughly Wilsonian ideal that believes like-minded democracies will opt to resolve difference through legal means and diplomacy. Therefore, when this is translated to the Middle East, a complete reordering of the political environment is desired in order to provide for regional stability in the long term. This is despite the transformation requiring a geopolitical overhaul which would create insecurity through socio-political changes. Indeed, this is in direct contrast to the Clinton administration's approach.

The nature of this pillar allows the charge that it is exceptionally optimistic and ambitious. Indeed, it goes well beyond the revolutionary vision Wilson articulated in the aftermath of the First World War. But for Bush, the 9/11 attacks marked an opportunity to restructure the world order. Bush remarked that "history has called us into action, and we are not going to miss that opportunity to make the world more peaceful and more free".[13]

With regard to the invasion of Iraq in March 2003, it was viewed by Bush as serving dual purposes commensurate with this pillar: firstly, it allowed the removal of Saddam Hussein's dictatorship and the installation of democratic polity; and secondly, a democratizing Iraq was viewed as fostering pressures for democratic reform within neighbouring authoritarian states within the region.[14] In some respects this is akin to the Cold War Domino Theory. Bush remarked in the aftermath of the Iraq invasion that "I believe that a free Iraq can be an example of reform and progress to all the Middle East."[15] Indeed, with Iraq serving as a beacon for democracy, the Bush administration believed that it would foster pressure within the civil society of neighbouring states for democratic reforms to be implemented.[16] This highlights that this pillar fostered a wider geostrategic agenda for the Middle East which is in direct contrast to the Clinton era.

Therefore, the promotion of social and political change towards the adoption of the very values, deemed universal, on which the American republic was based, now serves the mantle of a foreign policy fused with the formerly distinct pillars of crusading morality and a *realpolitik* national interest. The evolution of this tension between selfish conceptions of the national interest and universalistic moralism had previously never been harmoniously merged, but given the nature of threat in the War on Terror, this has now successfully been accomplished by the Bush administration. For the Middle East, it is therefore possible to understand that the long-standing US definition of Persian Gulf security has now been redefined from maintenance of the status quo towards political reform. Whilst such change risks instability and insecurity in the flow of hydrocarbon resources, this is now seen by the US as a necessary, but temporary evil, until the long-term goal of a Middle East based on an American conception of universalistic norms is realized. Achieving political change has therefore become the cornerstone of US foreign policy towards the region.

Concluding Observations

When taking a long-term view on US foreign policy, it is clear that the very principles, which are deemed to be universal, on which the republic was founded have gradually evolved to play a more assertive role in US diplomacy. Whilst originally such values were subordinated by a clear upholding of Westphalian notions of sovereignty, the evidence indicates that this principle began to break down for the United States during Wilson's presidency. Whilst America temporarily retreated back to isolationist zeal in the interwar period, what can be deduced is that there has been an inherent tension in US diplomatic history between a crusading universal moralism and a *realpolitik* pursuit of the national interest – both struggling to dominate the conduct of foreign policy. Nevertheless, in times of national threat a synergy develops between the two and serves a mutually reinforcing role but, however, for different reasons.

The War on Terror poses a new stage in this evolutionary process –

one that does not allow for a clear historical parallel to be drawn. Unlike the Cold War era where Wilsonians and *realpolitik* strategists saw a common enemy – the latter military and the former moral – in the War on Terror, the nature of the threat, and how to counter it, differs in a key respect. The root causes of Islamic terrorism are seen to be the very absence of free speech, democracy and equality which is seen to be a product of colonialism and US interests in maintenance of the status quo for a secure flow of hydrocarbon resources. Therefore, the prognosis of countering Islamic terrorism and thus securing US national security has a synergy with the crusading moralism ethic. So whilst Wilsonians may focus more on the moral obligation to promote such values, the key point is that even the more selfish Jacksonians, who seek to ensure US national security, see the lack of such values being at the root of the problem. The final analysis is that US foreign policy has entered into a fundamentally new era where its main strands of thought are wholly mutually reinforcing.

The conclusions that may be drawn from this are that the current agenda of promoting such values towards the Islamic world is likely to be a long-lasting strategy. Indeed, this will crosscut both political parties in the US. Saying that, the unfolding carnage induced by the war in Iraq and the failure to properly resolve the key security question of Iran's nuclear programme is likely to lead to more insecurity in the region for the medium term: the lack of security is a fundamental factor that will hinder the adoption of the values the US seeks. Indeed, the universal moralism in American foreign policy in the Middle East is likely to be increasingly equated with causing insecurity and thus such values may be rejected by many as alien and leading to suffering rather than seen as being universalistic by the region's people.

The key challenge for US diplomacy towards the Islamic world is to recognize that there are two main streams of thought in the currently dominant neoconservative school, both moving towards the same endgame but for differential reasons: a global moralism and a *realpolitik* assessment of the national interest. Here it needs to be recognized that this new strategic context is shaping two key debates on US foreign policy. The first point of debate is: should the United States uphold a crusading moralism as a determining force in its foreign policy? What relationship should moral values have in foreign policy to a *realpolitik* concept of the national interest?

For this debate, an initial observation from this chapter is that US diplomacy has not learnt the historical lesson that an *unchecked* global moralism, as a determining factor in its foreign policy, is both an unwelcome and counterproductive force. Although US administrations do have genuine benevolent intentions premised on America's own experience with enlightened rationalism, an unhindered and crusading moralism leads to perceptions of imperialism and orientalism, and makes the prospect of military force being used more likely as it justifies action politically on a moral plateau. So whilst it may be morally justified, its use as a guiding force in foreign policy runs counter not only to its own theoretical objectives, but in the War on Terror its crusading nature also makes, on a practical level, such factors less likely to be adopted and thus serves to undermine US national interests in countering terrorism for the long term.

The second main debate for US foreign policy in the War on Terror is: how can political changes in Islamic countries most effectively be promoted in order to counter the root causes of Islamic terrorism? Whilst this proposition rests on the basis that the political structure is the key problem, the importance of this question for US foreign policy is that it will help foster a more sophisticated *realpolitik* approach in US diplomacy towards the Middle East in order for US national security interests to be satisfied. Therefore it is crucial to develop an understanding of the true nature of Middle Eastern politics, what impact US policy is having, and how best change can be promoted in a productive manner, as this will be instrumental in countering the radicalism that has been inadvertently spawned historically from Western policies towards the Middle East.

NOTES

1   United States, 'The National Security Strategy of the United States of America', (Washington, D.C.: GPO, 2002), 35pp.

2   Kenneth N. Waltz, *The Spread of Nuclear Weapons: More May Be Better*, Adelphi Papers, No. 171 (London: International Institute for Strategic Studies, 1981) pp. 1–32; United States, *National Security Strategy to Combat Weapons of Mass Destruction* (Washington, D.C.: GPO, 2002); and also see United States, 'National Strategy for Combating Terrorism' (Washington, D.C.: GPO, 2003).

3   Paul R. Pillar, *Terrorism and US Foreign Policy* (Washington, D.C.: Brookings Institution Press, 2001), p. 164; David A. Kay, 'Wmd Terrorism: Hype or

Reality', in James M. Smith and William C. Thomas (eds.), *The Terrorism Threat and US Governmental Response: Operational and Organisational Factors* (Colorado: USAF Institute for National Security Studies, 2001), pp. 69–78.

4 George W. Bush, 'The President's State of the Union Address' (Washington, D.C.: GPO, 29 Jan. 2002), 20pp.

5 United States, 'The National Security Strategy of the United States of America' (Washington, D.C.: GPO, 2002), 35pp.

6 George W. Bush, 'West Point Commencement Speech', in Gideon Rose (ed.), *America and the World: Debating the New Shape of International Politics* (New York: Council on Foreign Relations, 2002), p. 367.

7 United States, 'The National Security Strategy of the United States of America'.

8 Walter B. Slocombe, 'Force, Pre-Emption and Legitimacy', *Survival*, Vol. 45, No. 1 (2003), pp. 123–128.

9 Robert F. Kennedy, *Thirteen Days: A Memoir of the Cuban Missile Crisis* (Norwalk, Connecticut: Easton Press, 1991), pp. 61–103; and John L. Gaddis, *Surprise, Security, and the American Experience* (Cambridge, MA: Harvard University Press, 2004) pp. 38–56.

10 Henry Kissinger, 'Consult and control: bywords for battling the new enemy', *Washington Post*, 16 September 2002, A19.

11 Fouad Ajami, *The Dream Palace of the Arabs: A Generation's Odyssey*, 1st edn (New York: Pantheon Books, 1998), pp. 133–158; and Bernard Lewis, *What Went Wrong?* (London: Phoenix, 2002) pp. 168–178; see also United Nations Development Programme, *The Arab Human Development Report 2004: Towards Freedom in the Arab World* (New York: United Nations Development Programme, Regional Bureau for Arab States, 2004).

12 Phillip H. Gordon, 'Bush's Middle East Vision', *Survival*, Vol. 45, No. 1 (2003), pp. 155–163.

13 George W. Bush, 'President, Vice President Discuss the Middle East', *Remarks by the President and the Vice President Upon Conclusion of Breakfast* (Washington, D.C.: GPO, 2002).

14 Gordon, 'Bush's Middle East Vision', pp. 155–163.

15 George W. Bush, 'President Discusses the Economy with Small Business Owners', *Remarks by the President in the Rose Garden* (Washington, D.C.: GPO, 2003); see also Colin Powell, 'The US–Middle East Partnership Initiative: Building Hope for the Years Ahead', *Remarks at the Heritage Foundation* (Washington, D.C.: GPO, 2002).

16 Stephen Cook, 'The Right Way to Promote Arab Reform', *Foreign Affairs*, Vol. 84, No. 2 (2005), pp. 92–96; and Marina Ottaway, et al., 'Democratic Mirage in the Middle East', in Thomas Carothers (ed.), *Critical Mission: Essays on Democracy Promotion* (Washington, D.C.: Brookings Institution Press, 2002), pp. 229–236.

12

Synergies in Reform: Case Studies of Saudi Arabia and Iran

Mahjoob Zweiri

"Everywhere in the Arab world, people are talking about reform . . . the wind is behind those who advocate free market, modern, Western-style reform."
Fareed Zakaria,
31 May 2004.

Political reform is an issue that has preoccupied political elites and intellectuals in the Middle East for over three centuries. Although reform has been to a large extent influenced by pressure from abroad, it is nevertheless difficult to deny the influence of certain internal factors too. This remains the case across the whole of the Middle East, regardless of whether the nature of the state in question is secular or religious. However, there is no doubt that discussing reform in secular environments is easier than discussing the same issue in religious atmospheres, simply because in the latter reformists face opposition from a power that can use God's decrees to prevent any kind of criticism.

This chapter aims to analyse the reasons for reform in both Saudi Arabia and Iran, and to explain whether reform in these countries was prompted from above or from below. The reason for choosing these two countries is that both consider themselves to be religious states and to some extent theocracies. Saudi Arabia uses the Sunni interpretation of Islam, while Iran on the other hand is based on the Shia interpretation. In both countries the *ulama* (religious scholars) have an unchallenged influence in the political life of the state, and in both countries it is accepted that the state should implement an Islamic way of life, the official understanding of which the public has no choice but to follow.

There are three main approaches to reform in Saudi Arabia and Iran:

1. The modernization approach, supported by many Arab regimes. This calls for increasing political participation, opening the door to more freedoms. However, the political elite keep their right to interfere as soon as they see new changes affecting their interests.
2. The secularization approach, aimed at establishing a secular state. This approach is popular among the reformist elite and secular intellectuals who believe that the traditional, old-fashioned state, which mixes religion with politics, is not qualified to govern in the modern world.
3. The 'Islamic' approach, which calls for limited reform and free elections. This strategy aims to tackle authoritarian regimes in a peaceful way. It is supported by Islamic movements such as the Muslim Brotherhood, as well as Saudi intellectuals seeking reform compliant with Islamic beliefs.[1]

It is very difficult to categorize Iran and Saudi Arabia using only one of these approaches. The historical backgrounds, the nature of state, the nature of the political elite and the many challenges which face every regime have affected the whole process of reform. There is a similarity in that both regimes and the reform elite believe reform is a necessity. However, each has their own understanding of what this process should achieve.

The Nature of Reform in Saudi Arabia and Iran

There are four main factors that help to explain the need for reform in both countries:

1. The nature of the state: the traditional political system.
2. Economic problems: unemployment, inflation, corruption, etc.
3. The technology revolution: the internet, satellite television, etc.
4. External pressures: the Second Gulf War, 9/11 and the so-called 'War on Terror'.

These factors have affected the mode of reform regardless of the starting date of reform.

The history of reform in Iran and Saudi Arabia goes back to the 1990s. In Saudi Arabia, like in other Gulf states, the revolution in Iran and its consequences led to several waves of reform in response to mass uprisings. Questions about the Saudi monarchy, dividing wealth and opening the political landscape were the main issues discussed by intellectuals, many of whom were later forced to leave the country or go to prison.[2] In spring 1991, a letter was signed by 435 religious scholars, judges and university professors asking for 12 political reforms, including a "consultative assembly, fair judiciary, redistribution of wealth, and an end to corruption".[3] The following year, a new *muthkarat al-nasiheh* (memorandum of advice) was signed by 107 religious scholars and issued to King Fahd, who refused to receive the document.[4] These two movements within Saudi society affirmed that the government could no longer ignore the demands of those calling for reform; the Saudi government had to respond quickly to calm the situation. The pressure for reform from Sunni Islamists and Shia opposition forced the Saudi government to launch a national dialogue on reform and announce its intention to hold the Kingdom's first nationwide municipal elections, in which half of the members of municipal councils would be elected.[5]

Previously, the government in Saudi Arabia had not accepted any criticism because of the nature of the state, which ruled based on *shariah* law. This meant that any attempt to reform might be challenged by the *ulama*, who believed that reform meant limiting the role of religion and might lead to secularization of the society.

The pressure which followed the First Gulf War in 1991 and Saudi Arabia's acceptance of US troops remaining in East Saudi Arabia was a first step towards encouraging the reformist elite to criticize the political situation, and mount a direct attack on the authoritarian monarchy. However, there was no real support from the international community for the reform attempts between 1991 and 2001, particularly from the United States. The reason for this was that the United States' involvement in the region was one of the factors causing problems for the regime, therefore the US government could not criticize the political situation without putting further pressure on the Saudi government.

The real juncture occurred post-9/11. American and Western pressure on the Saudi government increased and the government was asked to move on and respond positively to the waves of reform. The United States asked in particular that the educational system be reviewed, because many in the United States believed that the events of 9/11 were a result of the Saudi educational system, albeit indirectly.

Reformist elites used this opportunity to double the pressure on the government in Riyadh.

Criticizing the political situation involves criticizing the domination of the political process by the Saudi ruling family, the educational system, the division of oil wealth, human rights and the issue of women in Saudi Arabia. Each one of these issues has its own supporters. External players apply pressure, for instance, on education to be reformed as part of the War on Terror, and by asking for the liberalization of society, which is refused by the Saudi government and some traditional Saudis. Internal players, such as the Saudi reformists, ask for the opening up of the political atmosphere, more rights to be given to women (such as having an independent ID and driving licence), a fairer share in the country's wealth and the end of the use of religion as justification for the authoritarian regime.

As a consequence of increasing pressure from below, King (Crown Prince at that time) Abdullah Ibn Abdul Aziz announced in January 2003 that "internal reforms are just a matter of time"[6] and Prince Sultan Bin Abdul Aziz also confirmed "that political reform in Saudi Arabia is under study".[7] A petition entitled 'the vision' was submitted by Saudi intellectuals asking that an internal dialogue begin, in order to discuss the best means for internal reforms. The petition also focused on "developing the constitution of the ruling system towards a constitutional reform . . . the need to make a distinction between authorities and to establish a legislative authority, the Consultative Council (*Majlis al-Shura*)"[8] directly elected by the people and having monitoring authority over other authorities. It also called for public and basic rights of citizens to be guaranteed and for the situation of women in society to be dealt with so that they are given their due rights.[9]

However, the Saudi government maintains that Saudi society is not yet ready for fundamental changes to be made. In their view, the process needs more time, and reform needs to happen gradually.[10] The reform movement responds to this by arguing that they do not need 'big brother' to show them what is good and bad for them. The reformists want to be able to vote for an elected parliament with MPs who define their interests, this idea being understood as a step towards liberalizing or secularizing a country which currently gains its legitimacy from Islam and the Wahhabi interpretation of Islam. Those that believe in the Islamic version of the legitimacy in Saudi Arabia have started an anti-reform campaign supported by the *ulama* and traditional scholars. They have also attempted to put more pressure on the government to think seriously about the consequences of the reform process. There is no doubt that paying attention to the view of the *ulama* has helped the government to delay or reduce the speed of reform in the country.

The situation in Iran is not dissimilar. The Islamic Republic of Iran (IRI) as a revolutionary state is nearly 30 years old, and started its reform process in 1997 after Khatami was elected as the fourth President of the IRI. At that time, Iran was facing a situation which gave the Iranian political elite no option but to accept whoever had been elected by the people. More than 22 million of the Iranian public voted for Mohammad Khatami, a member of the clergy who was trying to create a link between what the people wanted and what the regime wanted. Aspects such as civil society, Islamic democracy, social freedoms and women's rights became a part of the daily debates of the Iranian people.

The origins of this reform can be traced back to the April 1992 parliamentary elections. This event established two new divisions within the revolutionary forces. The first group was 'the traditional conservatives', who had dominated politics in Iran since the revolution. The second group was the so-called 'Islamic left'. The latter emerged as a result of the political stability enjoyed by Iran following the end of war with Iraq. The priorities within Iranian society had changed: there was more focus on economic reconstruction, opening the doors to increased cooperation with other states, and most importantly changing the image of Iran. However, the Guardians Council prevented Islamic left candidates such as Behzad Nabavi and Ali Akbar Mohtashmipour[11] from running in the elections.

The reform process in Iran came to depend on three main forces:

- Firstly, individuals; Said Hajarian was a member of the reformist elite who worked for the Centre for Strategic Studies. This was linked with the Ministry of Foreign Affairs and a sub-committee of the Supreme National Security Council. Serving in such an organization helped Hajarian to attract some former officials of the security-intelligence apparatus who could push the reform movement ahead, such as Akabar Ganji,[12] Mohsen Armin,[13] Abbas Abdi,[14] Hamid-Reza Jalaipor,[15] Mohammaed Moussavi-Khoeiniha,[16] Ebrahim Asghar-Zadeh[17] and Mohsen Sazegaran.[18] Hajarian later paid the price for his views on reform after an assassination attempt left him disabled.

- Secondly, political groups; in addition to the thinkers mentioned above there were four main institutions: Sazeman Mojahedine Enghelabe Eslami (Organization of the Mojahedin of the Islamic Revolution – OMIR), the Majma'a Rohaneeyoon Mobarez (Forum of Militant Clergy – FMC), the Daftare Tahkeem Vahdat (Office for Fostering Unity – OFU)[19] and the Nehzat-e Azadi-e Iran (Freedom Movement of Iran – FMI).
- Thirdly, publications; two magazines, *Iran Farda* and *Kian*, reflected the opinions of the Islamic left. *Iran Farda* reflected the viewpoints of the FMI, while *Kian* was led by Mashallah Shamolvaezin.[20] Both magazines became an intellectual coordinating point for former senior officials and senior ex-Iranian Revolutionary Guard Corps personnel.

These three forces worked simultaneously to demand more changes within the political system, and at the same time create change which affected people's lives. It was clear that these changes would not be implemented unless there was a partnership between Khatami as President and the reform elite. This partnership involved each side playing a part in supporting the other side. The elite started to establish newspapers, strengthen the student movement, and unify all fronts to support the President in his suggested policies. On the other side, the President tried to put forward new legislation regarding the freedom of publishing, forming political parties, etc.

I believe that there are two key factors crucial to a real understanding of the reform movement in Iran. Firstly, the role of the elite and their initiatives, secondly the suggested new legislations concerning the freedom to publish new newspapers, limit the role of government in the publishing process, and produce movies and TV programmes, etc. The reformist elite believed that they were taking the initiative, and the growing number of newspapers (for example *Jameh*, *Rah-e No*, *Jameh Salem*, *Asr-e Ma* and *Tous*) and journalists was evidence of their move towards real reform. For his part, President Khatami was expected to counter the increasing pressure from the conservative front.

Khatami thus came to represent the increasing demands and hopes for freedom sought by Iranian society. He aimed to promote the role of law, liberalization and the democratic face of Iran. He believed that the only way to tackle the pressure from inside and outside was to open up

Iran's political landscape. In 1999, three months after students from Tehran were attacked by the police and *Basij* (popular military), and three students were killed, Khatami delivered a speech on what is called 'students day'. Here he defended his understanding of reform:

- that the system should be reformed from within, preserving the "Islamic" as well as the "Republic" basis of the government;
- that there should be a strategy of "tolerance" and "dialogue";
- that the achievements of the reform movement in creating a "criticizable" and "responsible" government and in reforming the intelligence system into one that worked for the safety of the citizens rather than against it should be recognized.[21]

What Khatami said in his speech was an attempt to respond to those who criticized him, those who wanted him to go 'head to head' with radical reformists and hardline groups[22] within the regime. Khatami blamed the radical groups for creating more problems and obstacles for his reform plan. At that time I was living in Tehran and witnessed the way in which many reformers were attacking Khatami, accusing him of weakness, and asking him to resign in protest. He was accused because he had closed several newspapers, detained and arrested journalists and also persecuted them for their writings.

Reform helped the Iranian regime to re-identify itself to the international community as a modern and democratic society based on the Shia interpretation of Islam. Many Iranian reformists were politicians who had originally taken part in establishing the Islamic Republic of Iran. However, they had now come to realize that the regime needed to show some flexibility in order to tackle new challenges from abroad and also from inside the country. Sadly for the reformists, the election of the neo-conservative president Mahmoud Ahmadinejad in June 2005 marked the end of the reform era. Nevertheless, this does not mean that the discourse of reform has disappeared completely. This can be seen in the flexibility with which Iran has dealt with its nuclear programme, for instance.

The division within Iranian society between reformists and conservatives shows there is a real gap between them. This has led to genuine political conflict, and accusations that the reformists are attempting to liberalize and secularize the society. However, the reformists had been responding to public opinion, as the Iranian people had become unhappy with the way of life in their country and the lack of political and social freedoms. Khatami as a politician was not against liberalization. As he said when speaking to the conservatives, "do not attack liberalization, but criticize it, deal with it as a challenge". Since the election of Ahmadinejad, this discourse is no longer prominent in Iran's politics, which is increasingly dominated by the neo-conservatives.

In both countries, Iran and Saudi Arabia, there are many limitations before reform can take place. Some of the problems connected with changing the nature of the regimes – from being religious to becoming secular – are created by the regimes themselves. Some politicians in both Iran and Saudi Arabia are concerned about the outcome of the reform process; therefore they use any means possible, whether legal or illegal, to prevent reformists relaying their agenda to the public. However, the politicians are prepared to address certain issues of reform in order to reduce the increasing pressure on them. They also insist that these reforms should be made through government channels.

Reform, Religion, and Regimes' Legitimacy in Saudi Arabia and Iran

The debate about the regimes' legitimacy is different in both countries. In Saudi Arabia, there are no specific issues surrounding the legitimacy question. Reformists are calling for reform within the regime and, to some extent, are allowing the regime to lead and become involved more in the reform process. Their aim is not regime change, whatever their own concerns about the regime's credibility for continuing on its path.

Since 1991, the game's rules have changed somewhat. The Saudi government has started to use religious authority to tackle reformists who want to marginalize the role of religion, or secularize Saudi society. This has occurred despite the fact that all the reformists had Islamic notions of some sort or another. This development has led to new calls for regime change, but from within the country. The Movement for Islamic Reform in Arabia (MIRA), which was headed by Dr Saad al-Faqih, who is close ideologically to the Muslim Brotherhood, has presented itself as a reform movement with aims to modernize Saudi society based on Islamic principles. By doing that, MIRA distances itself from being a secular reform movement, and faces down any attempt to undermine its role in Saudi politics. This movement was seen to put more pressure on the Saudi government and worked through its own radio station and later on satellite TV and their website to show the anger prevalent among ordinary people as a result of government limitations, corruption, and accusations that oil revenue has been exploited for personal purposes by members of the Saudi family. The MIRA leader thinks that the Saudi government has started to face a real challenge to its legitimacy since the 1991 Gulf War. The regime's religious legitimacy, which focuses on the Islamic dimension, has been called into question because of cooperation with the United States in the war on Iraq in 1991.[23]

The government in Riyadh did not want such a group to be active. Since London was at the centre of MIRA's activities, the Saudi government increased pressure on the British government to force the movement to stop its activities. The result of this pressure was that the movement was categorized as a terrorist group, which led to the banning of most of its activities in the UK.

In Iran, the reformist elite came from within the regime. The regime's religious legitimacy began to be questioned when the reformist elite realized that opponents of reform were using religious legitimacy – *Velayat-e Faqih* (the highest religious political authority in Iran) – to stop reform. The conservatives' perception of the reform agenda was that it was a step towards secularizing society, and had come as a result of a new wave of writings about the religious state in Iran, the role of Faqih, the source of legitimacy and authority, and the relationship between democracy and the *Velayat-e Faqih*. Since 1979, there has been a great deal of internal debate about the political theory behind Iran's regime. According to the Islamic Republic's constitution, the leader of the country must be *marji' al-taqlid "Faqih"*. Article 5 says,

> During the Occultation of the Wali al-Asr (may God hasten his reappearance), the wilayah and leadership of the Ummah devolve upon the just ('adil] and pious [muttaqi] faqih, who is fully aware of the circumstances of his age; courageous, resourceful, and possessed of administrative ability, he will assume the responsibilities of this office in accordance with Article 107.[24]

Being a Faqih, justice and piety are the essential qualifications for the leader.[25] Because of these qualifications, which include religious aspects, the leader has to have unlimited authority. He also has to monitor the political process in the country. These responsibilities become clear in Article 110 of the Iranian constitution.[26]

The role of *Velayat-e Faqih* was under investigation in the reform era in Iran from 1997–2005. The reason for this was that the wide authority of *Velayat-e Faqih* was seen as the main cause of obstacles to making real change in Iranian society. Not only that, but the role of *Velayat-e Faqih* has also opened the door to the regime becoming authoritarian. The debate, which started in 1997, discussed the extent to which Iran could modernize itself politically, socially and economically under this kind of authority. In other words, the question was: is *Velayat-e Faqih* compatible with the concept of democracy?

In November 1997, just four months after Khatami came to office, Ayatollah Hassan-e Ali Montazeri – Khomeini's successor designate – criticized the use of religious authority by the conservatives to destroy Khatami's attempts at reform. He published a 600-page memoir on his internet site and emphasized that the authorities in Iran have not been well received by the majority of Iranian people.[27] This criticism followed earlier comments he had made in his 1988 book,[28] in which he "put forward a somewhat modified interpretation of the theory of the Mandate of the Jurist that made the Supreme Jurist into an indirectly elected office".[29] Montazeri was aiming to put an end to the contradictions within the Iranian constitution. He believed that it should be clear whether the authority of the supreme leader came from the nation or from God. It also needed to be clear whether the *Velayat-e Faqih* should be supervisory (*nizart-e Faqih*) or be fully involved and have wide authorities.[30] This came as a direct and hard attack on the legitimacy of the regime in Iran. It also opened the door for more criticism, which was followed by Abdolkarim Soroush, Mohsen Kadivar and Hashem Aghagari.

As religion dominates the political atmosphere in both countries, the legitimacy of the two regimes has been directly linked to religion. Therefore, reformists' criticism of the regime is often perceived as criticism of religion itself, which has negative consequences on the reform process in both cases. Reform in both countries has opened the door for issues such as minorities and religious groups. Saudi Arabia and Iran have religious groups who disagree with the official reading of religion. In Iran, the Sunni minority lives among the Shia majority, while the Shia minority lives among the Sunni majority in Saudi Arabia. Minorities have found reform a chance to gain more rights. President Khatami appointed one of his advisers from the Sunni minority to deal with their issues in Iran; however, there are still feelings of discrimination against them. MPs in the Iranian Parliament have asked President Mahmoud Ahmadinejad to appoint some Sunnis as governors and deputy ministers.[31]

Economic challenges are also one of the main reasons behind reform waves in the Middle East. Reformist elites include oil revenue and how the current governments spend it as part of their reform project. The economies in Iran and Saudi Arabia are described as oil economies. Most criticisms in the two countries have focused on two main elements:

1. Oil revenue. There are an increasing number of voices asking for more transparency about oil contracts and the way oil money is spent and invested.
2. Governments have been invited to review their economic strategies and stop depending on oil. This example is clearer in Iran. Khatami's economic reform calls for economy without oil. In Saudi Arabia, the reformist elite accuse the government of corruption and using oil revenues for their own benefit.

There is a belief that oil revenues in Saudi Arabia and Iran have created a political generation who do not consider reform to be a priority. Oil money has been used to corrupt the media, intellectuals and academics. Oil revenue also made it difficult for strong civil society to develop in both countries.[32] Such a belief has led opponents of the two regimes to call for more transparency with regard to the spending of oil revenues.

These concerns were behind Khatami's suggestion for economic reform, which was based on increasing non-oil revenues and reducing the role of oil in the Iranian economy. It was also a strategy to strengthen the reform movement in general. After eight years under Khatami, the Iranian economy has gone back to a situation where more than 70% of its budget depends on oil. Khatami's successor, President Mahmoud Ahmadinejad, has promised to put oil revenue on every Iranian table.

Focusing on the political situation in the two countries led to reform attempts being identified as political reform rather than economic reform. Despite the existing debate about the role of the economy in reform projects in these two countries, there has not so far been any fundamental change in state control over the economies.

In addition, both countries have suffered from the rise of Islamist radicalism; whether it be Wahhabi Islam in Saudi Arabia, or traditional Shia in Iran. These radical movements perceive reform to be a threat. Therefore, they have often been used by the regimes as a way of countering reform. Reform in Iran has been marginalized by the neo-conservatives, who are now dominating politics in Iran after victories in the municipal elections in 2003, the (*Majlis*) parliamentary elections in 2004, and the presidential elections in 2005. The situation in Saudi Arabia looks different. The death of King Fahd, and the appointment of Prince Abdullah as King has reduced the pressure on the Saudi government from groups such as MIRA. It seems that the political activists are prepared to give King Abdullah, who had previously been presented as a moderate and open-minded leader, enough time for his intention to reform to be tested. However, he has to face the role of the *ulama*, who might interfere to stop the movement towards political reform.

Comparison Between Reform in Saudi Arabia and Iran

Saudi Arabia	Iran
The house of Saud leads with unlimited power	The supreme leader leads with unlimited power
The majority of Sunni *ulama* support the government	The majority of Shia *ulama* support the government
There are no signs of civil society institutions	Civil society had started to expand its activities by 1997, but suffering from serious problems making its activities very weak
One election in 70 years	24 elections in 25 years
Economy depends on oil revenues	Economy depends on oil revenues
Outside pressure from the United States and the West to liberalize itself socially and politically to endure	Outside pressure from the United States and the West to liberalize itself socially and politically to be accepted more by the international community

Conclusion

Iran and Saudi Arabia have many social, economic and political similarities. These similarities have led to the two countries being categorized politically as 'conservative states'. Being labelled as a conservative state means that there is more limitation in regards to political and social aspects of life. These limitations will affect, in one way or another, any progress these countries might make.

Moreover, it seems these cultural and social limitations have delayed any serious attempt to bring about reform in both countries.

There is no specific definition of reform in both countries, even among the reformist elite. Simplified reform in elections will lead to new political generations who become part of the old system. Approaches in both countries came as a result of pressure from below, and pressures from outside. Both governments have suggested a minimum of ideas which might diminish these pressures from below and outside. The steps which have been taken so far have led to some change; however, there is no major change in the political culture of society yet. Controlling governments have dominated the political process and the use of religious values has hampered any attempts to reform. Reformers in both countries have not suggested alternatives with regard to the leadership and its authorities. They have also suffered from a shortage of financial resources and lack of access to mass media communication in order to reach people and spread reform manifestos. For reform to take root in Iran and Saudi Arabia, it requires not only the development of a democratic culture and the activation of civil society but also constitutional law that could pave the way for the reformists to act.

NOTES

1 'Saudi Crown Prince: Constitutional Reforms are a Matter of Time', www.arabicnews.com, 2 January 2003. For more information see R. Looney, 'Middle East Reform Initiatives: A Stage-theory Perspective', *International Journal on World Peace*, Vol. 22, No. 1 (March 2005), pp. 13–34.

2 Ali Al-Demaini, Matruk Al-Faleh and Abdullah Al-Hamed were arrested after calling for an independent judiciary and limits on the power of the Saudi monarchy by adopting a constitution, www.arabnews.com, 2 December 2004; http://news.bbc.co.uk, 8 December 2004.

3   G. Okruhlik, 'Networks of Dissent: Islamism and Reform in Saudi Arabia', www.ssrc.org.

4   Ibid.

5   Amy Howthorne, 'Political Reform in the Arab World: A New Ferment?', *Carnegie Papers*, No. 52 (Oct. 2004), p. 7.

6   'Saudi Crown Prince: Constitutional Reforms are a Matter of Time', www.arabicnews.com, 2 January 2003.

7   'Political Reforms are Under Study in Saudi Arabia', www.arabicnews.com, 21 July 2003.

8   This *majlis* consists of 150 members selected by the King, who also has the power to restructure and dissolve it. For more see, 'Arab Political Systems, Baseline Information and Reforms – Saudi Arabia', www.carnegieendowment.org/arabpoliticalsystems.

9   'Saudi Crown Prince: Constitutional Reforms are a Matter of Time', www.arabicnews.com, 2 January 2003.

10   Prince Turki Al Faisal, 'Saudi Arabia Today', a talk at Durham University, 12 Oct. 2004.

11   Former Interior Minister.

12   Former Intelligence officer, Islamic Revolutionary Guard Corps (IRGC).

13   Former commander, IRGC, based in Lebanon.

14   One of the leaders who led the attack on the American Embassy in Tehran in 1979.

15   Former high-ranking IRGC officer.

16   The editor of *Salaam* newspaper, Tehran.

17   Prominent member of the students who attacked the American Embassy in 1979.

18   Former senior commander of IRGC, ground forces.

19   Wilfried Buchta, *Who Rules Iran: The Structure of Power in the Islamic Republic* (Washington: Washington Institute for Near East Policy, 2000), pp. 17–19.

20   He was sent to prison for 30 months for insulting Islamic values.

21   http://freethoughts.org/archives/0006665.php.

22   Ibid.

23   *Middle East Intelligence Bulletin*, Vol. 5, No. 11 (November 2003), www.meib.org.

24   Article 107: After the demise of the eminent *marji' al-taqlid* and great leader of the universal Islamic revolution, and founder of the Islamic Republic of Iran, Ayatullah al-'Uzma Imam Khumayni . . . who was recognized and accepted as *marji'* and Leader by a decisive majority of the people, the task of appointing the Leader shall be vested with the experts elected by the people. The experts will review and consult among themselves concerning all the *fuqaha'* possessing the qualifications specified in Articles 5 and 109. In the event they find one of them better versed in Islamic regulations, the subjects of the *fiqh*, or in political and social issues, or possessing general popularity or special prominence for any of the qualifications mentioned in Article 109, they shall elect him as the Leader. Otherwise, in the absence of such superiority, they shall elect and declare one of them as the Leader. The Leader thus elected by the Assembly of Experts shall assume all the powers of the *wilayat al-amr* and all the responsibilities arising there from. The Leader is equal with the rest of the people of the country in the eyes of law. http://www.salamiran.org/IranInfo/State/Constitution/.

25 Article 109: Following are the essential qualifications and conditions for the Leader: scholarship, as required for performing the functions of mufti in different fields of *fiqh*, justice and piety, as required for the leadership of the Islamic *Ummah*. Right political and social perspicacity, prudence, courage, administrative facilities and adequate capability for leadership. In case of multiplicity of persons fulfilling the above qualifications and conditions, the person possessing the better jurisprudential and political perspicacity will be given preference. http://www.salamiran.org/IranInfo/State/Constitution/.

26 Article 110: Following are the duties and powers of the Leadership: delineation of the general policies of the Islamic Republic of Iran after consultation with the Nation's Exigency Council, supervision over the proper execution of the general policies of the system, issuing decrees for national referenda, assuming supreme command of the armed forces, declaration of war and peace, and the mobilization of the armed forces, appointment, dismissal, and acceptance of resignation of: 1: the *fuqaha*' on the Guardian Council, 2: the supreme judicial authority of the country, 3: the head of the radio and television network of the Islamic Republic of Iran, 4: the chief of the joint staff, 5: the chief commander of the Islamic Revolution Guards Corps, 6: the supreme commanders of the armed forces. In addition to that: resolving differences between the three wings of the armed forces and regulation of their relations, resolving the problems, which cannot be solved by conventional methods, through the Nation's Exigency Council, signing the decree formalizing the election of the President of the Republic by the people. The suitability of candidates for the Presidency of the Republic, with respect to the qualifications specified in the Constitution, must be confirmed before elections take place by the Guardian Council, and, in the case of the first term [of the Presidency], by the Leadership; dismissal of the President of the Republic, with due regard for the interests of the country, after the Supreme Court holds him guilty of the violation of his constitutional duties, or after a vote of the Islamic Consultative Assembly testifying to his incompetence on the basis of Article 89 of the Constitution, and pardoning or reducing the sentences of convicts, within the framework of Islamic criteria, on a recommendation [to that effect] from the Head of judicial power. The Leader may delegate part of his duties and powers to another person.

27 www.shianews.com.

28 *Dirasa fi Vilayat Al-Faqih*, 2 Vols, Qum 1988.

29 Siad Amir Arjomand, 'The Reform Movement and the Debate on Modernity and Tradition in Contemporary Iran', *International Journal of the Middle East*, No. 34, 2002, p. 728.

30 Montazeri's booklet *Hukumat-i mardumi va qanun-i Asasi* (Popular Government and the Constitution) includes his thoughts about supervision of the jurist. See ibid., Christopher de Bellaigue, 'Iran's Last Chance for Reform', *Washington Quarterly*, Autumn 2001, pp. 73–75.

31 www.baztab.com, 27 June 2005.

32 See R. Looney, 'Development Strategies for Saudi Arabia: Escaping the Rentier State Syndrome', *Strategic Insights*, Vol. 3, Issue 3 (March 2004); A. Bishar, 'Reform and the Rentier State', http://weekly.alhram.org.eg; J. Louwa, 'Democracy, and the Rentier State', www.globalengagement.org.

Bibliography

Chapter 1 – Political Reform in the Gulf Monarchies: From Liberalization to Democratization? A Comparative Perspective

Aarts, Paul and Nonneman, Gerd, 'A Triple Nexus: Ideology, Economy, Foreign Policy and the Outlook for the Saudi Polity', in Aarts and Nonneman (eds.), *Saudi Arabia in the Balance: Political Economy, Society, Foreign Affairs* (New York/London: New York University Press/Hurst & Co., 2005).

AFP dispatch, 16 December 2006.

Almond, Gabriel and Verba, Sidney, *The Civic Culture: Political Attitudes and Democracy in Five Nations* (Princeton: Princeton University Press, 1963).

Anderson, Lisa, 'Dynasts and Nationalists: Why Middle Eastern Monarchies Survive', in Joseph Kostiner (ed.), *Middle East Monarchies: The Challenge of Modernity* (Boulder: Lynne Rienner, 2000).

Arab News, 21 December 2006.

——, 16 December 2006.

——, 13–29 April 2005

Arab Reform Bulletin, April 2006, Volume 4, Issue III, at http://www.carnegieendowment.org/publications/index.cfm?fa=view&id=18233. For the original in Arabic see the Brotherhood's website *Ikhwanonline*, at http://www.ikhwanonline. com/Article.asp?ID=19414&SectionID=113.

——, December 2004, Volume 2, Issue 11, at http://www.carnegieendowment.org/publications/index.cfm?fa=view&id=16242.

Arabian Business, 9 October 2006.

——, 16 October 2006.

Ayubi, Nazih, *Political Islam* (London: Routledge, 1988)

——, 'Islam and Democracy', in David Potter et al. (eds.), *Democratization* (Cambridge: Polity Press, 1997).

Baaklini, Abdo; Deneoux, Guilain; and Springborg, Robert, *Legislative Politics in the Arab World: The Resurgence of Democratic Institutions* (Boulder: Lynne Rienner, 1999).

Bahrain Rights report, at http://www.bahrainrights.org/files/albandar.pdf.

Barsalou, Judy, 'Islamists at the Ballot Box', USIP Special Report 144, July 2005.

Brumberg, Daniel, 'The Trap of Liberalized Autocracy', in Larry Diamond et al. (eds.), *Islam and Democracy in the Middle East* (Baltimore: Johns Hopkins University Press, 2003).

——, 'Liberalization versus Democracy: Understanding Arab Political Reform' (Washington: Carnegie Endowment, May 2003 [Working Papers, Middle East Series, No. 37]).

——, 'Authoritarian Legacies and Reform Strategies in the Arab World', in Brynen, Korany and Noble (eds.), *Political Liberalization and Democratization in the Arab World: Theoretical Perspectives* (Boulder: Lynne Rienner, 1995).

Brynen, Rex; Korany, Bahgat; and Noble, Paul, 'Introduction: Theoretical Perspectives on Arab Liberalization and Democratization', in Brynen, Korany and Noble (eds.), *Political Liberalization and Democratization in the Arab World: Theoretical Perspectives* (Boulder: Lynne Rienner, 1995).

Chazan, Naomi, 'Between Liberalization and Statism: African Political Cultures and Democracy', in Diamond (ed.), *Political Culture and Democracy in Developing Countries* (Boulder: Lynne Rienner, 1994).

Clapham, Christopher, *Africa in the International System* (Cambridge: Cambridge University Press, 1996).

Crooke, Alastair, 'Talking to Hamas', *Prospect Magazine*, June 2006 (also at http://www.prospect-magazine.co.uk/article_details.php?id=7481).

Crystal, Jill, *Oil and Politics in the Gulf: Rulers and Merchants in Kuwait and Qatar*, 2nd edn (Cambridge: Cambridge University Press, 1995).

Crystal, Jill and al-Shayeji, Abdullah, 'The Pro-democracy Agenda in Kuwait', in Bahgat Korany, Rex Brynen and Paul Noble (eds.), *Political Liberalization and Democratization in the Arab World, Vol. 2 – Comparative Experiences* (Boulder: Lynne Rienner, 1998).

Dahl, Robert, *Polyarchy: Participation and Opposition* (New Haven: Yale University Press, 1988).

Dalacoura, Katerina, *Islam, Liberalism and Human Rights* (London: I.B. Tauris, 1998).

Davidson, Christopher, *The United Arab Emirates: A Study in Survival* (Boulder: Lynne Rienner, 2005).

The Dialogue, at http://www.kacnd.org/. There is an English-language version at http://www.kacnd.org/eng/.

Diamond, Larry, 'Political Culture and Democracy' in Diamond (ed.), *Political Culture and Democracy in Developing Countries* (Boulder: Lynne Rienner, 1994).

——, 'Causes and Effects', in Diamond (ed.), *Political Culture and Democracy in Developing Countries* (Boulder: Lynne Rienner, 1994).

Diamond, Linz and Lipset, 'Introduction', in Ghassan Salamé (ed.), *Democracy without Democrats? The Renewal of Politics in the Muslim World* (London: I.B. Tauris, 1994).

Doorenspleet, Renske, 'Political Democracy: A Cross-National Quantitative Analysis of Modernization and Dependency Theories', in *Acta Politica: International Journal of Political Science*, Vol. 32 (1997), No. 4.

Dossari, Salman, 'Round-up: Bahrain Elections', in *Asharq al-Awsat* (English edition), 29 November 2006 (at http://aawsat.com/english/news.asp?section= 3&id=7176).

Economist Intelligence Unit, *Saudi Arabia Report*, May 2005.

Ehteshami, Anoushiravan, 'Power Sharing and Elections in the Middle East', in Sven Behrendt and Christian Hanelt (eds.), *Bound to Cooperate – Europe and the Middle East* (Gütersloh: Bertelsmann, 2000).

Eickelman, Dale, 'Introduction', in Norton, *Civil Society in the Middle East, Vol. II* (Leiden: Brill, 1995).

Al Fahad, Abdulaziz, 'Ornamental Constitutionalism: The Saudi Basic Law of Governance', paper for the Sixth Mediterranean Social and Political Research Meeting, Montecatini, 16–20 March 2005, Workshop 13.

Gause, Gregory, 'The Persistence of Monarchy in the Arabian Peninsula', in Kostiner (ed.), *Middle East Monarchies: The Challenge of Modernity* (Boulder: Lynne Rienner, 2000).

——, 'Regional Influences on Experiments in Political Liberalization in the Arab World', in Brynen, Korany and Noble (eds.), *Political Liberalization and Democratization in the Arab World, Vol. 1* (Boulder: Lynne Rienner, 1995).

Gulf News, 18 November 2006, 'What is the Federal National Council?'.

——, 24 April 2005, 'Citizens debate Islamists' win in municipal elections'.

Hamilton, N. and Kim, E., 'Economic and Political Liberalization in South Korea and Mexico', *Third World Quarterly*, Vol. 14 (1993), No. 1.

Hamzawy, Amr, 'The Saudi Labyrinth: Evaluating the Current Political Opening' (Carnegie Endowment, Middle East Series, No. 68, April 2006).

Al-Hayat, 21 October 2006.

Herb, Michael, 'Princes, Parliaments, and the Prospects for Democracy in the Gulf', in Marsha Pripstein Posusney and Michele Penner Angrist (eds.), *Authoritarianism in the Middle East* (Boulder: Lynne Rienner, 2005).

——, *All in the Family: Absolutism, Revolution and Democracy in the Middle Eastern Monarchies* (Albany: State University of New York Press, 1999).

Hertog, Steffen, 'Segmented Clientelism: The Political Economy of Saudi Economic Reform Efforts', in Aarts and Nonneman (eds.), *Saudi Arabia in the Balance: Political Economy, Society, Foreign Affairs* (New York/London: New York University Press/Hurst & Co., 2005).

Hinnebusch, Raymond, 'Calculated Decompression as a Substitute for Democratization: Syria', in Korany, Brynen and Noble (eds.), *Political Liberalization and Democratization in the Arab World, Vol. 2 – Comparative Experiences* (Boulder: Lynne Rienner, 1998).

——, 'Democratization in the Middle East: The Evidence from Syria', in Gerd Nonneman (ed.), *Political and Economic Liberalization* (Boulder: Lynne Rienner, 1996).

Hudson, Michael, 'The Political Culture Approach to Arab Democratization: The Case for Bringing it Back in, Carefully', in Brynen, Korany and Noble (eds.), *Political Liberalization and Democratization in the Arab World: Theoretical Perspectives* (Boulder: Lynne Rienner, 1995).

Huntington, Samuel, *The Third Wave: Democratization in the Late Twentieth Century* (Norman: University of Oklahoma Press, 1991).

Ibrahim, Hassanain Tawfiq, 'Internal Political Developments in the GCC States: An Overview', in *Gulf Yearbook 2005–2006* (Dubai: Gulf Research Center, 2006).

Ibrahim, Saad Eddin, *Al Mujtama' wa-d-dawla fi-l watan al-'arabi* (Beirut, 1988).

Ismail, Salwa 'Democracy in Contemporary Arab Intellectual Discourse', in Brynen, Korany and Noble (eds.), *Political Liberalization and Democratization in the Arab World: Theoretical Perspectives* (Boulder: Lynne Rienner, 1995).

Jones, Jeremy, *Negotiating Change: The New Politics of the Middle East* (London: I.B. Tauris, 2006).

Jones, Toby, 'The Iraq Effect in Saudi Arabia', in *Middle East Report*, No. 237, Winter 2005.

Kapiszewski, Andrzej, 'Elections and Parliamentary Activity in the GCC States', in Abdulhadi Khalaf and Giacomo Luciani (eds.), *Constitutional Reform and Political Participation in the Gulf* (Dubai: Gulf Research Center, 2006).

Khalaf, Abdulhadi, 'What do Gulf Ruling Families do when they Rule?', in *Orient*, Vol. 44 (20034), No. 4.

Kong, Tat Yan, 'The Origins of Economic Liberalization and Democratization in South Korea', in Nonneman (ed.), *Political and Economic Liberalization: Dynamics and Linkages in Comparative Perspective* (Boulder: Lynne Rienner, 1996).

Kostiner, Joseph (ed.), *Middle East Monarchies: The Challenge of Modernity* (Boulder: Lynne Rienner, 2000).

Krämer, Gudrun, 'Islam and Pluralism', in Brynen, Korany and Noble (eds.), *Political Liberalization and Democratization in the Arab World, Vol. 1* (Boulder: Lynne Rienner, 1995).

Kurzman, Charles (ed.), *Liberal Islam: A Sourcebook* (Oxford: Oxford University Press, 1998).

Lewis, Bernard, 'A Historical Overview', in Larry Diamond et al. (eds.), *Islam and Democracy in the Middle East* (Baltimore: Johns Hopkins University Press, 2003).

Lipset, Seymour Martin, 'Some Social Requisites for Democracy: Economic Development and Political Legitimacy', in *American Political Science Review*, Vol. 53 (1959), No. 1.

——, *Political Man*, 1st edn (Baltimore: Johns Hopkins University Press, 1981); 2nd edn (London: Heinemann, 1983).

Longva, Anh Nga, 'Citizenship in the Gulf States: Conceptualization and Practice', in Nils Butenschon et al. (eds.), *Citizenship and the State in the Middle East* (Syracuse: Syracuse University Press, 2000).

Lucas, Russell, 'Monarchical Authoritarianism: Survival and Political Liberalization in a Middle Eastern Regime Type', in *International Journal of Middle Eastern Studies*, Vol. 36 (2004).

Luciani, Giacomo, 'Democracy vs Shura in the Age of the Internet', in Khalaf and

Luciani (eds.), *Constitutional Reform and Political Participation in the Gulf* (Dubai: Gulf Research Center, 2006).

——, 'From Private Sector to National Bourgeoisie: Saudi Business', in Aarts and Nonneman (eds.), *Saudi Arabia in the Balance: Political Economy, Society, Foreign Affairs* (New York/London: New York University Press/Hurst & Co., 2005).

——, 'Allocation versus Production States', in Giacomo Luciani (ed.), *The Arab State* (London: Routledge, 1988).

Markoff, John, *Waves of Democracy: Social Movements and Social Change* (Thousand Oaks: Pine Forge Press, 1996).

Meijer, Roel, 'The Association of Muslim Scholars in Iraq', *Middle East Report*, No. 237, Winter 2005.

Milton-Edwards, Beverley, *Islam and Politics in the Contemporary Middle East* (Cambridge: Polity Press, 1999).

Moore, Barrington, *The Social Origins of Dictatorship and Democracy* (London: Allen Lane, 1967)

al-Muhanna, Mohammad, 'The Saudi Majlis ash-Shura: Domestic Functions and International Role' (PhD thesis, Institute of Middle Eastern & Islamic Studies, Durham University, 2005).

Murphy, Emma, 'Agency and Space: The Political Impact of Information Technologies in the Gulf Arab States', in *Third World Quarterly*, Vol. 27 (Sept. 2006), No. 6.

Al Najjar, Ghanim, 'Kuwait: Struggle over Parliament', in *Arab Reform Bulletin* (Carnegie Endowment), June 2006, Vol. 4, No. 5 (at http://www.carnegieendowment.org/publications/index.cfm?fa=view&id=18413&prog=zgp&proj=zdrl#kuwaitStruggle).

Al Naqeeb, Khaldoun, 'How Likely is Democracy in the Gulf?', in John Fox et al. (eds.), *Globalization and the Gulf* (New York: Routledge, 2006).

Nonneman, Gerd, *EU–GCC Relations: Dynamics, Patterns and Perspectives*, Gulf Papers Series (Dubai: Gulf Research Center, June 2006).

——, *Governance, Human Rights, and the Case for Political Adaptation in the Gulf* (RSC policy paper 01–3) (Florence: Robert Schuman Centre, European University Institute, 2001) (at http://www.iue.it/RSCAS/WP-Texts/01_03p.pdf).

——, 'Patterns of Political Liberalization: Explanations and Modalities', in Gerd Nonneman (ed.), *Political and Economic Liberalization: Dynamics and Linkages in Comparative Perspective* (Boulder: Lynne Rienner, 1996).

——, 'Linkages Between Economic and Political Liberalization', in Gerd Nonneman (ed.), *Political and Economic Liberalization* (Boulder: Lynne Rienner, 1996).

Norton, Augustus Richard (ed.), *Civil Society in the Middle East*, vols. 1 and 2 (Leiden: Brill, 1994, 1995).

——, 'The Challenge of Inclusion in the Middle East', in *Current History*, January 1995.

O'Donnell, Guillermo and Schmitter, Philippe, *Transitions from Authoritarian Rule: Tentative Conclusions about Uncertain Democracies* (Baltimore: Johns Hopkins University Press, 1986).

Parolin, Giovanni, 'Generations of Gulf Constitutions: Paths and Perspectives', in Khalaf and Luciani (eds.), *Constitutional Reform and Political Participation in the Gulf* (Dubai: Gulf Research Center, 2006).

The Peninsula, 28, 29, 30, 31 March 2005.

Peterson, John, 'Legitimacy and Political Change in Yemen and Oman', in *Orbis*, Vol. 27, No. 4 (1984).

——, 'The Emergence of Post-Traditional Oman', *Durham Middle East Papers*, No. 78 (Sir William Luce Fellowship Paper No. 5), Durham University, January 2005.

Pinkney, Robert, *Democracy in the Third World* (Buckingham: Open University Press, 1993).

Posusney, Marsha Pripstein, 'The Middle East's Democracy Deficit in Comparative Perspective', in Marsha Pripstein Posusney and Michele Penner Angrist (eds.), *Authoritarianism in the Middle East* (Boulder: Lynne Rienner, 2005).

Pridham, Geoffrey (ed.), *Encouraging Democracy: The International Context of Regime Transition in Southern Europe* (London: St Martin's Press, 1991).

Pridham, Geoffrey and Vanhanen, Tatu (eds.), *Democratization in Eastern Europe* (London: Routledge, 1994).

Przeworski, Adam, *Democracy and the Market: Political and Economic Reforms in Eastern Europe and Latin America* (Cambridge: Cambridge University Press, 1991).

Pye, Lucian and Pye, Mary, *Asian Power and Politics: The Cultural Dimensions of Authority* (Cambridge, MA: Harvard University Press, 1985).

Al-Rasheed, Madawi, *A History of Saudi Arabia* (Cambridge: Cambridge University Press, 2002).

Rathmell, Andrew and Schulze, Kirsten, 'Political Reform in the Gulf: The Case of Qatar', in *Middle Eastern Studies*, Vol. 36, No. 4 (October 2000).

Rustow, Dankwart A., 'Transitions to Democracy: Toward a Dynamic Model', in Comparative Politics, Vol. 2, No. 3 (April 1970).

Sager, Abdulaziz, 'Political Reform Measures from a Domestic GCC Perspective', in Khalaf and Luciani, *Constitutional Reform and Political Participation in the Gulf* (Dubai: Gulf Research Center, 2006).

Salamé, Ghassan, 'Small is Pluralistic', in Salamé (ed.), *Democracy without Democrats? The Renewal of Politics in the Muslim World* (London: I.B. Tauris, 1994).

Saudi Gazette, 13 April 2005.

——, 22 April 2005.

Saudi–US Relations, 'Third Round Balloting Marks End of Landmark Elections', 23 April 2005 (www.saudi-us-relations.org/newsletter2005/saudi-relations-interest-04-23.html).

Schmitter, Philippe, 'The International Context of Contemporary Democratisation', in *Stanford Journal of International Affairs*, Vol. 2 (1993), No. 1.

Schwedler, Jill, *Toward Civil Society in the Middle East* (Boulder: Lynne Rienner, 1995).

Sharabi, Hisham, *Neo-patriarchy: A Theory of Distorted Change in the Arab World* (New York: Oxford University Press, 1988).

Sisk, Timothy, *Islam and Democracy* (Washington, D.C.: USIP Press, 1992).

Sklar, Richard, 'Towards a Theory of Developmental Democracy', in Adrian Leftwich (ed.), *Democracy and Development* (Cambridge: Polity, 1996).

SPA dispatch, 13 April 2005.

Springborg, Patricia, 'Politics, Primordialism and Orientalism', in *American Political Science Review*, Vol. 80 (March 1986), No. 1.

Steinberg, Guido, 'The Wahhabi Ulama and the Saudi State: 1745 to the Present', in Paul Aarts and Gerd Nonneman (eds.), *Saudi Arabia in the Balance: Political Economy, Society, Foreign Affairs* (New York/London: New York University Press/ Hurst & Co., 2005).

Tetreault, Mary Ann, *Stories of Democracy: Politics and Society in Contemporary Kuwait* (New York: Columbia University Press, 2000).

Al-Thani, HH Shaikh Hamad Bin Khalifa, 'Address of HH Sheikh Hamad Bin Khalifa Al-Thani, Fourth Qatar Conference on Democracy and Free Trade, Doha, March 29, 2005'.

——, HH Shaikh Hamad Bin Khalifa, 'Mideast Reforms Cannot Wait, says Emir' [Sheikh Hamad's speech to the Fourth Qatar Conference on Democracy and Free Trade], *The Peninsula*, 6 April 2004.

——, 'Address of HH Sheikh Hamad Bin Khalifa Al-Thani, Third Qatar Conference on Democracy and Free Trade, Doha, 14 April 2002'.

Thope, Daniel and Meyer, Katherine, 'Religion and Democratic Support: Evidence from the World Survey', in *Democracy and Society*, Vol. 3, No. 1.

Vanhanen, Tatu and Kimber, Richard, 'Predicting and Explaining Democratization in Eastern Europe', in Geoffrey Pridham and Tatu Vanhanen (eds.), *Democratization in Eastern Europe: Domestic and International Perspectives* (London: Routledge, 1994).

Vitalis, Robert, *America's Kingdom* (pre-publication version, 2005, posted at http:// cas.uchicago.edu/workshops/cpolit/papers/vitalis.doc).

Waterbury, John, 'Democracy without Democrats?' in Ghassan Salamé (ed.), *Democracy without Democrats? The Renewal of Politics in the Muslim World* (London: I.B. Tauris, 1994).

Weaver, Mary Anne, 'Democracy by Decree', *The New Yorker*, 11 November 2002.

Chapter 3 – Patterns of Democratic Deficit: Is It Islam?

'Abd al-Fattah, Nabil and Rashdan, Diya (eds.), *A Report on the State of Religion in Egypt* (Cairo: Al-Ahram Center for Political and Strategic Studies, 1996) (in Arabic).

Abu al Magd, Ahmad Kamal, *A Contemporary Islamic Vision* (Cairo: Dar al-Shuruq, 1993) (in Arabic).

——, *The Dialogue of Confrontation* (Cairo: Dar al-Shuruq, 1988) (in Arabic).

al-'Awa, Muhammad Salim, *On the Political System of the Islamic State* (Cairo: Al-Maktab al-masri al-hadith, 1975) (in Arabic).

Ayubi, Nazih N., 'Islam and Democracy', in David Potter et al. (eds.), *Democratization* (Cambridge: The Polity Press, 1997).

Bellin, Eva, 'Coercive Institutions and Coercive Leaders', in Posusney and Angrist (eds.), *Authoritarianism in the Middle East* (Boulder: Lynne Rienner, 2005).

Ben-Dor, Gabriel, 'Prospects of Democratization in the Arab World: Global Diffusion, Regional Demonstration, and Domestic Imperatives', in Brynen, Korany and Noble (eds.), *Political Liberalization and Democratization in the Middle East, Vol. 1 – Theoretical Perspectives* (Boulder: Lynne Rienner, 1995).

al-Bishri, Tariq, *The Contemporary Legal Situation Between Shari'a and Positivist Law* (Cairo: Dar al-Shuruq, 1996) (in Arabic).

——, *What is Modernity?* (Cairo: Dar al-Shuruq, 1996) (in Arabic).

——, *The General Traits of Islamic Political Thought in Contemporary History* (Cairo: Dar al-Shuruq, 1996) (in Arabic).

Brownlee, Jason, 'Political Crisis and Restabilization', in Posusney and Angrist (eds.), *Authoritarianism in the Middle East* (Boulder: Lynne Rienner, 2005).

Brynen, Rex; Korany, Bahgat; and Noble, Paul (eds.), *Political Liberalization and Democratization in the Middle East, Vol. 2 – Comparative Experiences* (Boulder: Lynne Rienner, 1998).

——, *Political Liberalization and Democratization in the Middle East, Vol. 1 – Theoretical Perspectives* (Boulder: Lynne Rienner, 1995).

'Emara, Muhammad, *The Fall of Secular Extremism* (Cairo: Dar al-Shuruq, 1995) (in Arabic).

——, *Schools of Islamic Thought* (Cairo: Dar al-Mustaqbal al-'Arabi, 1983) (in Arabic).

——, *Islam and the Philosophy of Rule* (Beirut: Arab Foundation for Study, 1977) (in Arabic).

——, *Islam and the Bases of Rule* (Beirut: Arab Foundation for Study, 1972) (in Arabic).

Fattah, Moataz A., *Democratic Values in the Muslim World* (Boulder: Lynne Rienner, 2006).

Gause, F. Gregory III, 'Regional Influences on Experiments in Political Participation in the Arab World', in Brynen, Korany and Noble (eds.), *Political Liberalization and Democratization in the Middle East, Vol. 1 – Theoretical Perspectives* (Boulder: Lynne Rienner, 1995).

Huntington, Samuel, 'Democracy's Third Wave', in *Journal of Democracy, Vol. 2*, No. 3 (September 1991).

——, 'Will more Countries become Democratic?', in *Political Science Quarterly, Vol. 11*, No. 2 (Summer 1984).

Huwaidi, Fahmi, *Islam and Democracy* (Cairo: Al-Ahram, Center for Translation and Publication, 1993) (in Arabic).

Iraq Index, 30 January 2006 (Washington, D.C.: The Brookings Institution).

Kepel, Gilles, *Le Prophete et Pharaon: Les mouvements islamistes dans l'Egypte, contemporaine* (Paris: La Decouverte, 1984).

Khalid, Khalid Muhammad, *Memoirs: My Story with Life* (Cairo: Dar akhbar al-yom, 1993) (in Arabic).

——, *The State in Islam* (Cairo: Dar Thabet, 1981) (in Arabic).

Korany, Baghat, 'The Middle East After the Cold War: Torn between Geo-Politics and Geo-Economics', in Louise Fawcett (ed.), *International Relations of The Middle East* (Oxford: Oxford University Press, 2005).

——, 'Restricted Democratization from Above: Egypt', in Korany, Brynen and Noble (eds.), *Political Liberalization*, Vol. 2 (Boulder: Lynne Rienner, 1998).

——, 'Arab Democratization: A Poor Cousin?', in *Political Science and Politics* 27/3 (September 1994).

Mayo Newspaper (official organ of the governmental National Democratic Party), 4 May 1981.

Mustafa, Hala, *Political Islam in Egypt: From Reform to Violent Movements* (Cairo: Al-Ahram Center for Political and Strategic Studies, 1992) (in Arabic).

Posusney, Pripstein and Angrist, Michele Penner (eds.), *Authoritarianism in the Middle East* (Boulder: Lynne Rienner, 2005).

al-Qaradawi, Yusuf, *On the Jurisprudence of the State in Islam* (Cairo: Dar al-Shuruq, 1997) (in Arabic).

Walker, Edward et al., 'The Future of Egypt', A Panel Discussion, *Middle East Review of International Affairs* (MERIA), Vol. 10, No. 2 (June 2006) (electronic version).

Chapter 4 – Political Reform in Bahrain: The Changing Tide

Bahrain Centre for Human Rights, at http://www.bchr.net/sections/index.php?action=view&newsid=127.

'Bahrain: Four Political Societies Boycott Elections', at http://www.arabicnews.com/ansub/Daily/Day/020904/2002090418.html, 9 April 2002.

'Bahrain: Petition Detainees Released', at http://www.arabicnews.com/ansub/Daily/Day/040520/2004052012.html, 20 May 2004.

'Bahrain Warns the Opposition against Demanding Constitutional Amendments', at http://www.arabicnews.com/ansub/Daily/Day/040427/2004042710.html, 27 April 2004.

'Bahraini Groups Criticises New Political Law', in *Middle East International*, 21 July 2005, at http://www.middle-east-online.com/english/?id=14076=14076&format=0.

'Bahrainis Held a Peaceful March towards the US Embassy', at http://www.arabicnews.com/ansub/Daily/Day/020518/2002051815.html, 18 May 2002.

Boustany, Nora, 'In Bahrain, Doubts about Reform', in *Washington Post*, 24 June 2005, at http://www.washingtonpost.com/wp-dyn/content/article/2005/06/23/AR2005062301895.html?nav=rss_opinion/columns.

Energy Information Administration, at http://www.eia.doe.gov/emeu/cabs/Bahrain.

Evans, Brian, 'Moving backwards in Bahrain', in *Middle East International*, 7 July 2005, at http://meionline.com/features/378.shtml.

'Fraught Mood in Bahrain, Caught between Compromise and Continued Opposition', in *Gulf States Newsletter*, Issue 780, 28 April 2006.

Gulf Centre for Strategic Studies, 'Bahrain's Political Societies Profiled', in *Bahrain Brief*, Vol. 3, No. 4 (April 2002), at http://www.bahrainbrief.com.bh/english/april2002-issue1.htm.

——, 'Parliamentary Elections and the Future of Democracy in Bahrain', in *Bahrain Brief*, Vol. 3, No. 11 (December 2002), at http://www.bahrainbrief.com.bh/english/dec2002-issue.htm.

http://news.bbc.co.uk/1/hi/world/middle_east/389382.stm

http://news.bbc.co.uk/2/hi/middle_east/3691647.stm

http://www.bahrain.gov.bh/census/htm2/603.htm

http://www.transparency.org/policy_research/surveys_indices/cpi/

International Crisis Group, Bahrain's Sectarian Challenge, Middle East Report No. 40, 6 May 2005.

'Islamic Action Society', *Wikipedia*, http://en.wikipedia.org/wiki/Islamic_Action_Party.

Al-Jazeera, 'Anti-US Protests Shake Bahrain', Sunday 23 May 2004, at http://english.aljazeera.net/NR/exeres/5BB5398A-365A-414D-BD2D-19FEFB93918F.htm.

——, 'Bahrain Protest at Provocative Show', Tuesday 28 October 2003, at http://english.aljazeera.net/NR/exeres/1C7E7A67-C1EF-437F-A9B1-0319B974FE6C.htm.

Khalaf, Abd al-Hadi, 'Bahrain's Parliament: The Quest for a Role', in *Arab Reform Bulletin*, Vol. 2, No. 5 (May 2004), at http://www.carnegieendowment.org/publications/ index.cfm?fa=view&id=1536.

——, 'Political reform in Bahrain: End of a Road', in *Middle East International*, 19 February 2004, at http://meionline.com/features/194.shtml.

'King Hamad: Bahrain to Become a Modern Constitutional Democracy', 15 February 2002, at http://www.arabicnews.com/ansub/Daily/Day/020215/2002021534.html.

Mahdi, Mazen, 'Bahrain Warns Opposition after Pro-Reform Rally', in *Arab News*, 27 March 2005, at http://www.arabnews.com/?page=4&section=0&article=61126&d=27&m=3&y=2005.

Mansoor al-Jamri, 'State and Civil Society in Bahrain', in *Society for Gulf Arab Studies Newsletter*, Vol. 9, No. 1 (January 2000).

Al-Mdaires, Falah, 'Shi'ism and Political Protest in Bahrain', in *DOMES: Digest of Middle East Studies*, Vol. 11, No. 1 (Spring 2002).

Oxford Business Group Briefing, 'Bahrain: Labour Reform', 23 April 2006.

——, 'Bahrain: Sukuks on the Rise', 10 May 2006.

Peterson, J. E., 'Bahrain's First Reforms under Amir Hamad', in *Asian Affairs*, Vol. 33, Part 2 (June 2002).

'Political Party Reforms', in *Arab Reform Bulletin*, Vol. 2, No. 7 (July 2004), at http://www.carnegieendowment.org/publications/index.cfm?fa=view&id=1589.

Al-Qadumi, Ali; Abulhasan, Shila; and Muradi, Ali, 'Bahrain IM Sacked over Attack on Protest against Holy Sites Sacrilege', 23 May 2004, at http://www. jafariyanews.com/2k4_news/may/23_bahrainprotest.htm.

Reuters, 'Mass March Urges Reform in Bahrain', 26 March 2005.

'Rights Group Calls for Reform in Bahrain', in *Daily Star*, 1 July 2005, at http://www.dailystar.com.lb/article.asp?edition_id=10&categ_id=2&article_id=16385.

'Risk Management Report: Bahrain', in *Gulf States Newsletter*, Issue 777, 10 March 2006.

Sakr, Naomi, 'Reflections on the Manama Spring: Research Questions Arising from the Promise of Political Liberalization in Bahrain', in *British Journal of Middle East Studies*, Vol. 28, No. 2 (November 2001).

Schmetzer, Uli, 'Iraq Standoff Raising Anti-U.S.: Fever Protesters Turn Up Heat on Gulf States', in *Chicago Tribune*, 4 January 2003, at http://www.ccmep.org/2003%20Articles/010403_Iraq_standoff_raising_anti-us_Fever.htm.

'Steady Growth Expected in Non-oil Revenues with Current Strategy', in *Bahrain Tribune*, at Middle East and North Africa Financial Network, http://www.menafn.com/qn_news_story_s.asp?StoryId=76476.

Toumi, Habib, 'Bahrain Says New Law Will Help 'Sensible' Growth of Societies', in *Gulf News*, 17 August 2005.

——, 'New Controversy Brewing over Draft Anti-terrorism Law', in *Gulf News*, 19 August 2005.

US State Department, *Country Reports on Human Rights Practices: Bahrain*, 28 February 2005, at http://www.state.gov/g/drl/rls/hrrpt/2004/41719.htm.

Chapter 5 – Deconstructing Before Building: Perspectives on Democracy in Qatar

Abd al-Fadil, Mahmoud, *The Classes Formation in the Arab World* (Beirut: Centre for Arabic Union Studies, 1988).

Ayubi, Nazih, *Overstating the Arab State: Politics and Society in the Middle East* (London and New York: I.B. Tauris, 1995).

Bahry, Louay, 'Elections in Qatar: A Window of Democracy Opens in the Gulf', in *Middle East Policy*, Vol. 6, No. 4 (June 1999), at http://www.mepc.org/public_asp/journal_vol6/9906_bahry.asp.

Beblawi, Hazem and Giacomo Luciani (eds.), *The Rentier State* (Kent: Croom Helm, 1987).

Bill, James A., 'Class Analysis and the Dialectics of Modernization in the Middle East', in *IJMES*, Vol. 3 (1972).

Brumberg, Daniel, 'Democratization in the Arab World? The Trap of Liberalized Autocracy', in *Journal of Democracy*, Vol. 13, No. 4 (October 2002).

Burkhart, Grey E. and Susan Older, *The Information Revolution in The Middle East And North Africa* (Santa Monica: National Defense Research Institute and RAND, 2003).

Carothers, Thomas, 'Promoting Democracy and Fighting Terror', in *Foreign Affairs* (January 2003).

——, 'The End of the Transition Paradigm', in *Journal of Democracy*, Vol. 13 (January 2002).

Cordesman, Anthony, 'Saudi Security and the War on Terrorism: Internal Security Operations, Law Enforcements, Internal Threats, and the Need for Change' (Washington D.C.: Center for Strategic and International Studies, 2002), at http://www.csis.org/burke/saudi21/SaudiWaronTerr.pdf.

Dahl, Robert A., *On Democracy* (New Haven and London: Yale University Press, 1998).

Dobriansky, Paula J., 'The Core of US Foreign Policy', in *Foreign Affairs*, Vol. 82, No. 3 (May/June 2003).

Esposito, John and Voll, John, *Islam and Democracy* (Oxford: Oxford University Press, 1996).

Feldman, Noah, *After Jihad: America and the Struggle for Islamic Democracy* (New York: Farrar, Strauss and Giroux, 2003).

Foley, Sean, 'The Gulf Arabs and the New Iraq: the most to gain and the most to lose?', in *MERIA*, Vol. 7, No. 2 (June 2003).

Fukuyama, Francis, 'Do we really know how to promote democracy?', Speech in New York Democracy Forum, 24 May 2005.

Ghubash, Mohamed, 'The Gulf State: An Authority More than Absolute and Society Less than Crippled', in Ali Al-Kuwari et al., *Towards a Radical Reform in the GCC Countries*, Unpublished Manuscript, Development Forum, 25th Meeting, Doha, 2004.

Haass, Richard N., 'Toward Greater Democracy in the Muslim World', in *The Washington Quarterly*, Vol. 26, No. 3 (Summer 2003).

Ibrahim, S., *The New Arab Social Order: A Study of the Social Impact of Oil Wealth* (Colorado: Westview Press, 1982).

Khan, Muqtedar, 'Prospects for Muslim Democracy: the Role of U.S. Policy', at http://www.ijtihad.org.

——, 'Reflections on Islam and Democracy', in Muqtedar Khan (ed.), *American Muslims: Bridging Faith and Freedom* (Beltsville, MD: Amana Publications, 2002).

Lewis, Bernard, 'Islam and Liberal Democracy: A Historical Overview', in *Journal of Democracy*, Vol. 7, No. 2 (1996).

Mufti, Siraj, 'Muslims Love Democracy', in *Muslim Democrat*, Vol. 4, No. 2 (July 2002).

Naqeeb-Al, Khaldoun, 'Changing Patterns of Social Stratification in the Middle East: Kuwait 1950–70 as a Case Study' (PhD Dissertation, University of Texas, Austin, 1976).

——, *The State and Society in the Gulf and Arabia: A New Perspective* (Beirut: Centre for Arabic Union Studies, 1987).

Ottaway, Marina, 'Evaluating Middle East Reform: How Do We Know When It Is Significant?', Carnegie Papers, *Middle East Series*, No. 56, February 2005.

Przeworski, Adam, 'The Games of Transition', in Scott Mainwaring et al. (eds.), *Issues in Democratic Consolidation: The New South American Democracies in Comparative Perspective* (Notre Dame: Notre Dame University Press, 1992).

Saif, Ahmed A., *Arab Gulf Judicial Structures* (Dubai: Gulf Research Centre, 2004).

——, *Constitutionalism in the GCC States* (Dubai: Gulf Research Centre, 2004).

Chapter 7 – Economic Governance and Reform in Saudi Arabia

Abdul Ghafour, P. K., 'Seven new universities to be set up under 8th Plan', in *Arab News*, Jeddah, 24 November 2005.

——, 'WTO will open new markets for Saudi products', in *Arab News*, Jeddah, 21 December 2005.

Akeel, Maha, 'Mechanisms reviewed to implement employment strategy', in *Arab News*, Jeddah, 27 December 2005.

Borland, Brad, 'Arab world economies: prosperity amidst political uncertainty', in *Saudi–US Relations Information Service*, Washington, 23 September 2005.

——, *The Saudi Economy at Mid-Year 2005* (Riyadh: SAMBA Bank, 2005).

Bosbait, Mohammed and Wilson, Rodney, 'Education, school to work transitions and unemployment in Saudi Arabia', in *Middle Eastern Studies*, Vol. 41, No. 4 (July 2005).

Cordesman, Anthony, 'Saudi economics and Saudi stability: the facts behind the speculation', in *Free Muslims Coalition Press Corner*, Washington, 8 August 2005.

De Rato, Rodrigo, 'IMF Managing Directors statement at the conclusion of a visit to Riyadh', in *International Monetary Fund Press Release*, Washington, 24 October 2004.

Hanware, Khalil, 'Saudi stocks continue to fall', in *Arab News*, Jeddah, 18 October 2005.

——, 'Turning the economy into a global powerhouse', in *Arab News*, Jeddah, 30 December 2005.

Hassan, Javid and Al-Zahrani, Ali, 'Abdullah launches mega city project', in *Arab News*, Jeddah, 21 December 2005.

Hassan, Javid, 'SR 8.1 billion Shuaiba deal signed', in *Arab News*, Jeddah, 29 December 2005.

Henry, Clement M. and Wilson, Rodney, *The Politics of Islamic Finance* (Edinburgh: Edinburgh University Press, 2004).

Al-Kurdi, Usamah and Al-Sulaiman, Ghassan, 'Opportunities for economic and political reforms in the Kingdom of Saudi Arabia', in *Middle Eastern Institute Policy Brief*, Washington, 12 August 2005.

MEED staff writer, 'Emaar unveils King Abdullah Economic City', in *Middle East Economic Digest*, 23 December 2005.

Sabri, Sharaf, *The House of Saud in Commerce: A Study of Royal Entrepreneurship in Saudi Arabia* (New Delhi: I.S. Publications, 2001).

Saudi Arabian Monetary Agency, *Economic Developments First Quarter* 2005 (Riyadh: 2005).

Saudi Arabian Monetary Agency, *Monthly Bulletin of Statistics* (Riyadh: November 2005).

Sfakianakis, John, *Saudi Arabia: Third Quarter Economic Update* (Riyadh: SAMBA Bank, 22 October 2005).

Simmons, Matthew R., *Twilight in the Desert: the Coming Saudi Oil Shock and the World Economy* (New York: Wiley, 2005).

Soofi, Waheeb, 'Problems of Saudization', in *Al-Watan*, Riyadh, 18 December 2005.

Unnamed reporter, 'Companies rent names to beat Saudization rules', in *Al-Watan*, Riyadh, 20 December 2005.

Wilson, Rodney, *Banking and Finance in the Arab Middle East* (London: Macmillan, 1983).

Wilson, Rodney (with Al-Salamah, Abdullah; Malik, Monica; and Al-Rajhi, Ahmed), *Economic Development in Saudi Arabia* (London: Routledge Curzon, 2004).

Yamani, Mai, *Changed Identities: The Challenge of the New Generation in Saudi Arabia* (London: Royal Institute of International Affairs, 2000).

Chapter 8 – The Impact of Economic Reform on Dubai

Abu Dhabi Planning Department Economic Division, *Directive Documents for the Preparation of the Economic and Social Development Plan, 1977–1979* (Abu Dhabi: June 1976).

Bilal, Muhammad, *Changes in Population and Power among Immigrants and Citizens of the UAE, 1976–1980* (Sharjah: Sharjah Sociologist Society, 1990) (in Arabic).

Business Monitor International, *The United Arab Emirates*, second quarter report (London: 2002).

Crystal, Jill, *Oil and Politics in the Gulf: Rulers and Merchants in Kuwait and Qatar* (New York: Cambridge University Press, 1995).

Davidson, Christopher M., *The United Arab Emirates: A Study in Survival* (Boulder: Lynne Rienner, 2005).

Dawn Magazine, 28 October 2000, 'Arabs: a shrinking minority in the UAE'.

Dubai Chamber of Commerce and Industry, *Business in Dubai*, Volume 1, Issue 6 (June 2001).

——, *Business in Dubai*, Volume 2, Issue 15 (March 2002).

Dubai Department of Economic Development, *Development Statistics* (Dubai: 2001).

Dubai Government, 'Dubai Technology, Electronic Commerce and Media Free Zone Law No.1', issued by Sheikh Maktum Al-Maktum in 2000.

Dubai Internet City's official brochure.

Dubai Municipality Statistics Centre, 'Results of income and expenditure survey – Dubai city, 1997–1998' (Dubai: 1999).

Economist Intelligence Unit, *United Arab Emirates* (London: Economist Intelligence Unit, 2000).

Federation of UAE Chambers of Commerce, *The Components of Investment and the Methods of Promoting Investment Opportunities in the UAE* (Abu Dhabi: 1994).

Fenelon, Kevin, *The United Arab Emirates: An Economic and Social Survey* (London: Longman, 1973).

GCC Development Plans, *United Arab Emirates* (Abu Dhabi: 1982).

Gulf News, 11 January 2003, 'Majority of expats suffer from some sort of depression'.

——, 14 December 2002, 'New contract rule to benefit nationals'.

——, 3 September 2000, 'Mashriq Bank joins hand with NHR to promote Emiratization'.

——, 19 August 1998, 'Emaar flies high with mega project'.

——, 26 February 1998, 'Emaar ups project outlay'.

——, 25 November 1997, 'Emaar to set up Dh700 million complex'.

Hawley, Donald, *The Trucial States* (London: George Allen & Unwin, 1970).

Heard-Bey, Frauke, *From Trucial States to United Arab Emirates* (London: Longman, 1982).

Herb, Michael, *All in the Family: Absolutism, Revolution, and Democracy in the Middle Eastern Monarchies* (New York: State University of New York Press, 1999).

Khaleej Times, 26 July 2000, 'University Students take Al-Futtaim Trading Courses'.

——, 26 July 2000, 'Only Nationals to be Captains of Fishing Vessels'.

——, 25 October 1998, 'Dubai investment park excites Dubai investors'.

——, 13 May 1998, 'Dubai investments to lift returns assets'.

Middle East Economic Digest, 8 March 2002, 'Bridging the Gap'.

Oxford Business Group, *Emerging Emirates* (London: Oxford Business Group, 2000).

Peck, Malcolm, *The United Arab Emirates: A Venture in Unity* (Boulder: Westview Press, 1986).

Al-Sharhan International Consultancy, *UAE Country Report* (Dubai: 2001).

Al-Tamimi Consultancy, *The Development of the Dubai Internet City* (Dubai: 2001).

The Times, 5 January 2002, 'Biggest man-made isles rise from the Gulf'.

WAM, 17 May 2001, 'New avenues for UAE women'.

Chapter 9 – ICT and the Gulf Arab States: A Force for Democracy?

Abbott, Jason, 'Democracy@internet.asia? The Challenges to the Emancipatory Potential of the Net: Lessons from China and Malaysia', in *Third World Quarterly*, Vol. 22, No. 1 (2001).

Anderson, Jon W., 'Producers and Middle East Internet Technology: Getting beyond "Impacts"', in *Middle East Journal*, Vol. 54, No. 3 (Summer 2000).

Ayensu, Edward, 'International Management', quoted in Brian Murphy, *The World Wired Up* (London: Comedia, 1983).

Beblawi, Hazem and Luciani, Giacomo (eds.), *The Rentier State* (London: Croom Helm, 1987).

Bellin, Eva, *Stalled Democracy: Capital, Labour and the Paradox of State-sponsored Development* (Ithaca: Cornell University Press, 2002).

——, 'The Robustness of Authoritarianism in the Middle East: A Comparative Perspective', paper presented at *Bringing the Middle East Back In*, Yale University, December 2001.

Brumberg, Daniel, 'The Trap of Liberalised Autocracy', in *Journal of Democracy*, Vol. 13, No. 4 (October 2002).

Castells, Manuel, *The Internet Galaxy: Reflections on the Internet, Business and Society* (Oxford: OUP, 2001).

Chaudhry, Kiren, *The Price of Wealth* (Ithaca: Cornell University Press, 1997).

Crystal, Jill, 'Political Reform and the Prospects for Democratic Transition in the Gulf', in *Working Paper for Fundacion Para Las Relaciones Internacionales y el Diálogo Exterior* (July 2005).

'Digital Dilemmas: A Survey of the Internet Society', *The Economist*, 25 January 2003.

Ehteshami, Anoushiravan, 'Is the Middle East Democratising?', in *British Journal of Middle Eastern Studies*, Vol. 26, No. 2 (November 1999).

European Commission, 'eEurope: An Information Society for All' initiative, at http://europa.eu.int/ISPO/basics/I_europe.html.

Fandy, Mamoun, 'Information Technology, Trust and Social Change in the Arab World', in *Middle East Journal*, Vol. 54, No. 3 (Summer 2000).

Garfinkle, Adam, 'The New Missionaries', in *Prospect* (April 2003).

Ghadbian, Najib, 'Contesting the State Media Monopoly: Syria on al-Jazira Television', in *MERIA Journal*, Vol. 5, No. 2 (June 2001).

Ghareeb, Edmund, 'New Media and the Information Revolution in the Arab World – an Assessment', in *Middle East Journal*, Vol. 54, No. 3 (Summer 2000).

Herb, Michael, 'Emirs and Parliaments in the Gulf', in *Journal of Democracy*, Vol. 13, No. 4 (October 2002).

Huff, Toby E., 'Globalisation and the Internet: Comparing the Middle Eastern and Malaysian Experiences', in *Middle East Journal*, Vol. 3, Summer 2001.

Huntington, Samuel, 'Will More Countries become Democratic', in *Political Science Quarterly*, Vol. 99, No. 2 (Summer 1984).

International Crisis Group, 'Can Saudi Arabia Reform Itself?', in *ICG Middle East Report No. 28*, Cairo/Brussels, 14 July 2004.

International Telecommunication Union, press release 21/1/02, 'United Nations adopts resolution in the World Summit on the Information Society'.

——, *The Global Diffusion of the Internet*, March 1998.

James, Jeffrey, 'The Global Information Infrastructure Revisited' in *Third World Quarterly*, Vol. 22, No. 5 (2001).

Kamrava, Mehran, 'Non-democratic States and Political Liberalisation in the Middle East: A Structural Analysis', in *Third World Quarterly*, Vol. 19, No. 1 (1998).

Lyon, David, *The Information Society: Issues and Illusions* (Cambridge: Polity Press, 1988).

Murphy, Emma, 'Agency and Space: The Political Impact of Information Technologies in the Gulf Arab States', in *Third World Quarterly*, Vol. 27, No. 6 (2006).

Lefebvre, Henri, *The Production of Space* (Oxford: Blackwell, 1991).

Lust-Okkar, Ellen, 'Divided They Rule: The Management and Manipulation of Political Opposition', in *Comparative Politics*, 2002.

McPhail, Thomas, *Electronic Colonialism: The Future of International Broadcasting and Communication* (London: Sage, 1981).

Main, Linda, 'The Global Information Infrastructure: Empowerment or Imperialism?', in *Third World Quarterly*, Vol. 22, No. 1 (2001).

Mandaville, Peter G., 'Reimagining the ummah? Information Technology and the Changing Boundaries of Political Islam', in Ali Mohammadi (ed), *Islam Encountering Globalization* (London: Routledge Curzon, 2002).

Martin, William, *The Information Society* (London: Aslib, 1988).

Middle East Digest, 27 May 2005.

Middle East Economic Digest, 27 May 2005.

——, 18 February 2005.

——, 24 September 2004.

——, 27 June 2003.

——, 19 April 2002.

——, 23 November 2001.

Middle East International, 6 February 2004.

Perrit Jr, D. H., 'The Internet as a Threat to Sovereignty? Thoughts on the Internet's Role in the National and Global Governance', in *Indiana Journal of Global Legal Studies*, Vol. 5, No. 2 (1998).

Perthes, Volker (ed.), *Arab Elites: Negotiating the Politics of Change* (Boulder: Lynne Rienner, 2004).

Romer, Paul, 'Endogenous Technological Change', in *Journal of Political Economy*, Vol. 98, No. 5 (1990).

Schleifer, S. Abdallah, 'Satellite TV and Democracy' in *bitterlemons-international.org Middle East Roundtable*, Ed. 19, Vol. 3 (26 May 2005).

Seznec, Jean-François, 'Stirrings in Saudi Arabia', in *Journal of Democracy*, Vol. 13, No. 4 (October 2002).

Stepan, Alfred with Robertson, Graeme, 'An Arab More than a Muslim Electoral Gap', in *Journal of Democracy*, Vol. 14 (July 2003).

Sussman, Gerald, *Communication, Technology and Politics in the Information Age* (London: Sage, 1997).

United Nations Global E-Government Readiness Report (New York: United Nations, 2004).

Vandewalle, Dirk, *Libya Since Independence: Oil and State-Building* (Ithaca: Cornell University Press, 1998).

Volpi, Frédéric, 'Pseudo-democracy in the Muslim World', in *Third World Quarterly*, Vol. 25, No. 6 (2004).

Warf, B. and Gromes, J., 'Counterhegemonic Discourses and the Internet', in *The Geographical Review*, Vol. 87, No. 2 (1997).

Wilhelm, Anthony, *Democracy in the Digital Age* (London: Routledge, 2000).

Yale University, 'Yale University Information Society' project, at http://www.law.yale.edu/isp/strongdem/overview.html.

Chapter 10 – The Future of Reform in the Societies of the GCC Countries

Al Bana, Jamal, paper on Islamic reservations concerning democracy.

Al Feisal, Saud, paper presented to the Janadiria festival in Riyadh, 2004, part of which was reproduced in *Al Hayat*.

Hamad, Abdulatif, 'Political and Economic Reforms in the GCC Countries and Their Future Horizons', paper presented to a roundtable held by the Kuwaiti parliament under the title 'The Region and the Future', 15–17 May 2004.

Hiji, Tariq, 'Hawamish ala Daftar al Islah', in *Al-Ahram* of Egypt, 21 February 2004.

Al Kawari, Ali, 'Mutatalibat Tahkik Agenda Al Islah Jazri min al Dakhel fi itar Majlis Al Tawon', paper presented at the 25th Development Forum meeting, February 2004.

Al Nueimi, Abdurrahman, paper presented to the 25th meeting of the Development Roundtable, February 2005.

Al Rumaihi, Mohammad, paper presented to the Conference on Democracy and Reform held in Doha, Qatar, 3–4 June 2004.

Al Thani, Sheikh Hamad Bin Khalifa, speech given during the opening of the Conference on Democracy and Reform in the Arab World, Doha, 3–4 June 2004.

Zanubian, Vinan, 'It is Time for Historical Decisions in the Gulf Area', paper presented to the Center of Strategic and Futuristic Studies, Kuwait University, November 2002.

Chapter 11 – US Foreign Policy and the Changed Definition of Gulf Security

Ajami, Fouad, *The Dream Palace of the Arabs: A Generation's Odyssey*, 1st edn (New York: Pantheon Books, 1998).

Bush, George W., 'President Discusses the Economy with Small Business Owners', in *Remarks by the President in the Rose Garden* (Washington, D.C.: GPO, 2003).

——, 'The President's State of the Union Address' (Washington, D.C.: GPO, 29 January 2002).

——, 'West Point Commencement Speech', in Gideon Rose (ed.), *America and the World: Debating the New Shape of International Politics* (New York: Council on Foreign Relations, 2002).

——, 'President, Vice President Discuss the Middle East', in *Remarks by the President and the Vice President Upon Conclusion of Breakfast* (Washington, D.C.: GPO, 2002).

Cook, Stephen, 'The Right Way to Promote Arab Reform', in *Foreign Affairs*, Vol. 84, No. 2 (2005).

Gaddis, John L., *Surprise, Security, and the American Experience* (Cambridge, MA: Harvard University Press, 2004).

Gordon, Phillip H., 'Bush's Middle East Vision', in *Survival*, Vol. 45, No. 1 (2003).

Kay, David A., 'Wmd Terrorism: Hype or Reality', in James M. Smith and William C. Thomas (eds.), *The Terrorism Threat and US Governmental Response: Operational and Organisational Factors* (Colorado: USAF Institute for National Security Studies, 2001).

Kennedy, Robert F., *Thirteen Days: A Memoir of the Cuban Missile Crisis* (Norwalk, Connecticut: Easton Press, 1991).

Kissinger, Henry, 'Consult and control: bywords for battling the new enemy', in *Washington Post*, 16 September 2002.

Lewis, Bernard, *What Went Wrong?* (London: Phoenix, 2002).

Ottaway, Marina et al., 'Democratic Mirage in the Middle East', in Thomas Carothers (ed.), *Critical Mission: Essays on Democracy Promotion* (Washington, D.C.: Brookings Institution Press, 2002).

Pillar, Paul R., *Terrorism and US Foreign Policy* (Washington, D.C.: Brookings Institution Press, 2001).

Powell, Colin, 'The US–Middle East Partnership Initiative: Building Hope for the Years Ahead', in *Remarks at the Heritage Foundation* (Washington, D.C.: GPO, 2002).

Slocombe, Walter B., 'Force, Pre-Emption and Legitimacy', in *Survival*, Vol. 45, No. 1 (2003).

United Nations Development Programme, *The Arab Human Development Report 2004: Towards Freedom in the Arab World* (New York: United Nations Development Programme, Regional Bureau for Arab States, 2004).

United States, *National Strategy for Combating Terrorism* (Washington, D.C.: GPO, 2003).

United States, *National Security Strategy to Combat Weapons of Mass Destruction* (Washington, D.C.: GPO, 2002).

United States, *The National Security Strategy of the United States of America* (Washington, D.C.: GPO, 2002).

Waltz, Kenneth N., *The Spread of Nuclear Weapons: More May Be Better*, Adelphi Papers, No. 171 (London: International Institute for Strategic Studies, 1981).

Chapter 12 – Synergies in Reform: Case Studies of Saudi Arabia and Iran

'Arab Political Systems, Baseline Information and Reforms – Saudi Arabia', at http://www.carnegieendowment.org/arabpoliticalsystems.

Arjomand, Siad Amir, 'The Reform Movement and the Debate on Modernity and Tradition in Contemporary Iran', in *International Journal of the Middle East*, No. 34 (2002).

Bishar, A., 'Reform and the Rentier State', at http://weekly.alhram.org.eg.

Buchta, Wilfried, *Who Rules Iran: The Structure of Power in the Islamic Republic* (Washington: Washington Institute for Near East Policy, 2000).

Constitution of the Islamic Republic of Iran, at http://www.salamiran.org/IranInfo/State/Constitution/.

de Bellaigue, Christopher, 'Iran's Last Chance for Reform', in *Washington Quarterly*, Autumn 2001.

Dirasa fi Vilayat Al-Faqih, 2 Vols (Qum, 1988).

Al Faisal, Prince Turki, 'Saudi Arabia Today', a talk at Durham University, 12 October 2004.

Howthorne, Amy, 'Political Reform in the Arab World: A New Ferment?', *Carnegie Papers*, No. 52 (Oct. 2004).

http://freethoughts.org/archives/0006665.php.

http://news.bbc.co.uk, 8 December 2004.

http://www.arabnews.com, 2 December 2004.

http://www.baztab.com, 27 June 2005.

http://www.shianews.com.

Looney, R., 'Middle East Reform Initiatives: A Stage-theory Perspective', in *International Journal on World Peace*, Vol. 22, No. 1 (March 2005).

——, 'Development Strategies for Saudi Arabia: Escaping the Rentier State Syndrome', *Strategic Insights*, Vol. 3, Issue 3 (March 2004).

Louwa, J., 'Democracy, and the Rentier State', at http://www.globalengagement.org.

Middle East Intelligence Bulletin, Vol. 5, No. 11 (November 2003), at http://www.meib.org.

Okruhlik, G., 'Networks of Dissent: Islamism and Reform in Saudi Arabia', at http://www.ssrc.org.

'Political Reforms are Under Study in Saudi Arabia', 21 July 2003, at http://www.arabicnews.com.

'Saudi Crown Prince: Constitutional Reforms are a Matter of Time', 2 January 2003, at http://www.arabicnews.com.

Index

Tables are indicated by italic page numbers followed by "*t*". End note page numbers are followed by an "n".